Mission Statement

To empower the serving and retired members of Gyan Chakra in the field of strategic thinking by providing a forum for incubation of ideas and the collation of wisdom of elders in the form of articles; creating an environment of discussion and exchange of ideas which leads to the creation of a more informed, educated and mature military leadership.

Gyan Chakra, Senior Veterans Home
Sector-2 Panchkula, Haryana, India
t: 0172 2587305 **e:** gcttch@gmail.com
w: www.gyanchakra.org

Gyan Chakra on India's Military Strategy

Also by Gyan Chakra:

Gyan Chakra on Indian Strategic Thought 2021

Also by Fauji Days:

Drummers Call:
An Anthology of Writings While Following the Drum

The POW Who Saved Kashmir:
Unsung Saga of Sher Bachha Brig Pritam Singh, MC

The General Called Tsunami:
Memoir of a Sapper

Engineering the Victory March:
Bangladesh Liberation War 1971

Forthcoming Titles by Fauji Days:

Military Pensions Simplified:
Commentary, Case Law & Provisions

Illustrated Military History of India

The Crossover Girl and Other Stories

Gyan Chakra
on
India's Military Strategy

Edited by

Maj Gen Amarjit Singh

GYAN CHAKRA THINK TANK
A Western Command Initiative

THE BROWSER | FAUJI DAYS

Title: Gyan Chakra on India's Military Strategy
Edited by: Maj Gen Amarjit Singh
Gyan Chakra Think Tank (A Western Command Initiative)

ISBN: 978-93-92210-18-1

Edition: I

Published by:
J.G.S. Enterprises Pvt Ltd
Imprint: The Browser

Publisher's Address:
SCO 14-15, Sector 8-C, Chandigarh 160 009

Website: www.thebrowser.org
Email: service@thebrowser.org

Printed in India.

Editing, Layout and Cover Design by beagles
www.99beagles.com

Disclaimer:
The views and opinions expressed in this book are the authors' own and the facts are as reported by them, and the editors and publishers are not in any way liable for the same.

THE BROWSER
www.thebrowser.org
Publishers & Booksellers

FAUJI DAYS
www.faujidays.com
Oral History and Military Publishing

Dedicated to

All the Strategic Military Minds who have kept and will keep India secure.

Contents

2

The Strategic Future

3

The Strategic Neighbourhood

4

The Strategic World

From the Chairman's Desk

Military Strategy is an essential component of a Nation's quest towards realising its vision and safeguarding its National Interests. As Military Strategy is also a component of the Grand Strategy involving different constituents of National Power, it needs to be studied in earnest both by the soldier and the academician. It is with a sense of satisfaction that I bring to you the *Gyan Chakra Journal 2023* with the theme 'India's Military Strategy'. Rarely will you find the collation of wisdom in one book of such experienced and intellectual veterans of India's military strategy.

This book covers the evolution of India's military strategy from 1947 to date and has been authored by officers who have actually been part of the process. In my view, it would be necessary for all students and executors of strategy to read this compilation to draw vital lessons as they move ahead towards attaining the National Goals.

The global security environment has become extremely complex with the ongoing war in Europe as also the emerging situation in the Indo-Pacific. In the regional arena, India stands between two nuclear-powered nations with whom the relationship today is extremely disturbed. The emergence of India as a reckonable power also leads to pulls and expectations in the global arena. Thus it becomes extremely important for India to chart a course that ensures the safeguarding of National Interest and comprehensive development. I convey my gratitude and thank all our esteemed elders for sharing their wisdom with us.

Their collective wisdom not only makes this journal an interesting read but also serves as a fountainhead for strategic discourse for all officers and students of defence studies. The Gyan Chakra Think Tank is doing a magnificent task of inculcating the art of strategic thinking in our future leadership, and this book is a step in that direction.

Happy reading!

Jai Hind!

Lieutenant General Nav K Khanduri,
PVSM, AVSM, VSM
GOC-in-C
Western Command

From the Editor's Desk

Military strategy is the *raison d'être* of military generalship. It is they who devise and execute a winning strategy for nations in times of war. Its success is a matter of life and death for the people of the country. India, since independence, has seen many wars and has experienced both victory and defeat. The experience of the military leaders who have planned and fought these wars is vital to the present generation, for it takes a wise man to learn from his mistakes but a wiser man to learn from others. Humans have the unique ability to learn from the experiences of others, but they also fall prey to oversight because of high self-worth. This collation of wisdom of retired experts and specialists who have been at the nation's helm of decision-making aims to document experiences and advice for a wise man to learn from.

The fundamental blocks of a nation's strategic culture fall in the spheres of military and politics. In a democracy, both these spheres must be balanced with sufficient overlap of responsibility and a clear understanding of the precedence of politics. This is important because a vacuum in one sphere should be immediately filled by the other. In Pakistan, the political sphere developed a huge void after Jinnah and Liaquat Ali Khan, which was filled by the military. In India, we have a third power centre that comes into play: the bureaucracy. Fortunately or unfortunately, the bureaucracy fills the voids in the military and political sphere to retain the balance. The question I raise here is whether the Indian military leadership has adequately occupied the military sphere. In 1971, 1999, and recent surgical strikes, the military has shown its prowess to prevail. However, the perceptible divergence in understanding of a common military strategy in peace and war, and the process of conducting daily business between the

Army, Navy, and Air Force creates a space for non-military professionals to step in matters of command and control, which seriously affects military decision-making and the construct of strategy.

Indian military leadership has been outstanding in war, where personalities have stood over the bureaucratic red tape to shape victory. But learning never exhausts the mind, and there are always better ways to discover. New paths will be found if there is a quest for research and humility to acknowledge gaps in our knowledge. One of the learning methods is analysing the wisdom of past leadership. If this wisdom is to be studied, then it must be documented. I agree that old soldiers fade away, but their wisdom certainly must not. This book is the collation of the knowledge of military leaders who have experienced military challenges first-hand and have been tested on the touchstone. The more military thought we generate, the more we contribute to the education of the younger generation.

In this book, we concentrate on military strategy. It was such a wonderful experience interacting with our veterans on this subject. We have been able to cover all the wars, internal security, military reforms, and extension of experiences into the future and also look at world politics. Each of the articles has been written by an expert who has actually been responsible for steering the outcome of our security challenges. Till now, such a galaxy of military leaders had not come together in one book to pen down their thoughts. So I must thank each of them for their valuable contribution.

The Gyan Chakra Think Tank has been trudging along in creating an environment for exchanging views and providing a platform for educating the younger generations of officers and students of defence studies. Our discussions are webcast over all stations of Western Command as well as Panjab University, Punjabi University, and Chitkara University. We have also been interacting with the Rashtriya Raksha University and the Department of Defence at Shimla University.

I firmly believe that strategy and defence studies are seriously neglected in our country. Due to the lack of formal education in strategy, the actual working knowledge of strategy and defence comes to officers in their last two years of service when there is limited time for learning and putting it to practice. Military analysts and defence researchers are spending far too much time on current events rather than analysing the strategies of nations to acquire power. In India, we are only following trends. It has been my wish that Indian leadership must create trends and get into the habit of staying ahead of others in the field of strategy. The Military Commanders,

Vice Chancellors of universities and education policymakers must take serious note of this gap in our strategic education. The greatness of a nation will arise only from the strategic understanding of military power and world politics and not by merely stating 'India's rightful place in the comity of nations'.

I thank the Army Commander, Western Command and the Chief of Staff for supporting Gyan Chakra's venture. I sincerely thank all the veterans for contributing their wisdom to this book. A special thanks also to the controlling staff at the Command Headquarters for sparing their time to assist us in this publication. I also extend my appreciation to my editorial team for working tirelessly in producing the manuscript and collating all the data required for this book.

Major General Amarjit Singh
Director
Gyan Chakra Think Tank

Abbreviations

(I)	Independent
(I) Inf Bde	Independent Infantry Brigade
AD	Air Defence
ADB	Army Design Bureau
AEW&C	Airborne Early Warning & Control System
AGPL	Actual Ground Position Line
AI	Artificial Intelligence
ANI	Andaman and Nicobar Islands
AOC	Air Officer Commanding
AOR	Areas of Responsibility
ARN	Army Reserve North
ASAT	Anti-Satellite
AWACS	Airborne Warning and Control System
AWS	Autonomous Weapon Systems
Bde	Brigade
BCE	Before the Common Era
BRI	Belt and Road Initiative
BTG	Battalion Tactical Group
C-in-C	Commander-in-Chief
C4	Command, Control, Communications, Computers
C4I	Command, Control, Communications, Computers, and Intelligence
CAIR	Centre for Artificial Intelligence and Robotics
CBM	Confidence-Building Measures
CCP	Chinese Communist Party
CCS	Cabinet Committee on Security
CDS	Chief of Defence Staff
CE	Common Era
CENTO	Central Treaty Organisation
CGI	Corrugated Galvanised Iron

CGS	Chief of General Staff
CIA	Central Intelligence Agency
CMC	Central Military Commission
CMI	Civil Military Integration
CMLA	Chief Martial Law Administrator
CNP	Comprehensive National Power
CNS	Chief of Naval Staff
CO	Cyberspace Operations
COAS	Chief of the Army Staff
CORPAT	Coordinated Patrol
COS	Chief of Staff
COSC	Chiefs of Staff Committee
CPEC	China-Pakistan Economic Corridor
CRPF	Central Reserve Police Force
DAIC	Defence Artificial Intelligence Council
DAIPA	Defence Artificial Intelligence Project Agency
DAP	Defence Acquisition Procedure
DCAP	Defence Capital Acquisition Plan
DDR&D	Directorate of Defence Research & Development
DE	Directed Energy
DGIS	Directorate General of Information Systems
DGMO	Director General of Military Operations
DIA	Defence Intelligence Agency
Div	Division
DM	Decision-Making
DMA	Department of Military Affairs
DPC	Defence Planning Committee
DPSU	Defence Public Sector Unit
DRDO	Defence Research and Development Organisation
DSC	Defence Security Corps
DSSC	Defence Services Staff College
DSTI	Defence Science, Technology, and Industry
EC	European Commission

ECOSOC	United Nations Economic and Social Council
EEZ	Exclusive Economic Zone
EW	Electronic Warfare
FCNA	Force Command Northern Areas
GBAD	Ground-Based Air Defence
GHQ	General Headquarters
GOC	General Officer Commanding
GOC-in-C	General Officer Commanding-in-Chief
GPS	Global Positioning System
HADR	Humanitarian Assistance and Disaster Relief
HAL	Hindustan Aeronautics Ltd
HQ	Headquarter
HRC	Human Rights Council
IAF	Indian Air Force
IAS	Indian Administrative Service
IB	Intelligence Bureau
IB	International Border
ICAT	Institute of Computer Accounts
ICC	International Criminal Court
ICDP	Integrated Capability Development Plan
ICT	Information and Communication Technologies
IDS	Integrated Defence Staff
IED	Improvised Explosive Device
IHL	International Humanitarian Law
IN	Indian Navy
Inf Bde	Infantry Brigade
Inf Div	Infantry Division
INS	Indian Naval Ship
IO	Information Operations
IONS	Indian Ocean Naval Symposium
IOR	Indian Ocean Region
IoT	Internet of Things
IPKF	Indian Peace Keeping Force

IPS	Indian Police Service
ISI	Inter-Services Intelligence
ISIS	Islamic State of Iraq and Syria
ISPR	Inter-Services Public Relations
ISR	Intelligence, Surveillance, and Reconnaissance
ISRO	Indian Space Research Organisation
IT	Information Technology
IUU	Illegal, Unreported and Unregulated (fishing)
J&K	The erstwhile state of Jammu and Kashmir
JeM	Jaish-e-Mohammed
JIC	Joint Intelligence Committee
JIT	Joint Investigation Team
JOC	Joint Operations Command
JSSF	Joint Strategic Support Force
KK	Karakoram
KP	Khyber Pakhtunkhwa
LAC	Line of Actual Control
LAWS	Lethal Autonomous Weapon Systems
LeT	Lashkar-e-Taiba
LoC	Line of Control
LPD	Landing Platform Dock
LTIPP	Long Term Integrated Perspective Plan
LWE	Left Wing Extremists
MDA	Maritime Domain Awareness
MDO	Multi-Domain Operations
MINUSCA	United Nations Multidimensional Integrated Stabilisation Mission in the Central African Republic
MINUSMA	United Nations Multidimensional Integrated Stabilisation Mission in Mali
MoD	Ministry of Defence
MONUSCO	United Nations Organization Stabilization Mission in the Democratic Republic of the Congo
MoU	Memorandum of Understanding
MRLS	Multiple Launch Rocket Systems

NAB	National Accountability Bureau
NATO	North Atlantic Treaty Organisation
NCO	Network-Centric Operations
NCW	Network-Centric Warfare
NDA	National Democratic Alliance
NDC	National Defence College
NEFA	Northeast Frontier Agency; now Arunachal Pradesh
NLAW	Next generation Light Anti-tank Weapons
NLI	Northern Light Infantry
NM	Nautical Miles
NPA	Non-Performing Assets
NPC	National People's Congress
NSA	National Security Advisor
NSAB	National Security Advisory Board
NSCS	National Security Coordination Secretariat (a unit under the Prime Minister's Office for national security planning and coordination)
NSS	National Security Strategy
NTRO	National Technical Research Organisation
NWNP	No War No Peace
OF	Ordnance Factory
OGWs	Over-Ground Workers
OODA	Observe, Orient, Decide, Act
Op	Operation
PAF	Pakistan Air Force
Para Bde	Parachute Brigade
PKO	Peacekeeping Operation
PLA	People's Liberation Army
PLAAF	People's Liberation Army Air Force
PLAN	People's Liberation Army Navy
PLASSF	People's Liberation Army Strategic Support Force
PM	Prime Minister
PMO	Prime Minister's Office
PMO	Project Management Organisation

PMSC	Private Military and Security Companies
PNS	Pakistan Naval Ship
PoGB	Pakistan-occupied Gilit Baltistan
PoJK	Pakistan-occupied Jammu & Kashmir
PoK	Pakistan-occupied Kashmir
POTUS	President of the United States
PP	Patrolling Points
PTI	Pakistan Tehreek-e-Insaf
QAT	Quick Action Team
QUAD/ QSD	Quadrilateral Security Dialogue (comprising India, USA, Japan, and Australia)
R&D	Research & Development
RAW	Research and Analysis Wing
RIAF	Royal Indian Air Force
RMA	Revolution in Military Affairs
ROK	Republic of South Korea
RPG	Rocket-propelled Grenade
RR	Rashtriya Rifles
SAGAR	Security and Growth for All in the Region
SAM	Surface-to-Air Missile
SCS	South China Sea
SDGs	Sustainable Development Goals
SLOC	Sea Lanes of Communication
SLR	Self-Loading Rifle
SME	Small and Medium-sized Enterprise
SOP	Standard Operating Procedure
SP	Superintendent of Police
SSG	Special Service Group
SSW	Sub Sector West
TIIs	Terrorist Initiated Incidents
TPCR	Technology Perspective and Capability Roadmap
TRP	Targeted Attack Protection
UAF	Ukraine Armed Forces

UAV	Unmanned Aerial Vehicle
UN	United Nations
UNGA	United Nations General Assembly
UNIMISS	United Nations Mission in South Sudan
UNSC	United Nations Security Council
USA	United States of America
UT	Union Territory
VA	Vulnerable Area
VCOAS	Vice Chief of the Army Staff
VKS	Russian Aerospace Forces (Vozdushno-Kosmicheskiye Sily)
VP	Vulnerable Point
WAC	Western Air Command
WESEE	Weapons and Electronics Systems Engineering Establishment
WHO	World Health Organisation
WMD	Weapons of mass destruction
WTO	World Trade Organisation
WWI	First World War
WWII	Second World War

1

The Strategic Past

1

Military Strategy in the Kargil War

General V.P. Malik

Kargil was the biggest blunder committed in the history of Pakistan.
–Benazir Bhutto

After this (Kargil) operation, it's going to be either a Court Martial or Martial Law.
–Air Commodore Abid Rao, Pakistan Air Force,
when briefed about the operation in May 1999

In her book, *From Kargil to the Coup*, Pakistani journalist Nasim Zehra reveals that Pakistan's 1971 surrender in East Pakistan had inflicted the deepest of cuts on the Pakistani psyche. For some, the shame and anger had lingered. India's preemptive occupation of the Siachen Glacier in 1984 became yet another embarrassment – a thorn in the flesh of the Pakistan Army. Since the late 1980s, a military coterie of senior army officers comprising General Pervez Musharraf (who had once commanded the Special Services Group troops in Siachen and made several futile attempts to capture Indian posts), Lieutenant General Mohammad Aziz Khan, Lieutenant General Mehmood Ahmad, and Major General Javed Hasan, believed that an offensive in the Dras-Kargil-Batalik and the adjoining Sub Sector West (SSW) of the Siachen Glacier would enable them to avenge earlier defeats. Their refrain was that Siachen had to be avenged and military pressure on India would force India to settle Kashmir in favour of Pakistan. However, the political and senior military leaders had denied permission for such an action due to operational logistics, geopolitical, and strategic reasons.

In October 1998, when Pakistan's Prime Minister Nawaz Sharif appointed Pervez Musharraf as the COAS superseding two of his senior colleagues, the coterie, under Musharraf, got its chance to implement their long-term obsession. After taking over, Musharraf made some quick changes in the top echelons of the army to position his coterie. He brought in Lieutenant General Mehmood Ahmad as GOC, 10 Corps, in-charge of all Pakistan Army deployments in PoK. Lieutenant General Mohammad Aziz Khan from the ISI, without commanding a corps as per the usual practice, was appointed Chief of General Staff (CGS), Pakistan Army. From ISI, Javed Hasan was already GOC, Force Command Northern Areas (FCNA) and was commanding troops that were deployed in the northern areas of Pakistan.

Geostrategic Backdrop

On 11 and 13 May 1998, the newly-formed NDA Government in India stunned the world by carrying out nuclear weapons tests, thus, terminating its nuclear ambiguity. This step marked the implementation of a decision taken after decades of discussions within several Indian Governments. Pakistan followed the Indian example 15 days later. That was not a surprise. After the events, governments in both countries received massive domestic support, but both nations faced sharp criticism from foreign countries.

Pakistan's nuclear tests unleashed two simultaneous and parallel developments in the country's two well-known power centres. At the political level, Pakistan decided to join India in developing Confidence-Building Measures (CBMs) and to attempt to resolve disputes through peaceful dialogues. The negative development was within its army – to make use of the nuclear threshold for initiating a limited war against India.

The Lahore Declaration

The international flak faced by India and Pakistan and the imposition of sanctions on both countries engendered a new sense of responsibility in New Delhi and Islamabad. The political authorities realised the non-viability of an all-out war in future. In the next few months, direct and back-door diplomacy between India and Pakistan became hyperactive.

This resulted in Indian Prime Minister Atal Behari Vajpayee's historic bus journey to Lahore and the signing of the Lahore Declaration with Pakistan's Prime Minister Nawaz Sharif on 20–21 February 1999. In the declaration, both prime ministers recognised that the nuclear dimension had added 'to their responsibility for avoiding a conflict between the two countries'. They reiterated their determination 'to implement the Shimla Agreement in letter and spirit' and agreed 'to intensify their efforts to resolve all issues, including the issue of J&K'.

A significant part of the Lahore Declaration was made up of an MoU signed by the Foreign Secretaries of India and Pakistan for the two nations 'to engage in bilateral consultations on security concepts and nuclear doctrines to develop measures for confidence-building in the nuclear and conventional fields aimed at avoidance of conflict'. The MoU listed seven significant clauses on nuclear and conventional CBMs, mutual consultations, and communication between the two sides.

On the day the Lahore Declaration was signed, violence erupted in the city. The *jehadi* elements (Jamaat-i-Islami), which had a long-standing alliance with the Pakistan military, started riots in many parts of the city to protest the Vajpayee visit. Indian military intelligence also intercepted several radio messages from across the border exhorting all *jehadi* elements inside J&K to increase the levels of violence. As a result, there was a sudden spurt in the *jehadi* elements' activities in J&K. Between February and April 1999, there were 618 incidents of violence in which 487 civilians, security forces' personnel, and terrorists were killed.

Captured documents and diaries of the Pakistanis during the Kargil War have revealed that Pakistan Army under Musharraf had put into motion the battle procedure for the Kargil War well before the Lahore Declaration. Since November 1998, it had been busy planning and carrying out reconnaissance and logistic preparations for its 'infiltrate and capture' operation across the LoC in the Kargil and Siachen sectors.

Terrain

Beyond Zoji La, the LoC is along the Ladakh Range at heights ranging from 16,000 ft to 21,000 ft where the mountain sides are barren, steep, and rugged. The terrain gets more rugged from Chorbat La to Turtuk, an ancient trade-route village on the LoC, captured by India during the 1971 War. In 1999, there was no foot track connecting Batalik to Turtuk across Chorbat La. Turtuk was connected to Leh by a vehicular road which passes over Khardung La.

On the Pakistan side, the road coming from Burzil towards Boyil and beyond passed over the Great Himalayan Range through the Burzil Bai pass. Another road came from Skardu, a feeder opposite the Batalik and Kargil sectors. Other feeder roads supported the Pakistani troop deployment along the Actual Ground Position Line (AGPL).

It is interesting to note that Dras has a mostly Sunni population. Kargil, Batalik and Turtuk have 80 per cent Shia Muslims and the rest are mostly Buddhists. The majority population in the rest of Ladakh is Buddhist.

India's Deployment in the Kargil Sector

In May 1991, after the Kashmir Valley got engulfed in militancy, 28 Inf Div and 53 Inf Bde had been moved from Western Ladakh to the Kashmir Valley. In Mar 1997, before J&K's State Assembly elections, 70 Inf Bde of 3 Inf Div was also moved to the Valley and got sucked into counter-militancy or terrorism operations. As a result, there were no reserves for any offensive or defensive operations in Kargil and Ladakh. In September 1998, after an improvement in the operational situation in the Valley, HQ 70 Inf Bde, with one battalion, was moved back to Ladakh. The brigade had to leave behind two battalions as the reorganisation of the sectors in the Valley could not be completed before the winter closure of the Zoji La Pass.

In early 1999, this entire area was part of 3 Inf Div under HQ 15 Corps. As per the zone threat analyses of the 15 Corps, due to terrain and climatic conditions, large-scale movement of forces was not expected. It was, thus, considered the lowest priority sector. Only main approaches were held by 121 Inf Bde between Kaobal Gali and Chorbat La. This pattern of deployment, with long gaps between defences, was followed on both sides of the LoC. The deployment had acquired a traditional pattern over the last 52 years. Neither side had tried to occupy these gaps due to the difficult nature of the terrain and limited threat perception. Gaps in the 121 Inf Bde sector were as follows:

Turtuk-Chorbat La	26 km
Chorbat La-Shangruti	25 km
Point 5299-Bimbat	9 km
Bimbat LoC-Marpo La	9.5 km
Marpo La-Kaobal Gali	36 km

During my tenure as Vice Chief and Army Chief, till the outbreak of the Kargil War, no recommendation was ever made to Army HQ for the deployment of additional formations in this sector.

Pakistan's Deployment and Operational Plan

In Pakistan, Rawalpindi-based HQ 10 Corps, which planned and executed the Kargil operation across the LoC, is responsible for the entire Kashmir area, including Siachen, with two divisions and the FCNA. The planning and execution of the operation in Batalik pivoted around the FCNA. Under its GOC, Major General Javed Hasan, there were three brigades:

80 Inf Bde at Minimarg under Brig Masood Aslam.

62 Inf Bde at Skardu under Brig Nusrat Sial.

323 Inf Bde at Siachen under Brig Salahuddin Satti.

A key arm of the FCNA was the Northern Light Infantry (NLI), with 11 battalions of troops from the northern areas. These battalions could be placed under any one of the three FCNA brigades. The NLI officers were posted from the army. The uniform of NLI forces was khaki, like that of the regular army.

In a first-hand account, Air Commodore M. Kaiser Tufail, then Director of Air Operations in the PAF, has stated, 'In early May 1999, Kaiser Tufail accompanied Air Commodores Abid Rao and Saleem Nawaz to attend a briefing on the "Kashmir Contingency" by Lieutenant General Mehmud Ahmed, GOC 10 Corps, responsible for Pakistani military deployments opposite the J&K valley, Kargil and Ladakh. During this briefing, Mehmud Ahmed informed the Pakistan Air Force contingent that a "limited operation" had been started in the Kargil sector. He said that a few vacant Indian posts had been occupied on the heights across the LoC, overlooking the Dras-Kargil Road. Field artillery guns had been heli-lifted to these heights, piecemeal, and re-assembled over the previous few months when the Indians had been off-guard due to winter conditions. Stinger surface-to-air missiles had been deployed on these heights to ensure that the Indian Air Force could not intervene. These forces, he said, would block and cut off India's crucial lifeline, which carried the bulk of supplies needed for daily consumption as well as annual winter-stocking in India's Leh-Siachen Sector. He was hopeful that this stratagem could choke off the Indians in this vital sector for up to a month, after which the monsoons would prevent vehicular movement due to landslides and suspend all airlift by the Indian Air Force. Mehmud Ahmed summed up the briefing by saying, "Come October, we shall walk into Siachen – to mop up the dead bodies of hundreds of Indians left hungry, out in the cold."'

According to Kaiser Tufail, 'It seemed from the Corps Commander's smug appreciation of the situation that the Indians had been tightly straitjacketed in Dras-Kargil Sector and had no option but to submit to our operational design. More significantly, an alternate action like a strategic riposte by the Indians in another sector had been rendered out of question, given the nuclear environment. Whether resort to an exterior manoeuvre (diplomatic offensive) by the beleaguered Indians had crossed the planners' minds, it was not discernible in the Corps Commander's elucidation... Perhaps it was the incredulousness of the whole thing that led Air Commodore Abid Rao to quip "After this operation, it's going to be either a Court Martial or Martial Law."'

According to Lieutenant General Shahid Aziz of the Pakistan Army, 'There were no Mujahideen (in Kargil); only taped wireless messages, which fooled no one. Our soldiers were made to occupy barren ridges, with hand-held weapons and ammunition. There was no way to dig in, so they were told to make parapets with loose stones and sit behind them, with no overhead protection.'

As per Nasim Zehra's book, *From Kargil to the Coup,* the original plan was that about 200 Pakistani troops would cross the LoC to dominate the Indian supply lines from Srinagar to Leh (NH-1A) beginning from the Zoji La Pass. This was to be explained as an exercise which involved manning levels in the winter months and ensuring the forward movement of local reserves to deny any possible Indian offensive. These troops would occupy dominating heights up to India's NH-1A. The planners had thought of occupying 10 or 12 posts but noting the vast unheld areas, the scope of the operation was expanded. More FCNA troops—primarily of the NLI—were made to cross the LoC to include areas from Kaobal Gali up to SSW in the Siachen Sector. 'An operation which expanded on detection of an opportunity by military men at the planning and implementation stage precluded any intra-institutional deliberations and more importantly, on the merits and demerits of such an expanded operation.'

Surprise and Deception Measures

Some of the measures taken by the Pakistan Army to achieve surprise and deception for the Kargil War were:

The whole plan was based on stealth and deception and kept a closely guarded secret among select commanders and military planners. Other Service Chiefs and Corps Commanders were briefed on a need-to-know basis, mostly after Pakistani troops had infiltrated the LoC.

In the beginning, troops were sent in the garb of the *jehadis* wearing black salwar and kameez.

As a deception measure, deliberate radio transmissions in Balti and Pashto languages were made to convey an impression that it was the *jehadis* who had intruded across the LoC. In fact, there were no *jehadis* on the scene throughout the war.

The deception that the *jehadis* were capturing Indian areas and that the Pakistan Army was not involved became the official line for civil and military spokespersons of the Pakistan Government.

Battalions of the NLI, which were involved up-front, were already located in the northern area. They were fully acclimatised and had good knowledge of the terrain.

Pakistan Army chose the winter season to carry out initial reconnaissance of the area of operations and to establish firm bases. Ammunition and stores for the operation were put in place gradually over months. The bulk of the troops infiltrated in small groups when the snow began to thaw in the upper reaches of the mountains.

The northern areas were placed under army rule to deny access to the media and to facilitate optimal exploitation of local resources.

India's Intelligence and Surveillance Failures

In India, none of the assessments by the JIC, RAW, or NSCS had given any indications that the Pakistan Army was preparing for an intrusion or attack by infiltration. The focus of all intelligence reports and assessments was on the ongoing militancy. Some IB reports indicated that additional groups of *jehadis* were being trained with a view of infiltrating them across the LoC. But these reports were not area specific. The intelligence reports also indicated an enhanced level of artillery fire exchanges in Kargil in the forthcoming summer. The possibility of a conventional conflict with the Pakistan Army was consistently negated though. All inputs and assessments reflected a lack of preparedness on Pakistan's part for a direct military conflict.

The *Kargil Review Committee Report* has stated, 'The Committee had overwhelming evidence that the Pakistani armed intrusion in the Kargil sector came as a complete and total surprise to the Indian Government, army, and intelligence agencies as well to the J&K State Government and its agencies. No agency or individual had been able to realise before the event the possibility of such a large-scale Pakistani intrusion.'

The military intelligence agencies at brigade, division, and corps levels spent considerable time and resources to accomplish militancy-oriented intelligence missions. In 3 Inf Div, incidents reported in different brigade sectors were neither linked together nor properly assessed. Most of the newly-created intelligence teams remained obsessed with staff work and tended to neglect the fieldwork. Formation and unit commanders did not maintain close contact with the civil population to obtain a ground-level feel in their areas of responsibility. In some cases, there was a 'strained relationship' between the locals and the men in uniform.

By May 1999, four Pakistan NLI battalions with additional troops had infiltrated across the LoC. Tactical intelligence should have picked up some tell-tale signs. The brigade, division, corps, or command had not been able to obtain any such intelligence and, thus, prepare for any assessment anticipating the events that followed.

Those responsible for safeguarding this sector considered 'that the threat was limited to infiltration of *jehadi* militants along with heavy firing to interdict the road'. Attack by infiltration, a usual tactical technique in mountain warfare, had not been considered. As late as 19 May 1999, GOC 15 Corps stated to a newspaper, 'A local counter-insurgency operation… *jehadis* in Kargil backed by the Pakistani Army want to revive the defeated proxy war and to internationalise the situation by building up war hysteria… the local situation is to be dealt with locally…. It will be a time-consuming operation for which no specific timetable could be given. Media reports about the use of helicopters, gunships and aircraft by India were not correct. I am hopeful that all groups (of infiltrators) would be eliminated in a few days… they were on a suicidal mission.'

Pakistan Army's Strategic Planning

In Pakistan, when General Pervez Musharraf took over as Army Chief, two policy approaches towards India came into play. The Nawaz Sharif Government opted for diplomacy and dialogue (Lahore Declaration). But Pervez Musharraf and his coterie wanted to intensify proxy war and conflict with India. These Generals had not gotten over the defeat in the 1971 War and the loss of Siachen. Musharraf and his close team started planning to send troops to cross the LoC to pay back in kind to India for Siachen. His team believed that under pressure, India, at the very least, would be forced to give up Siachen.

The decision to go ahead with the operation was based on several factors. Some important ones were:

> Pakistan's security apparatus had received a major boost after the successful nuclear tests.
>
> A section within Pakistan's national security establishment noted the weakening of the insurgency inside J&K and was unhappy with it.
>
> The Pakistan-India dialogue led by the two Prime Ministers was proceeding ahead rapidly. The idea that the civilian leadership should decide to overhaul Pakistan's Kashmir policy worried the Generals. Many senior military officers believed that the Kashmir issue was being omitted from the draft of the Lahore Declaration.
>
> They believed that India and its army did not have the stomach to oppose them and dislodge them from those dizzy heights when occupied by Pakistani troops.

The operation was expanded with the belief that it would result in control of a bigger chunk of the strategic heights across the LoC—the bigger the territory, the more diplomatic and political advantage would accrue to Pakistan during negotiations. India would be under pressure to enter into negotiations for two reasons. One, the Indians would be desperate to end the near siege of NH-1A. Two, the international community had no stomach for military conflict in South Asia and would urgently encourage negotiation. These factors would put Pakistan in an advantageous position at the negotiating table. In addition to preventing another Indian operation from further occupying territory across the LoC, the minimum gain would be India's withdrawal from the Siachen area. The maximum gain would be an Indian commitment to enter into a serious dialogue on Kashmir. Pakistan's military operation would also reinvigorate the Kashmir's political struggle.

Pakistan's planners calculated an incremental Indian response to their operation. Initially, the Indians would only react locally with a limited incursion and build defensive positions along the ingress areas. Later, the Indian Army may also counter-attack using local forces to reclaim the heights, which would be an impossible task. The military planners ruled out an all-out war across the International Border (IB). GHQ, Pakistan Army was certain that with forces tied down in Kashmir, the Indians did not have the force structure to execute an all-out offensive against Pakistan elsewhere.

The Kargil plan was also based on the belief that Indians do not fight. Once Pakistani troops successfully choked the lifeline of the Indian troops based in Leh and Siachen, by interdicting NH-1A and by setting up posts and pickets in the Drass-Kargil sector, the Indian response would not be determined and decisive.

In the minds of the Pakistani military leadership, Delhi's reaction of anger and panic would attract global attention. Due to nuclear overhang, world powers would be forced to seek a quick political settlement. Pakistan would have a distinct advantage; with its troops having cut off the NH-1A and occupied strategic heights. They would then be able to dictate its terms for the settlement of Siachen and the Kashmir issue. In other words, India's military vulnerability in Ladakh would be used to pressurise India to enter into serious negotiations to settle the Kashmir dispute. At the very least, India would be forced to vacate the Siachen area.

The beginnings of the operation lay in a strong hurt due to past military defeats, which made the planners follow unconstitutional practices, institutional indiscipline, faulty linear outlook and maverick ways.

Pakistan adopted the diplomatic and political positions that the Kargil planners had intended – that these are not Pakistani troops but freedom fighters; the LoC is not well-defined, we need to sit down and define it better; our troops are on our side of the LoC; the international community must encourage the Indians to resolve the Kashmir dispute; if the Indians agree on dialogue, we can influence the freedom fighters to vacate Kargil. They were convinced that the global community, especially the USA, would have no tolerance for a confrontation between the two nuclear powers.

Fog of War in India

In Kargil and Siachen Sectors, often there was a frequent exchange of small arms and infrequent artillery shelling. But a physical intrusion by Pakistani personnel into Indian territory was not detected till early May 1999. An intelligence input by a local Tashi Namgyal to the local unit of 121 Inf Bde indicating the presence of some unidentified people wearing black salwar kameez in the higher reaches of the Batalik sector and the subsequent patrol clashes was handled at the formation level and not reported to the Army HQ. The DGMO who visited Kargil on 4–5 May 1999 and GOC-in-C Northern Command who visited HQ 15 Corps on 8 May did not get the impression of Pakistani intrusion in their interaction with formation commanders.

On 12 May, when I was on an official trip abroad, the DGMO informed me that about 100 to 150 *jehadi* militants appeared to have infiltrated Kargil, mostly in the Batalik sector. He said that it was a localised infiltration and HQ 15 Corps was taking action to evict them. On that day, the Defence Minister, GOC-in-C Northern Command, and GOC 15 Corps were visiting Partapur (Shyok Valley), Leh and Kargil. On 15 May, the assessed number of infiltrators was increased to 250–300. On 19 May, the VCOAS visited Srinagar. GOC 15 Corps addressed a press conference in Srinagar. He described the situation as a local counter-insurgency operation. This was 'a local situation to be dealt with locally.' He was hopeful that all the groups of infiltrators would be eliminated in a few days as they were simply on a 'suicidal mission'. Till the end of May, the intelligence agencies assessed that the composition of the intruders was 70 per cent *jehadi* militants backed by some elements of the Pakistan Army. The exact number of intruders, their identity and deployment were not clear. Despite additional troops sent from the Valley, 121 Inf Bde was employing anti-militancy 'rules of engagement' to evict the intruders wherever identified occupying mountain tops.

On return from abroad (20 May), I visited HQ Northern Command and 15 Corps. The briefings and question and answers gave me the following impressions:

> Movement of additional units and sub-units to 121 Inf Bde sector had been done in haste – neither did they have adequate strength nor logistic support. Tasks were given to battalions in an ad hoc manner without adequate planning.

> The intrusion had been deliberately planned and executed. Pakistan Army appeared fully involved. It had taken the initiative and achieved tactical surprise leading to penetration from Mushkoh to SSW (Siachen). There was the need to establish the identity of intruders soonest and to collect information about their precise locations.
>
> Pakistan's political or military objectives were not clear. We needed more information in that context. Meanwhile, the Pakistan Army had to be stopped from making further moves into the Kargil sector or anywhere else.
>
> One division-level effort to evict the intruders from Kargil-Ladakh was not sufficient. We needed to react strategically where our strength lay. It was essential to be prepared for all contingencies which may arise either due to enemy action or to achieve our own objectives.
>
> The CCS had been exercising excessive restraint by denying the use of air power (in the meeting held on 18 May) fearing that the situation would escalate. The situation demanded greater military effort to create a strategic asymmetry on the Indo-Pakistan front and to achieve escalation dominance.

Working on Military Strategy

For any combat situation, we must employ all services optimally in an integrated manner. The allocation of exact missions is a matter of detailed coordination, keeping in view, characteristics and capabilities of the assets available with each service.

Over the next two days, I, with my colleagues in the Chiefs of Staff Committee (COSC), worked on the military strategy to handle the adverse ground situation in Kargil. Although certain that the Pakistan Army was involved in the intrusion, we did not have authentic evidence to indicate the extent of their involvement. The intruders wore the civilian clothes of the *jehadi* militants but conducted themselves as well-trained army personnel. Their count appeared to be in the thousands now. They were well-armed and supported with mortars and artillery. Having occupied dominating heights, they were interfering with our movements not only on the NH-1A but also on the smaller roads and tracks going up to our posts on the LoC. None of our posts on the LoC or in the rear areas had spotted infiltration by the intruders. There had been no encounters on or near the posts.

After I briefed the situation, the COSC took a unanimous decision to work on a joint military strategy, including the use of naval and air power. In working out our military strategy, some relevant questions which we considered were:

> We needed much greater forces in the West to prevent Pakistan from doing any more damage and to undo the present situation.
>
> What political objectives will be given to us? Will the Government be prepared to declare a 'war' and go the whole hog? Will the Cabinet Committee on Security (CCS) allow conflict escalation and induction of the Air Force and Navy?
>
> How will escalation dominance work in Indo-Pak nuclear environment? We were considered a nuclear rogue nation with severe sanctions imposed on us. How will the Government handle international opinion?
>
> Unless political leadership declares a war, how do we achieve large-scale mobilisation without causing alarm in the country and abroad?
>
> How soon could we launch an offensive, if and when permitted?
>
> How would the monsoon climate (June-July) impact our war effort?
>
> We needed to take stock of our inventories; and review urgently our capabilities for defensive as well as offensive operations.

CCS Briefing and Mandate

On 24 May, I briefed the CCS. In my presentation, I informed them about the situation on the ground and my assessment.

The Pakistan Army elements intruded into the areas of Batalik, Kaksar, Dras and Mashkoh with the aim of holding ground permanently to interdict the strategic Srinagar-Kargil highway and the road from Kargil to Leh along the Indus River. They had entrenched themselves at strategic locations along the dominating heights. The intruders were supported by an array of armaments such as artillery, air defence weapons, machine guns and other heavy-calibre weapons. This intrusion could change the alignment of the LoC and affect our movement along these roads. In the Turtuk Sector, the Pakistan Army was attempting to outflank our defences in the SSW by moving up the Mian Lungpa (a gully in the mountains across the LoC) to the Ladakh Range and then rolling down the Turtuk Lungpa. Such movement could render our defences untenable in this area and enable the Pakistanis to capture Turtuk and dominate the road along the Shyok River. There were some reports that Pakistan was planning to initiate insurgency in Turtuk.

Pakistan's political objectives appeared to be to internationalise the Kashmir issue and create a situation that would enable them to negotiate on J&K from a position of strength. From a military viewpoint, their objective appeared to be to:

Cut off the strategic Srinagar-Leh road;

Alter the status of the LoC permanently for strategic and territorial gains;

Divert our attention from anti-terrorist operations in Kashmir Valley;

Revive insurgency in J&K; and

Capture Turtuk and a part of the Siachen Sector.

Our response, so far, had been to ensure that we did not lose any existing post to the intruders, keep the road communications open, and locate, isolate and evict intrusions.

I, then, informed the CCS about the discussions held in the COSC on the previous day. It was necessary, I emphasised, to gain the strategic initiative to facilitate operations of the 15 Corps and Northern Command. We had to be prepared for war escalation, either by Pakistan or by us, and in such a situation, all three services must be prepared and act cohesively.

I sought permission for the use of air power and the deployment of the Navy. (I had been told that, at the political level, the Minister of External Affairs, Jaswant Singh, had opposed the use of air power in the CCS meeting on 18 May. While seeking permission this time, I recall, looking more at him than at the Prime Minister or anyone else. To my surprise and great relief, there was no objection from anyone.) The CCS approved the proposal and asked that the intrusions along the LoC must be cleared at the earliest. Jaswant Singh, however, insisted that our forces should *not* cross the LoC or the international border. The National Security Advisor, Brajesh Mishra, on behalf of the CCS, reiterated this statement as a term of reference.

Although it came as a bit of a surprise, this restraint at this juncture was understandable. Pakistan's political motives were not clear and the identity of the intruders was doubtful. Due to sustained inputs given by all intelligence agencies, and owing to the Pakistani radio deception, no one was in a position to authenticate whether the Pakistan Army was using *jehadi* militants or carrying out the operation by itself.

A war effort at the national level requires a great deal of preparation. A considerable amount of work had to be done on the diplomatic front because only the previous year India and Pakistan had blasted their way out of nuclear ambiguity, thus, upsetting the US and other powers. The nuclear factor must have been weighing on the mind of the Prime Minister and his CCS colleagues.

The CCS had been conveyed an unambiguous picture of the ground realities and the military and political implications. If there were doubts in anyone's mind these were clarified; if there were expectations from Track-2 dialogues, these were dispelled. I wrapped up my briefing by informing the CCS that the Army had codenamed the operation in the Kargil sector as Operation Vijay. We would take all necessary actions to ensure that ultimately *vijay* would be ours.

That night, Prime Minister Vajpayee spoke to Nawaz Sharif. Vajpayee told him that 'we will not allow any intrusion to take place in our territory. We will clear our territory'.

India's Joint Military Strategy

The crux of our military strategy was to adopt an aggressive posture in the air, on the seas, and all along the LoC and International Border to prevent Pakistan from focusing on Kargil only and to maintain the capability to undertake defensive and offensive operations. Why?

Even though we were politically mandated not to cross the border or the LoC, in a dynamic situation like war, one must consider all possible contingencies. In this situation, further escalation of the war could not be ruled out either due to Pakistani action or for us to achieve the given objective. My instructions, therefore, were that our forces should be deployed in such a state of readiness so that at six days' notice we should be able to launch an offensive operation anywhere across the LoC and International Border. This deployment was to be achieved with maximum security and minimum disturbance to normal air, rail and road traffic and other civilian activities along the border.

We decided to abide by the political terms of reference but to keep our military options open and to some extent make them visible to Pakistan. If Pakistan pumped in more troops in the Kargil-Siachen Sector to strengthen its position or took the initiative elsewhere, we would retaliate and cross the LoC or International Border. Also, if we could not evict Pakistan from Kargil by the end of the monsoon season, we should be prepared to cross the International Border in September-October.

Broadly, the military strategy was:

A military posture all along the Western border to prevent Pakistan from reinforcing its forces opposite Kargil.

Threaten and maintain pressure on Pakistan throughout our land, air, and sea borders. Try and create a strategic imbalance for the Pakistani Armed Forces.

Be prepared to launch forces across the border or LoC at short notice.

Retain balance on borders with China and Bangladesh.

Activate an information war effort. Pakistani claims about militants and vague LoC were to be demolished through media and diplomacy.

I, then, visited all formations on the Western border and finalised outline plans of all corps for defensive and offensive missions. Two separate sets of operational instructions were issued for operations in J&K and on the rest of the Western border. I also visited different formations in Kargil and SSW sectors at least once every week.

Telephone Intercept

On 26–27 May, we obtained the most invaluable intelligence: an intercept of a telephonic conversation between the Pakistani CGS (Chief of General Staff), Lieutenant General Muhammad Aziz Khan and his Chief, Pervez Musharraf, who was then in Beijing. After a few days, the CCS decided to send a copy of the tapes on which the telephone conversation had been recorded to Prime Minister Nawaz Sharif.

The Juggernaut Gets Moving

Our military build-up along the Western border went along smoothly. Along with the concerned Army Commanders, I visited every Corps HQ to discuss and lock in their operational plans. Gradually, military operations and operational logistics staff in the Army HQ redeployed the strike and reserve formations and issued instructions for stocking forward logistics bases in accordance with approved operational plans. 108 Inf Bde from the Andaman and Nicobar Islands was brought to the West coast for training and possible amphibious operations.

In the COSC and in the Military Operations Room, we monitored the situation closely, keeping our escalation option open. Although the political term of reference not to cross the LoC or border was clear, my colleagues in the COSC and I never considered it as non-reviewable. We were prepared for all contingencies. Around mid-June, I again warned all Army Commanders to be prepared for escalation—sudden or gradual—along the LoC or International Border and go to full-scale conventional war at short notice.

In the first week of June, Prime Minister Vajpayee made a public statement that India would not cross the International Border or LoC. I raised the issue with him and Brajesh Mishra and requested that our Prime Minister should not make such a statement. When the Prime Minister gave me an enquiring look, I told him that we were following the directions stipulated by the CCS. But suppose we could not throw the intruders out from Kargil, the military would have no alternative except to cross the International Border or LoC. Vajpayee did not respond to my statement. But in the evening, Brajesh Mishra arranged an interview with a TV channel. In the interview, he stated, 'Not crossing the border and the LoC holds good today. But we do not know what may happen tomorrow.'

The middle of June was the most anxious period of the war, possibly the closest when we came to enlarging the conflict area. Bitter fighting was going on in all sub-sectors but we had not won any battle. This was also the period when we felt that the Pakistani Army had started showing some signs of nervousness.

Around this time, Brajesh Mishra informed the US National Security Advisor Sandy Berger that India would not be able to continue with its policy of restraint for long and that our military forces cannot be kept on leash any longer. He added that the Goverment of India may have to let them cross the LoC or International Border any day. According to Brajesh Mishra, the US Administration took this message quite seriously.

Throughout the war, the communications between Prime Ministers and DGMOs remained open. The DGMOs would talk on fixed days every week, and sometimes on additional occasions too. When we pointed out the intrusions, the Pakistani DGMO stated that the LoC in this area was defined vaguely and the Pakistan Army and intruders were on the Pakistani side and not across the LoC. We then faxed him the unambiguously marked LoC on the map which had been signed by Lieutenant General P.S. Bhagat, VC and the Lieutenant General from Pakistan Army. On 15 June, Pakistan's DGMO asked our DGMO as to why India was escalating the situation along the International Border by deploying troops including armour and artillery. He then complained that the Indian Air Force had fired rockets at a Pakistan village in Kel, opposite the Machhal Sector. After some further conversation, he raised the issue of escalation once again and said that both Directors Generals needed to sit down together and analyse the maps pertaining to the LoC and International Border. One could make out that now Pakistan did not want to escalate but defuse the situation. There were repeated suggestions from Pakistan's DGMO to keep the operational activity confined to the LoC. Having started the war, he was now advising us on how to conduct it!

On 20 June, Nawaz Sharif once again stated, 'Kargil is an aspect of [the] Kashmir issue… If the Kashmir issue is not resolved once and for all according to the wishes of the Kashmiri people, many more Kargil-like issues can crop up.' This rhetorical threat and its implications were discussed in the CCS. It was obvious that we had to remain prepared for an escalation. The National Security Council Secretariat (NSCS) staff was asked to prepare an intelligence assessment on Pakistan's intentions and options on top priority.

However, the need to escalate the situation by us got reduced after our forces recaptured Tololing and Point 5140 in the Dras sector. Thereafter, operations in all sectors progressed smoothly and we began achieving steady success. A few days later, Air Chief Anil Tipnis sought permission from the CCS for fighter pilots to cross the LoC to engage the Pakistani logistic base Munthodhalo, which was located very close to the LoC but inside our territory in the Batalik sector. The fighter pilots were facing difficulty in going through their flying circuit within our territory to engage this important target due to its proximity to the LoC. Tipnis' request had been supported in the COSC. But the CCS rejected our request for the fighters to cross the LoC even by a few kilometres.

Movement of Formations: What Did it Involve?

We had a complex situation. Unless the precautionary stage of the War Book is declared and financial powers decentralised, large-scale movements of troops and materials are difficult. Many essential activities for the preparation of the war effort hinge on other ministries; railways, surface transport, petroleum, natural gas, and so on. The preparation process was severely constrained. However, regular CCS meetings enabled us to get over most of the bureaucratic hassles. Movement of combat as well as combat support formations to and within Northern Command were given high priority.

The Navy had issued instructions for an alert even before the CCS meeting held on 24 May. INS *Taragiri* had been deployed on a barrier patrol off the coast of Dwarka. The Navy added two information warfare Dornier aircraft and deployed INS *Veer* and INS *Nirghat* near Okha. Instructions were issued by the Government so that our shipping fleet stood warned. The Navy Chief decided to supplement the Western Naval Fleet with selected units of the Eastern Naval Fleet and moved the latter to the Arabian Sea. This step enabled the Navy to extend the range of its deployment.

Naval staff carried out an analysis of Pakistan's oil vulnerability and planned to interdict Pakistani oil tankers. The naval projection of reach and mobility had an immediate impact. Pakistan started providing escorts to its oil tankers as they moved out from the Gulf to Karachi.

The IAF had been providing aircraft, including Mi-17 helicopter sorties, for airlifting of army troops for redeployment. On 21 May, a Canberra, on a reconnaissance mission, while flying along the LoC, was hit by enemy fire, but it was able to return safely. The IAF responded very quickly after the CCS approved the employment of air power on our side of the LoC. It launched its first close-support air strikes with MiGs and armed Mi-17 helicopters on the morning of 26 May.

Sartaj Aziz's Visit

Soon after 24 May, diplomatic pressure from Pakistan and the international community had been building on India and Pakistan to discuss this issue bilaterally. Initially, Nawaz Sharif suggested that air strikes (within our own country) be stopped as a precondition for talks. When this suggestion was rejected by India, he offered to send Foreign Minister Sartaj Aziz to New Delhi. The Government accepted this offer. But this was worrisome for me. If attempts to seek a diplomatic solution at this point resulted in a militarily disadvantageous position, it would lead to humiliation as had happened in 1962. Till then, we had not been able to recapture any tactically significant area in the Kargil sector. On 5 June, while returning from HQ Northern Command, I decided to address the Army through a special log.

> Log number 198/05 June 99/MO3 (.)
> From COAS to all ranks (.)
>
> Firstly (.) the enemy has violated the Line of Control in the 3 Infantry Division Sector in the area Batalik to Dras and made some intrusions into our territory with a strategic and political aim (.) in the last few days, our troops, some of whom had to be inducted from outside this sector, have managed to stall the enemy's operations thus denying him the fulfilment of his mission (.) we have succeeded not only in containing the enemy but also in pushing him back from his original forward positions (.) hard battles are being fought all along in the Kargil sector (.)
>
> Secondly (.) this intrusion by the enemy has thrown a big challenge before us (.) we have a very clear and precise task and that is to get our territory vacated and liquidate the intrusion (.)
>
> Thirdly (.) while our operational plans are being put into action and preparations are afoot, the Ministry of External Affairs is having a diplomatic dialogue with Pakistan (.) This process, however, should not distract us from our mission (.) our challenge clearly remains to rid our land of intruders (.)

> this mission has to be accomplished with all the resolve and fortitude at your command (.)
>
> Fourthly (.) May God be with you!

On 7 June, the Prime Minister addressed the nation and said:

> I do want to make it plain: if the stratagem now is that the intrusion should be used to alter the Line of Control through talks, the proposed talks will end before they have begun... Have confidence in the ability of our Armed Forces. The Armed Forces shall accomplish this task and ensure that no one dares to indulge in this kind of misadventure in future.

The Situation in July 1999

Nawaz Sharif visited China to obtain support for a cease fire. Later, prompted by Musharraf, he met US President Clinton in Washington, D.C. on 4 July. That morning, Tiger Hill had been captured before their meeting was held. Nawaz Sharif requested Clinton to intervene or persuade India to ceasefire. Pakistan accepted the inviolability of LoC and agreed with Clinton's advice to pull back troops from the remaining areas on our side. Our operations, however, continued. By 10 July, Pakistanis had been evicted from most of Batalik and Ras, and some areas of Kaksar. In Mushkoh, 50 Para Bde was poised for mopping up.

Vice Admiral Khattak (Retd) of the Pakistan Navy in his paper *Investigating Kargil* has written, 'During much of the eight weeks preceding the 4 July meeting in Washington, we had looked helplessly at TV images of pinpoint artillery shoots and resultant instant pulverisation of some of the nation's bravest sons on a such mountainous salient in the war zone as Point 5140 (Dras), Point 5203 (Batalik), Three Pimples (Dras) and Tiger Hill.'

On 10 July, after day-long discussions with Prime Minister, we agreed to allow Pakistani troops to withdraw, if they accepted our plan of withdrawal. At Pakistan PM's request, a meeting of the DGMOs was arranged at Attari on 11 July. Pakistani DGMO was given proof of his Army's total employment in the intrusion and shown captured documents and marked maps. Pakistani DGMO agreed to withdraw troops from the remaining areas as per the plan given by us. Their withdrawal commenced on 14 July. However, three enemy pockets close to LoC were not vacated as per the given plan. These positions were attacked and captured between 23–25 July. On 26 July, we informed the CCS (and the public) that the task given to the Armed Forces had been achieved.

Strategic Lessons

Kargil war broke out within two months of the Prime Ministers of India and Pakistan signing the Lahore Declaration with much fanfare. It proved Admiral J.C. Wylie's first basic assumption in his paper *Military Strategy: A General Theory of Power* that 'despite whatever effort there may be to prevent it, there may be a war'. Military history tells us that nations who neglect this historical fact make themselves vulnerable to military surprise and defeat. This assumption, therefore, is a reminder to politicians and strategists to visualise security threats, the possibility and nature of conflict, and to always remain prepared.

Another basic assumption for war planning is that we cannot predict with certainty the pattern of war for which we prepare ourselves. It has seldom been possible to forecast the time, place, scope, intensity, or the general tenor of a conflict. This assumption implies that our security plans should cater to the complete spectrum of conflict. Our military strategies and doctrines, therefore, must be flexible and capable of application in any unforeseen circumstances. As military history very often tells us, planning for uncertainty is less dangerous than planning for certitude!

Other important lessons were:

> There may be remote chances of a full-scale conventional war between two nuclear weapon states, but if there are territory-related disputes—currently we have them with China and Pakistan—the adversary can indulge in a proxy war, a limited border war, or both. A proxy war, too, can lead to a limited war.
>
> A major military challenge in India is the political reluctance to a proactive grand strategy or engagement. This disadvantage is enhanced manifold because no loss of territory is acceptable to the public and the political authority. This is a strategic handicap and a risk in any war setting, which increases in a limited war scenario. It is, therefore, essential to have credible strategic and tactical intelligence and assessments,

and effective surveillance. For commanders, it often leads to a temptation to deploy more forces along the border or the LoC at the cost of reserves.

Information operations are important due to the much greater transparency of the battlefield. A military operation requires moral high ground. The adversary must be exposed and denied any moral justification. This needs a comprehensive media and information strategy.

The successful outcome of a border war depends upon our ability to react rapidly.

The new strategic environment calls for faster decision-making, versatile combat organisations, rapid deployment and synergy amongst all elements involved in the war effort, particularly the three services.

A proactive grand strategy and capability to wage a successful conventional and nuclear war is a credible deterrent. A conventional war may remain limited because of credible deterrence or escalation dominance—when one side has overwhelming military superiority at every level. Such deterrence may prevent war; it gives more room for manoeuvre in diplomacy and conflict.

Any war in the future will require close political oversight and politico-civil-military interaction. It is, therefore, essential to keep the military leadership in the security and strategic decision-making loop.

Conclusion

The Kargil War set yet another example of informed and enlightened cooperation between the politicians, civil services and the Armed Forces, backed by public support. It constituted a unique example of a security and strategic exercise by India.

My focus in this chapter has been on strategic planning and implementation. It needs to be remembered, however, that tactical actions and the implementation of operational plans are more important than strategic planning. The test of any plan is how it ends, never how it begins. Most of the credit for victory in Kargil, quite deservedly, goes to the bravery and dedication shown on the battlefield by soldiers and young officers. They were upfront, not hesitating to make any sacrifice to uphold the regimental and national pride, and dignity. Based on great determination, high morale, and brilliant junior leadership, our troops performed superbly.

It was not the first time that Pakistan had initiated a war, and we cannot assume that it would be the last. Every good military would like to be proactive. However, it also has to develop the will and capability to react. The essence of military leadership lies in the way we react to restore a situation, howsoever adverse the circumstances of the battle.

General V.P. Malik, PVSM, AVSM, was commissioned into the Sikh LI Regiment and rose to be the Indian Army's 19th COAS. He has vast experience of, among other things, commanding an Infantry Brigade in J&K, a Mountain Division, a Corps in Punjab, and the Southern Army. Subsequently, General Malik served as the Vice Chief, COAS, and the Chairman of the COSC. He was instrumental in guiding the Indian Army to victory in the Kargil War against Pakistan in 1999. A well-respected author of several books and articles on military subjects, he has been acknowledged by several academic and civil society awards for excellence in leadership.

2

Evolution of Naval Strategy and the Geostrategic Importance of IOR

Admiral Sunil Lanba

The vital feature which differentiates the Indian Ocean from the Atlantic or the Pacific is the subcontinent of India which juts out far into the sea for a thousand miles. It is the geographical position of India that changes the character of the Indian Ocean.

–K.M. Pannikar

India is a country with a rich maritime tradition spanning over 4,000 years. The Indian seaboard has always witnessed peaceful maritime activity with trade as the prime driver. Indian folklore, ancient Indian texts, and Buddhist *Jatakas*, all allude to the fact that the Indus Valley Civilization of Mohenjodaro, Lothal, and Harappa thrived due to maritime activity between ancient India and the countries of Africa, Arabia, Mesopotamia, and the Mediterranean. Trade and navigation, both oceanic and riverine, grew significantly in the fourth century BCE. Indian cultural and religious interplay was naturally intertwined with trade. Accompanying traders, Buddhist and Hindu philosophers travelled to Southeast Asia and the resultant cultural and religious integration gave a distinct Indian flavour to the region. The ensuing period of Indian history witnessed significant maritime activity in the form of trade, naval expeditions, and pilgrimage (*Haj*) which is illustrative of sound navigational techniques.[1]

The landing of Vasco da Gama at Calicut in 1498 was followed by the introduction of a new dimension of maritime power to India—the military component. The Portuguese were followed in quick succession by the Dutch, British, and French, who rode into Indian waters on the back of blue water naval capability. Between the sixteenth and eighteenth centuries, extra-regional naval forces were challenged by the brown water coastal navies of Indian kingdoms. During the colonial period, however, Indian kingdoms focused a greater part of their energies on land. India's preoccupation with a continental strategy also led to its failure to develop new shipbuilding and other nautical technologies for long-legged ocean transit by naval ships and warfighting. The lessons of ignoring the ability to control the seas around India are, thus, embedded in the colonisation of India and three centuries of European, mostly British, rule. Post independence, India has attempted to regain its maritime moorings. With its rapidly increasing dependence on the seas for its economic and social well-being, it is now laying adequate emphasis on developing commensurate maritime-military power.[2]

Importance of IOR

The Indian Ocean is the third largest ocean in the world, and the nations along its periphery and hinterland account for over 35 per cent of the global population.[3] These are some of the fastest-growing economies in the world. The economic centre of gravity is shifting back to Asia[4] and with young population, significant untapped reserves, growing domestic demand and growing regional cooperation, economic growth in the Indian Ocean Region (IOR) is set to increase exponentially. Countries of the IOR are emerging as significant drivers of global economic growth in the years ahead.

Additionally, the region's hydrocarbon energy reserves have fuelled global growth for decades and even today, two-thirds of all global oil shipments traverse through the Indian Ocean.[5] Furthermore, the international sea lanes of the region are also transited by half the world's container traffic and one-thirds of bulk cargo shipments. It is pertinent that almost three-quarters of the traffic passing through the Indian Ocean is headed for destinations outside the region.[6]

What sets the Indian Ocean apart from the other oceans is that it is bordered by land on three sides. Consequently, access to these waters is through a limited number of narrow passages, which have acquired the telling name of 'choke-points,' and are viewed as a source of potential vulnerability by many. These include vital international waterways like the Straits of Hormuz and Malacca, which if disrupted, could trigger cascading effects on the global economy. Consequently, keeping all parts of the Indian Ocean safe, secure, and open for international maritime activity is imperative for countries across the globe. While this objective is well-defined and shared by most countries in the region, several challenges must be addressed.

Emerging Challenges in the Maritime Domain

Most challenges of the world stem from the uncertainty that arises from a global order that is rapidly undergoing transition. To put it simply, for decades during the Cold War, there was a bipolar world which became unipolar after the collapse of the Soviet Union. We are now witnessing a shift towards a multi-polar world, with the responsibility for global security and prosperity being shared among a wider group of nations spread across the world.

Consequently, there has been a return of interstate rivalry as a predominant aspect of international affairs. As this rivalry has intensified, it has triggered a competitive action-reaction chain in a wide range of sectors. Assertive actions to gain strategic advantage by China and the need to find new ways to sustain economic growth have led to an increasingly transactional nature of inter-state interactions. Traditional considerations are regularly being overlooked in favour of meeting these objectives. Consequently, we have had many disruptive events in international relations which have undermined long-standing arrangements as well as given shape to new ones.

The IOR has also witnessed a growing competition among countries, both regional and extra-regional, to establish and expand their footprint across the region. While such competition, expectedly, encompasses all aspects of national power—diplomatic, economic, information, and military—the way these have been integrated and wielded has been a cause for concern.

Like any other part of the world, the IOR, too, has a number of traditional fault lines based on historical, political, cultural, ethnic, and economic issues. While nations in the region have, to a large extent, limited the fallout from these differences, there is a growing tendency of some parties with vested interests to exploit these issues to promote their agenda. This has resulted in a further strain on the region's stability and given rise to pockets of potential volatility.

Although these issues originate on land, they invariably spill over into the maritime domain. In the Indian Ocean itself, we have seen how governance issues in Somalia led to a rise in maritime piracy—the effects of which were felt globally. Maritime nations across the world have responded by stepping up their military presence in the region, and over 60 ships from extra-regional navies operate in the IOR around the year.[7] While most nations are working in coordination to overcome common challenges to security, China has taken this as an opportunity to increase its military footprint in the region. The establishment of military bases, dual-use infrastructure as well as the deployment of permanent forces could have serious ramifications on the regional security paradigm.

Another challenge emerges from the rapid pace of technological evolution, particularly, in the security domain. New technologies have enabled a wide proliferation of precision weapons as well as weapons of mass destruction (WMD).[8] Non-state and irregular actors are capable of causing damage at an unprecedented scale through the use of cyberspace, commercially available unmanned platforms, and malicious information campaigns to name a few. The challenges from Artificial Intelligence-based systems are another issue of vital importance which will become increasingly important in the future.

An associated domain that is evolving very rapidly is information—particularly its access and dissemination aspects. Individuals across the world are deeply interconnected today, and large-scale, real-time information sharing is possible across geographical divisions to an extent that is unprecedented in human history. It is, therefore, a reality today that war in the information domain is perennial and in the absence of internationally implementable regulatory frameworks, only likely to expand.

Adherence to International Law and respect for the various mechanisms established to enforce these laws has come under pressure in the past decade. It is the shared duty of all responsible nations to uphold these constructs and abide by them to ensure peace, inclusive growth, and widespread prosperity.

In addition to these traditional challenges, which concern interactions between states, there are also a number of non-traditional threats in the maritime domain. The gravest among these is, undoubtedly, terrorism. Maritime piracy continues to be a threat to shipping in some regions of the IOR and many maritime security forces are participating in efforts to counter it. Although the threat has diminished, there is the possibility of a resurgence due to ongoing unrest in the Horn of Africa. With the effects of climate change on the oceans becoming more pronounced, there are several challenges which need to be addressed in the coming decade. Severe weather events are likely to intensify and become more frequent. Low-lying and coastal areas will be affected by rising sea levels, which is a serious concern as approximately 50 per cent of the global population lives in the coastal region.[9] Lastly, Illegal Unreported and Unregulate (IUU) fishing continues to affect the region, particularly in countries which have limited capability to secure their maritime zones.

Successfully addressing this wide range of threats and challenges requires a very high degree of situational awareness, and readiness to respond to any contingency across the spectrum of maritime operations.

India's Approach and IN Strategy

India, due to its geographical centrality within the IOR as well as its traditional role as the region's security provider, has shouldered the responsibility for enhancing maritime security across the region. Our national commitment to this mission is encapsulated in the Prime Minister's vision of Security and Growth for All in the Region (SAGAR), which demonstrates our belief that the seas are the medium through which this can be best achieved. Efforts of the Indian Government towards realising this vision are guided by the 'Neighbourhood First' and 'Act East' policies. Cooperative arrangements based on mutual interests, shared ownership and long-term sustainability form the mainstays of all our international efforts. India seeks a cooperative solution to common and shared challenges.[10]

As India moves forward in the twenty-first century, its development and prosperity will remain closely linked to the maritime domain. History bears out the role and contribution of maritime power in the growth and prosperity of great nations. The effective exercise of maritime power and employment of its primary instruments, especially the Navy and Coast Guard, requires an overarching strategy for achieving the maritime strategic goals.

Development of Strategic Maritime Thought

The first important paper about Indian strategy in the IOR was, *The Naval Plan 1948,* which was an analysis of India's strategic location in the Indian Ocean and the force level required to secure India's maritime interest. This is a classified document which had the foresight to lay out the force structure of the Navy. In the 1980s, there was a need felt to have a document which included a broader policy and plan which led to the publication of another classified document, *The Maritime Military Strategy*. The decade of the 1990s saw a greater thrust and support for conceptual thinking and doctrine development. A Doctrine Study Group was formed in 1996 which was tasked to articulate a Maritime Doctrine. The first *Indian Maritime Doctrine* was published in 2004—an unclassified document which was published as a book of reference and made available to Naval officers and select members of the Government and the public. This document aimed to provide a book, which advocated a common vocabulary, and a uniform understanding of maritime concepts applicable to the IN.[11] In 2006, the Navy published *The Strategic Guidance for Transformation* which provided a roadmap for the future Navy. In 2007, the Navy published its first unclassified maritime strategy in a document called the *Freedom to Use the Seas: India's Maritime Military Strategy.* It emphasised the growing importance of the maritime environment, and the centrality of maritime security for national development. It provided insight and rationale for the resurgence of Indian maritime power and postulated a strategy underpinned by 'freedom to use the seas for our national purposes, under all circumstances,' with a central role for the Navy. The strategy brought out the various ways in which the Indian Navy could serve as a catalyst for peace, security and stability in the IOR.[12]

The above maritime strategy document provided long-term direction and guidance to the IN in a dynamic environment for over a decade. The last decade witnessed India's dependence on its maritime environment expanding substantially as its economic, military, and technological strength grew, its global interactions widened and its national security imperatives and political interests stretched to the Indo-Pacific region. There seems little doubt today that the twenty-first century will be the 'Century of the Seas' for India and that the seas will remain a key enabler in its global resurgence. The IN today remains the principal manifestation of India's maritime power and plays a central role in safeguarding and promoting its security and national interests in the maritime domain. The Navy's roles and responsibilities have also expanded significantly over the years in response to changing geoeconomic and geostrategic circumstances. *The Indian Maritime Doctrine*, promulgated in 2004 and revised in 2009, and the *Freedom to Use the Seas: India's Maritime Military Strategy,* articulated the Navy's maritime strategic outlook, defined the parameters of its employment, and provided overarching guidance for its evolution as a combat force. The two documents served their role well.

Considering the changing geostrategic environment and changes in the strategic imperatives, in 2015, a revised document, *Ensuring Secure Seas: Indian Maritime Security Strategy,* was published.[13]

The overarching strategy enunciated in the *Indian Maritime Security Strategy* 2015 consists of five foundational strategies—Strategy for Deterrence, Strategy for Conflict, Strategy for Shaping a Favourable and Positive Maritime Environment, Strategy for Coastal and Offshore Security, and Strategy for Maritime Force and Capability Development.[14]

The fundamental pillar of our 'Strategy for Deterrence' is, of course, high preparedness for conflict, the core of which is:

> To prevent conflict and coercion, the Navy is committed towards deterrence by strengthening its capabilities, readiness posture and communication to resolve, and the intention to make conflict unviable for the adversary in economic, military and political terms.
>
> To achieve this credible deterrence by maintaining adequate force levels, sustained presence in our areas of maritime interest and maintaining a very high degree of preparedness through regular training, quality maintenance, and strategic situational awareness.

The 'Strategy for Conflict' is based on the ability to undertake swift and decisive maritime military operations in complete synergy with our Army and Air Force, as well as other arms of the Government. This entails the directed and efficient application of force to enable early termination of conflict on terms favourable to India. To achieve such an outcome a high tempo of operations has to be achieved.

Actions taken to ensure the physical security of coastal and offshore assets are guided by the 'Strategy for Coastal and Offshore Defence'. The IN works in close coordination with the Indian Coast Guard, Central Ministries and agencies, State Governments, port authorities, coastal communities and several other stakeholders to ensure security in waters close to our coast and the island territories.

To address common challenges faced by nations in the region, the IN has adopted a cooperative approach guided by the 'Strategy for Shaping a Favourable and Positive Maritime Environment'. These efforts are closely aligned with our foreign policy as well as the overarching vision of SAGAR. Joint maritime exercises form the principal means of engagement between the navies at the operational level. The IN has actively engaged various regional and extra-regional countries and conducted bilateral as well as multilateral exercises to improve interoperability. The experience accrued from such interactions, as well as the mutual understanding achieved, is invaluable in promoting an environment of trust and transparency among like-minded maritime forces. It also yields a high degree of interoperability, which will allow more effective coordination, when faced with common threats or challenges.

Since 2017, the Navy has been maintaining a near-continuous presence of mission-ready task forces in some vital areas of our maritime neighbourhood. This presence and readiness have enabled rapid response to emerging contingencies. This has been aptly demonstrated in relief efforts in recent times, where the Indian Navy responded promptly and effectively to several emergencies across the IOR. A prime example is the availability of a ship to repatriate our citizens from Sudan. India and the Navy have established a reputation as the first responder in the region in times of need. Our active participation in anti-piracy operations off the Horn of Africa in coordination with all other navies deployed in the region was instrumental in mitigating the threat. We also deploy assets to patrol the waters of the Maldives, Seychelles, and Mauritius, based on their request, and undertake Coordinated Patrols (CORPATs) with Bangladesh, Myanmar, Thailand, Bangladesh, and Indonesia in the Bay of Bengal, which have helped secure these regions against a range of common maritime security threats.

In keeping with the vision of SAGAR, the Navy has also helped in capacity building and capability enhancement for a large number of IOR littorals so that they can look after their own Exclusive Economic Zones (EEZs) adequately and also contribute towards the larger regional aim of preserving peace and stability. Our outreach to maritime friends is not limited to hardware assistance but also covers training, technical support, hydrography and several other domain-specific areas. One such domain is shared situational awareness which is the prerequisite for ensuring maritime security. To effectively integrate our resources, India has operationalised merchant shipping information agreements with over 20 countries. In addition, the IN supports various multilateral initiatives such as the Indian Ocean Naval Symposium (IONS).

'Strategy for Maritime Force and Capability Development' describes the ways to develop and maintain a combat-ready, technology-driven, network-enabled navy, capable of meeting India's maritime security needs into the future. The Capability Development covers conceptual, human resource and force-level aspects. The major thrust areas for Force Development have been defined with a focus on indigenisation, Maritime Domain Awareness (MDA), Network-Centric Operations (NCO), force projection and protection, maintenance and logistics, and new technologies.[15]

Naval Strategy in 1965 and 1971 Wars

In the 1965 War, the Government wanted to limit the extent of the war to the restoration of the status quo in Kashmir. Despite the attack by Pakistan in September 1965, a war was not declared by the Government. During the planning stage, no role was envisaged for the Navy. On commencement of hostilities, the MoD issued directives to the Navy that 'the Navy is not to operate north of the latitude of Porbandar and is also not to take or initiate offensive action at sea against Pakistan unless forced to do so by offensive action by Pakistani forces'.

In the 1971 Bangladesh War, the leadership of the Navy planned to exploit the full gambit of maritime capability. In New Delhi, joint war plans were made and a combined Operational Directive was issued to the three Service Headquarters by the COSC. At the Naval Headquarters, the plan for the Arabian Sea (Western Theatre) and the Bay of Bengal (Eastern Theatre) was drawn up and Operational Directives were issued by the CNS to the C-in-Cs.

The Operational Directives issued to the Eastern Command were to destroy enemy forces and shipping, strike enemy ports and bases and, where possible, provide support to ground forces, deny access to East Bengal to ships of all nations by contraband control, and blockade when ordered, and secure own ports and bases, including the Andaman and Nicobar Islands. Whilst the main thrust of the Western Naval Command was to engage and destroy as many Pakistani main naval units as possible, the second and complementary aim was to attack Karachi and carry out bombardment of Gwadar, Pasni, and along the coast, up to Karachi, and also to blockade Karachi to prevent petroleum and other essential supplies needed for war from reaching there.

In the west, attacks on naval units and harbour installations were launched by missile boats (Osa Class of Soviet origin). Being designed for harbour defence, they had limited endurance, so the Navy conceived of a novel plan of towing them and letting them loose south of Karachi. Two attacks were carried out on the night of 4–5 December and 7–8 December. The first attack led to the sinking of the destroyer PNS *Khaiber*, the minesweeper *Muhafiz*, and a merchant ship. The second attack damaged the tanker *Dacca*, sank a merchant ship, and set ablaze the Karachi fuel tank farm. These attacks succeeded in bottling up the Pakistani Navy, as well as merchant ships seeking safe passage from India, in the Karachi harbour.

In the east, INS *Vikrant's* air wing of Sea Hawk jet fighters and Alize ASW aircraft attacked airfields, ports, merchant shipping, and riverine traffic. Along with other units, East Pakistan was cut off from supplies from the sea and seaward escape routes for Pakistani forces were blocked, which hastened their surrender. The Navy also mounted covert operations in East Pakistan. Over 400 Mukti Bahini volunteers were trained in diving, combat swimming, demolition and sabotage. Indian and Mukti Bahini naval commandos destroyed nearly 1,00,000 tons of shipping in ports and rivers, leaving Pakistan short of riverine transport to support operation, movement and logistics.

The important spin-off of the 1971 War was that the maritime world accepted India's naval predominance in the Arabian Sea and Bay of Bengal. Also, this served as a realisation for the Government of the effectiveness of sea power and the relevance of a navy. The war in the Eastern Theatre emphatically underlined the importance of carrier-borne air power for a blue-water navy. This initiated a political commitment and support for the Navy's growth.

Conclusion

The last two decades have seen major changes in the global geostrategic and security environment, the contours of which continue to change. The present international security scenario is in a state of flux and is likely to remain characterised by uncertainty and ambiguity in the coming decade. The centre of gravity and focus of activity is shifting from the West towards Indo-Pacific. India has also undergone significant changes. India would need to maintain an external environment that is friendly, with due security and safety for its citizens to freely pursue national and individual development, and growth. The basic attributes and characteristics of warships enable multiple roles and objectives for the IN, ranging across military, diplomatic, constabulary, and benign. The IN would have to prepare itself for increased effort and ability in discharging these roles. The core role of the Navy, however, will be its military function. The Navy's policies, tactics and strategies would need to evolve to meet the growing challenge.

Admiral Sunil Lanba, PVSM, AVSM, rose to be the 23rd Chief of the Naval Staff of the Indian Navy. Graduating from the DSSC, CDM and Royal College of Defence Studies, UK, Admiral Lanba has a distinguished record on frigates, destroyers, aircraft carrier, and in training establishments—imparting skills, and laying down coastal security frameworks. He has been the Commandant of the tri-service NDC, FOC-in-C of the Southern as well as the Western Fleet and the Chairman of the COSC. He has been the Chairman of the National Maritime Foundation and has been conferred the Meritorious Military Service Medal by the Government of Singapore for enhancing bilateral defence relationship between the two Navies. A thinker on training, operational, and international military diplomacy, Admiral Lanba continues to contribute ideas on naval strategy at various fora such as military literature festivals, think tank panel discussions and seminars.

Endnotes

1. Indian Maritime Doctrine 2009 available at https://www.indiannavy.nic.in/sites/default/files/Indian-Maritime-Doctrine-2009-Updated-12Feb16.pdf
2. Ibid.
3. IOR population is around 3 billion and global population is 7.7 billion –38 per cent approximately.
4. The Economist. "The World's Shifting Centre of Gravity." *The Economist*, 28 June 2012, https://www.economist.com/graphic-detail/2012/06/28/the-worlds-shifting-centre-of-gravity.
5. Minister, External Affairs. Remarks by External Affairs Minister. https://www.mea.gov.in/Speeches-Statements.htm?dtl/30327/Remarks_by_External_Affairs_Minister_at_the_3rd_Indian_Ocean_Conference_Vietnam_August_27_2018. 3rd Indian Ocean Conference.
6. Ibid.

7. Remarks by Chief of Naval Staff at Navy Day press conference 3 December 2022 New Delhi available at https://www.the statemen.com.
8. *Global Strategic Trends: The Future Starts Today.* 6th ed., Ministry of Defence UK, 2018, https://assets.publishing.service.gov.uk/government/uploads/system/uploads/attachment_data/file/1075981/GST_the_future_starts_today.pdf.
9. Ibid.
10. Modi, Narendra. *Creating a Shared Future in a Fractured World.* https://pib.gov.in/PressReleasePage.aspx?PRID=1517596. World Economic Forum.
11. Promulgation Page, *Indian Maritime Doctrine,* Integrated Headquarters Ministry of Defence (Navy) 2004.
12. *Freedom to Use the Seas: India's Maritime Military Strategy,* Integrated Headquarters Ministry of Defence (Navy).
13. Page 8, *Ensuring Secure Seas: Indian Maritime Security Strategy An Overview,* October 2015, Integrated Headquarters Ministry of Defence (Navy).
14. *Ensuring Secure Seas: Indian Maritime Security Strategy* (IMSS 2015), Integrated Headquarters, Ministry of Defence (Navy) New Delhi, October 2015, p. 1 available at https://www.indiannavy.nic.in/sites/default/files/Indian_Maritime_Security_Strategy_Document_25Jan16.pdf
15. Ibid

3

Indian Air Force Strategies: Past, Present, and Future

Air Marshal Anil Khosla

The art of winning a war can be learnt by understanding some rules (Strategies) and then applying them in a practical manner.

—Chanakya and the Art of War

Aerospace power is a decisive factor and a game-changer in the current context of geostrategic uncertainties. Although it looks simple, the application of aerospace power is a complex process. Major roles of aerospace power during war include shaping the environment, offensive force application, and synergising the operations with surface forces. Aerospace power also plays a pivotal role during peace and transition from peace to war.

Military Strategy refers to the art and science of planning and directing military operations and campaigns. It involves the development of plans and tactics for the use of military force in achieving specific objectives, whether in a single battle or a larger campaign. Military Strategy is based on the analysis of the strengths and weaknesses of both—one's own forces, and those of the enemy, as well as the political and social context of the conflict. Military Strategy typically involves several components including objectives, force structure, deployment, logistics, tactics, intelligence, communications, risk assessment, etc. Effective Military Strategy requires careful planning and execution, as well as flexibility and adaptation based on changing circumstances. Successful military leaders must be able to think creatively, make quick decisions under pressure, and inspire and motivate their troops to achieve their objectives.

Air Warfare Strategy, a subset of Military Strategy, is the art of planning and directing overall air operations. It depends on several factors. Effective Air Strategy requires careful consideration of these factors and needs to adapt to changing circumstances and situations.

The Air Strategy of the IAF has evolved, reflecting changes in strategic priorities, operational environment, doctrine and technology. While it is worthwhile to trace the evolutionary process of the past, it is also valuable to look at the ones to deal with existing challenges and suggest some future strategies.

Air Strategies and Influencing Factors

> *Strategy is a broad concept that embraces objectives, resources and a plan for using those resources to achieve the objective.*
>
> *—William P. Snyder*

Air Strategy is the process of coordinating the development, deployment, and employment of aerospace power assets to achieve national security objectives. It flows through the joint military strategy and is laterally interlinked with the land and maritime strategies. Air Strategy should cover and must be specific to the entire spectrum of war, No War No Peace (NWNP), and peace. Air Warfare Strategy typically involves conceptualisation and articulation of several key campaigns focussed on effectively and efficiently achieving stated military objectives and could include offensive counter-air to achieve the desired degree of control of the air, defensive counter-air for protection, strategic air operations, force application to shape the battlefield, Intelligence, Surveillance, and Reconnaissance (ISR), Electronic Warfare (EW), etc. Effective Air Warfare Strategy requires the integration of these components into a cohesive plan that can be executed efficiently and effectively. Air Warfare Strategy also requires careful consideration of the risks involved, including the possibility of collateral damage and the potential for escalation of the conflict besides imponderables like weather.

Aerospace power could be applied to deter, deny, coerce, or punish during NWNP situations. The strategies employed would be for external or internal security operations, shaping the zone of operation, and information dominance to improve situational awareness, and command and control. The peacetime strategy of aerospace power deals essentially with sovereignty protection, deterrence, air diplomacy, and nation-building by assisting the Government and other agencies during Humanitarian Assistance and Disaster Relief (HADR) situations.

Factors Influencing Air Strategy

Several factors dictate Air Strategy. Effective Air Strategy requires careful consideration of these factors, as well as the ability to adapt to changing circumstances, to take advantage of new opportunities as they arise. These factors include:

Political Considerations: Political factors, such as the potential impact on civilians, international relations, and public opinion can also influence Air Strategy.

Military Objectives: The overall objectives of the military campaign or operation will determine the specific tasks that air power needs to accomplish.

Capability Comparison: Relative capability comparison between the warring sides including doctrinal precepts, the quantum and quality of equipment, technological disparity, infrastructure, and human resource dictate the scope and nature of the air campaign.

Geographic Factors: The terrain, weather conditions, and other geographic factors can impact the effectiveness of air operations, such as visibility, range, and access to targets and form a part of Air Strategy deliberations.

Evolution of IAF Strategies

Historic Perspective

Like the role of air power in the last century, the air strategy of the IAF has evolved, reflecting changes in technology, doctrine, and strategic priorities. Some key milestones in the evolution of the air strategy of the IAF are given in the succeeding paragraphs.

Genesis and Early Years: The IAF was established in British India as an Auxiliary Air Force of the Royal Air Force on 8 October 1932, with four Westland Wapiti biplanes and five Indian pilots. The then Royal Indian Air Force (RIAF) grew during the WWII to, eventually, ten squadrons. In the early years of the IAF, the primary focus was on providing air support to British and Commonwealth ground forces. During WWII, the IAF played a significant role in the Burma campaign by halting the advance of the Japanese army by providing air cover and support for ground troops. IAF evolved, initially, in a tactical role, primarily to support surface and maritime wars.

Partition in 1947: The IAF of independent India came into being with seven squadrons (six fighter squadrons and one transport squadron). By then, it had a well-established professional ethos and a reputation to live up to.

The Indo-Pakistan War of 1947: Almost immediately after Independence, India and Pakistan clashed over the future of Kashmir. On the first day itself, on 27 October 1947, an infantry battalion was airlifted from Delhi to Srinagar. The IAF, thereafter, carried out air operations (airlift of troops and supplies, photo-reconnaissance, bombing, strafing, and interdiction), in support of surface forces. The air power usage was tactical and reactionary to emerging situations.

Initial Growth: The decade of the 1950s saw the induction of aircraft and support systems, both in quantity and quality, into the IAF. During this period, the IAF acquired its first jet fighters and transport aircraft, and India began to develop its own indigenous aircraft and weapons systems. The IAF began to shift its focus to defending India's borders and air space, and its capabilities started developing beyond the limited scope of the support role.

The Indo-Sino War of 1962: The ground reality in 1962 was that the IAF had relatively potent air power with Western aircraft *vis-a-vis* old Russian aircraft with China. Despite a clear combat edge, the fighter component of the Air Force was not used during the Sino-Indian conflict of 1962. There has been a general reluctance to use air power due to the perceived fear of escalation of conflict, which was evident even up to the 1999 Kargil conflict, and has changed since the Balakot strike in 2019. However, post-war, it was decided to build up the IAF strength to 45 squadrons.

The Indo-Pakistan War of 1965: In 1965, the IAF gave a good account in the skies and in support of ground operations. Air superiority in specific terms was not contested by either side. It provided close air support to help with the Pakistan Army's armoured thrusts. Eventually, the Pakistan offensive was stopped, and the war ceased. After the war, the IAF continued to acquire modern combat aircraft and had 39 combat aircraft squadrons by 1971. It also improved tactics and techniques based on the lessons of the 1965 War. IAF decided the war priorities, in sequence, to be air defence, support to surface forces, and offensive action to counter or neutralise the enemy air.

The Indo-Pakistan War of 1971: In 1971, the IAF was in much better shape in qualitative and quantitative terms than the PAF. This was the first time the IAF actively engaged the enemy air force. IAF achieved complete air superiority over the eastern wing of Pakistan within a few days. Air operations included close air support and air cover to the Indian Army, independent raid missions against the PAF bases, assistance to Indian Navy in maritime operations, offensive attacks on enemy armour, and strategic bombing. The IAF played a pivotal role in the victory, leading to the liberation of Bangladesh, and it was, probably, the high point for the IAF. In this war, IAF carried out all air campaigns in parallel.

Modernisation and Expansion (1980–2000): To retain relevance in the evolving operational environment, with the induction of modern aircraft and systems in the immediate neighbourhood, in the 1980s and 1990s, the IAF modernised itself with advanced aircraft, weapons, and sensors, and expanded its capabilities to include strategic airlift.

Power Projection Abroad: During 1987–1990, the IAF was involved with operations in Sri Lanka and Maldives. It established an air bridge between the mainland of India and Sri Lanka for the IPKF. Although combat aircraft were not used, IAF helicopters provided fire support for the Army. In 1988, the IAF undertook Operation Cactus, wherein, it flew at least a battalion of paratroopers more than 1,000 miles away to the Maldives when rebels attempted to overthrow the Government. In these operations, the IAF demonstrated its ability to project forces on short notice.

The Kargil War of 1999: Kargil's operations demonstrated, once again, the impact of air power in the achievement of objectives. The IAF flew hundreds of strike missions supported by combat patrols and escorts. Air power was employed in a very innovative way in high altitudes. The Kargil War forced the IAF to rethink aerial strategies as it attempted to orchestrate an aerial campaign at altitudes of 14,000–18,000 ft against well-camouflaged targets.

Balakot Strike: A game-changer shift took place on 26 February 2019, when India decided to use offensive air power by carrying out deep strikes against targets in Pakistan even beyond the PoK. The myth about the use of air power being escalatory in nature was broken.

Strategic Transformation: Originally, the IAF had been formed purely to meet the requirements of British interests and its empire. Its roles and responsibilities were limited to tactical applications of air power. Post independence, the application of air power continued to remain tactical. It was only in 1971 that the IAF carried out strategic effect-based operations with air campaigns in parallel. In the first decade of this century, IAF inducted airborne early warning and aerial refuelling capability leading to an increase in strategic reach along with conventional deterrence. The transformation of the Indian Air Force from a tactical air power to a strategic one had begun, and subsequently, the pace picked up for it to become a broad-spectrum air force in future.

Doctrinal Evolution

The IAF formally formulated and published its first doctrine in 1995. It was the basic doctrine covering air assets, tasks, and campaigns. Thereafter, the doctrine was revised in 2012, and the latest version has been released in 2022. The salient aspects of these editions are in the succeeding paragraphs.

The IAF Doctrine of 1995: The IAF was the first among the three services in India to formulate a doctrine in 1995.

> The first IAF doctrine provided an exhaustive description of the basics of air power. It covered topics such as the theory of war, characteristics of air power and its relationship with strategy, aspects related to prosecuting an air war, various air campaigns, and combat support operations.

The doctrine laid emphasis on the importance of offensive air operations, the increase in technology levels, the role of combat support operations by force multipliers, and the network-centric environment.

It stressed on modernisation of air defence and communications networks and C4I (Command, Control, Communications, and Intelligence) structures.

The IAF Doctrine of 2012: This version of the doctrine went beyond outlining what air power is, to establish a connection between air power and national security. It brought out the greater role of air power in the full spectrum of national security and diplomacy. Relevant additions were as follows:

It provided a clear vision of how it could contribute to sub-conventional operations including counter-terrorism missions.

It brought into focus the enabling characteristics of air power such as air mobility, helicopter support for Special Forces operations, casualty evacuation, and HADR.

Aspects related to nation-building, aerial diplomacy, and perception management were also added.

It included the strategic significance of space (and space-enabled capabilities).

It also covered maritime air operations and how air power could be used in the maritime domain for many of its roles and functions.

It highlighted the importance of modernisation of the Air Force's transport and training aircraft, helicopters, the induction of force enhancers, modern armaments and weapon systems, space-based systems, bolstering of air defence systems, information or electronic warfare abilities, secure communication set-ups, and upgradation of training facilities.

It highlighted the strategic aspect of the control of the air by suggesting that deterrence and control of the air were inextricably intertwined.

It pointed out that the classification of an offensive air operation as 'strategic' is not determined by range, platform type, or the weaponry used, but is determined by the objective or the purpose served.

The IAF Doctrine of 2022: The major differences from the previous doctrine were as follows:

It proposed a larger regional role for IAF beyond territorial defence.

The 2022 doctrine, unequivocally, advocated the shift from air power to aerospace power and stressed greater space exploitation for the achievement of national objectives.

It asserted that aerospace power is the foundation for sustained surface operations.

It recommended increased bilateral and multilateral exercises with extra-regional actors as part of military diplomacy.

It elucidated a NWNP strategy, based on kinetic (including punitive strikes) as well as non-kinetic responses.

It explained how the technology had transformed core characteristics of reach, flexibility and versatility, mobility, responsiveness, offensive lethality, and trans-domain capabilities.

It contained an exhaustive chapter on Air Strategy which covered its doctrinal and structural engagement across the entire spectrum and levels of conflict, with the nations' joint military strategy, and land and maritime strategies.

Peace time strategy constituted sovereignty protection, deterrence, air diplomacy, and nation-building.

The first NWNP strategy covered the employment of aerospace power in the continuum between peace and war for information dominance, shaping operations, and external and internal security operations.

The Wartime Strategy and the campaigns were covered comprehensively for the employment of aerospace power in the unique multi-domain-multi-spectrum Indian security context.

The doctrine also elaborated on multi-domain operations, and the importance of battle-space transparency, combat networking, cyber and information warfare, electronic warfare, techno-logistics, administration and human resource management, and training, in this scenario.

Air Strategies to Deal with the Current Situation

Challenges

India faces two nuclear-powered inimical neighbours. China is emerging as a major regional power with the aspiration to be a global power, and its desire to dominate Asia and, finally, the world has implications for India. India's relations with China are changing from cooperative to competitive to combative. China also continues to enhance its strategic presence in regions of the Indian Ocean and is investing in the littoral countries to achieve a foothold and extend its influence. China sees India as a competitor and would like to keep India off-balance. China's warfare strategy is focused on developing a modern and capable force that can support its national security interests and regional or global ambitions. The Chinese forces are undergoing significant modernisation and expansion at a rapid pace with particular emphasis on developing advanced technologies and capabilities. Some key elements of China's warfare strategy include:

Developing expeditionary capability by enhancing the capabilities of the PLAAF (People's Liberation Army Air Force) and the PLAN (People's Liberation Army Navy).

Infusion of existing and future technologies.

Reorganisation to deal with future challenges in all domains of warfare including cyber, space, electronic, and information.

Mastering the art of Grey Zone Warfare using anything and everything as a weapon.

Investing in long-range vectors (including hypersonic weapons) and unmanned platforms to resort to no-contact warfare.

Military-civil fusion for a whole-of-government approach.

A string-of-pearls strategy to develop and support logistic bases in the Indian Ocean Region.

Salami slicing and cabbage strategy to achieve objectives without serious military action.

A robust defence industry producing indigenous platforms, weapons, and systems (including developing and producing modern fifth and sixth-generation stealth aircraft).

When it comes to Pakistan, it remains a security threat and continues to use non-state actors to maintain a situation of unrest. Asymmetric warfare will remain an instrument of its state policy. Pakistan's strategy would continue to be to wage proxy war and, in the event of an escalation, use the nuclear card.

China-Pakistan Collusive Challenge: China's increasing economic and political ties with Pakistan influence the geostrategic balance of the region. China has strategic interests in using Pakistani territory to reach West Asia and Africa and has invested in the China-Pakistan Economic Corridor (CPEC) that connects the Xinjiang region in West China to the China-built-and-operated Gwadar Port near the Gulf of Hormuz. In case of a conflict between India and Pakistan, China would posture along the northern and eastern border to keep the Indian military divided. Pakistan openly boasts of collusive support from China in case of a war with India. These two countries have a close and longstanding strategic partnership that includes co-operation even in areas of defence and security. China has even helped Pakistan militarily to acquire technologies for its nuclear weapons and missile program. In the context of air warfare, there are many ways in which China and Pakistan collaborate to enhance their respective capabilities. This includes joint development of aircraft (JF-17 *Thunder*), supply of advanced aircraft (including the J-10 and J-11), supplying defence systems and technologies, and training and exercises.

Lessons from the Recent Wars

At this juncture, it is important to pick up lessons from various conflicts going around the globe to evolve a suitable strategy for the Indian operational environment.

Recent wars, such as the conflicts in Iraq, Afghanistan, Syria, Libya, and Ukraine have provided several important lessons for Air Strategy. Some key lessons include:

> Effect-based, offensive application of air power yields faster results due to the shock and awe effect that it creates.
>
> Restrictions in the of air power increase the cost (in terms of time, money, and life) of achievement of objectives.
>
> The offensive counter-air and defensive counter-air campaigns are enmeshed with each other. These cannot be planned and executed independently in isolation.
>
> A no-fly is viable and effective only if it is backed up by the wherewithal to implement it.
>
> Stealth technology is essential for undetected penetration of enemy airspace with minimal risk of interception and attrition.
>
> Networked air environment (including AWACS [Airborne Warning and Control System] and AEW&C [Airborne Early Warning and Control System] aircraft) provides comprehensive situational awareness, and command and control capabilities.

A high degree of situational awareness is of utmost importance and can be achieved by good ISR capability and effective information-sharing mechanisms.

Air warfare is witnessing the enhanced role of unmanned platforms, drones, and swarms.

Shoulder-fired air defence systems can cause prohibitive damage to enemy aerial platforms in urban areas and hilly terrain.

The efficacy of airborne operations (using fixed-wing or helicopters) is doubtful in a contested air space proliferated with Air Defence (AD) weapons.

Precision and stand-off capabilities are important for punitive air strikes in urban areas.

Protection of own assets by protective infrastructure, dispersal, and passive measures is essential to safeguard own assets from enemy attack, especially during the opening phases of the conflict.

Intangible factors like morale, training, tactics, and leadership are very important for military success.

Coordinated application of surface and air force is very important. The operations need to be planned and executed jointly.

Suggested Strategies

Orchestrating an air war, especially with multiple threats and limited resources, needs some innovative strategies that maximise the use of available resources. These strategies are somewhat applicable even when adequate resources are available but are more important with limited resources. Some suggestions are as follows:

Integrated Conceptualisation: Conflicts demand multi-domain responses and to optimise resource utilisation, integration of all capabilities is necessary at conceptual and strategic levels before making a comprehensive plan to chalk out national military objectives and pursuant strategies. Land, maritime and air strategies need to germinate in an integrated manner.

Resource Allocation: Providing resources (platforms, sensors, and weapons) to the Command Headquarters for fighting the air war is the responsibility of the Service Headquarters. These resources are allotted *ab initio*, and reallocation is done during the war depending on the situation. No problem is faced if the resources are adequate, with the possibility of keeping some as a reserve. However, with limited resources, the principle of sharing poverty rather than the distribution of riches needs to be followed. Air assets of other services and civil aviation too need to be factored in the overall allocation matrix.

Active Monitoring: In the orchestration of air war, the roles of the Service Headquarters include conveying higher directions, monitoring the progress of operations in all zones or fronts, and providing the required wherewithal. Active monitoring means not only listening out or observing, but collecting data continuously, analysing, anticipating, and proactively providing resources by transferring from one zone to the other. The principle followed would be providing milk before the baby cries. A dynamic resource allocation model for various sectors can help optimise resource utilisation and this is possible with high-speed high volume data transfers between various entities.

Swing Force Concept: Generally, fighter squadrons can operate from two to three operational locations. These locations are predecided and have a certain amount of supporting infrastructure and equipment. Even the aircrew are familiar with the area of operation. In the swing force concept, some of the capability-based assets would swing from one front to the other depending on how the situation is developing.

Seamless Operations: The air command area of responsibilities is delineated with earmarked boundaries. The targets and resources for air operations are planned accordingly. More resources, if needed, are sought from the Service Headquarters. In the concept of seamless operations, a higher degree of synergy, cooperation, and teamwork between the Command Headquarters would have to be exercised.

Effect-based Force Application: Air war entails effect-based operations. However, with limited resources, the available resources would have to be employed judiciously to obtain maximum effect. Some of the relevant aspects include selective dominance rather than attempting to achieve air superiority, selective targeting to hit where it hurts the most, parallel operations (on a tactical, operational, and strategic level), and conservative risk-taking.

Protection of Assets: Protection of assets becomes a priority in a limited assets scenario. The air assets would be the first ones to be targeted by a standoff through precision weapons and missiles. Various measures need to be employed to ensure the protection of assets. These would include the dispersal of assets following the principle of not keeping all eggs in one basket, need-based induction of resources, protective infrastructure, and passive measures of deception, camouflage, and concealment. To increase survivability in the air, the self-protection suite and systems of the platforms would be essential besides the use of tactical routing. Besides platforms, the protection of networks would be equally vital.

Effective Air Strategies: These would include developing multi-role capabilities, a networked air defence system, investing in unmanned aerial platforms, focused training and readiness, and interoperability with air forces of friendly foreign countries.

Strategy Enablers: The success of the suggested strategies depends upon several factors. Some of these include integrated air and surface forces plans, prioritised joint target lists, AI-supported multi-domain, and multi-sensor for a high degree of situational awareness, a network environment with efficient information sharing mechanisms, rapid mobility capability, and adequate supporting equipment and infrastructure.

Future Air Strategies

Technology has had a profound influence on and is a major driver of innovation and evolution in Air Strategy. Future strategies would generally depend upon the influence of technology on warfare and the changing nature of warfare, besides the prevailing threats. Some of these aspects are discussed in the succeeding paragraphs:

Investment in Technology: Air Force is a technology-intensive service and converting technology into capability is a time-consuming process. To stay on top of the challenges, there is a need to invest in emerging technologies and ideate about their utilisation in warfare. Some of the future technologies that are impacting the air war are:

Quantum computing;

Hypersonic weapon systems;

Artificial intelligence;

Robotics;

Nanotechnology;

Unmanned platforms, drones, and swarm technology;

Network-centric environment or Internet of Things or System of Systems.

Situational Awareness and Decision-making: One of the effects of advanced technology on air warfare is the increased pace and intensity of air operations. In such a scenario the decision-making process must be quick to keep up with the OODA (Observe, Orient, Decide, Act) cycle. The three most important contributing factors are—a high degree of situational awareness, a robust and fast, network system for information sharing, and AI-based decision support systems.

Unmanned Platforms: The use of unmanned platforms and systems is growing in warfare. This shift is expected to continue as technology advances and the capabilities of unmanned systems improve further. Drones of various sizes and capabilities are taking over the tasks of conventional platforms. Their utilisation is spread across the entire spectrum of threats ranging from sub-conventional and conventional to long-range attacks. Investment in anti-drone systems is also a need of the hour.

Loyal Wing Man Concept: Both manned and unmanned platforms have their respective advantages and disadvantages. The thought process for the next generation of platforms is to harness the advantages of both and develop networked systems, wherein, both can work in an integrated manner. Research is going on in many countries on the loyal wingman concept. Hindustan Aeronautics Ltd (HAL) in India is also working on the Institute of Computer Accounts (ICATs) program on similar lines.

Sixth Generation Aircraft: Sixth-generation aircraft are still in the development phase. However, based on current trends in air technology, sixth-generation aircraft will likely have several key features that will shape Air Strategy in the future. They are likely to have increased automation with advanced AI and machine learning algorithms that will enable autonomous decision-making and allow them to adapt to changing situations quickly. They would also have enhanced stealth capabilities making them virtually invisible to radar and other detection systems. Integrated sensor systems in these aircraft will provide comprehensive situational awareness and the ability to engage targets with great precision. Overall, sixth-generation aircraft are expected to have a significant impact on Air Strategy in the future, with their advanced capabilities enabling air forces to operate with greater autonomy, and strike enemy targets with unprecedented precision and speed. However, as with any new technology, there may also be challenges associated with the introduction of sixth-generation aircraft, including the need to develop new tactics, training programs, and support infrastructure to fully realise their potential.

Hypersonic Weapons: The development of hypersonic weapons is likely to have a significant impact on Air Strategy. Hypersonic weapons provide new opportunities for rapid response and long-range strike capabilities with precision. They also pose new challenges in terms of protection and air defence. The high speed and unpredictability of hypersonic weapons will require the development of new air defence strategies, as traditional air defence systems may be unable to detect or intercept these weapons. This could lead to the development of new technologies, such as directed energy weapons or advanced sensors, to counter the threat posed by hypersonic weapons. Also, protective infrastructure would be required which can withstand the destructive power of these weapons.

New Domains of Warfare: The domains like cyber, space, electronics and information are coming into the influence of warfare. China's formation of a Joint Strategic Support Force (JSSF) as a separate service, with defensive and offensive capabilities, in the above-mentioned four domains, indicates future challenges. Reorientation is required in IAF to deal with these changes.

Grey Zone Operations: Grey Zone operations are operations in the contested arena somewhere between routine statecraft and open warfare. These are becoming a norm in modern-day warfare. Both the adversaries of India are resorting to these operations regularly. Air power, besides offensive use, can also be effectively utilised in many ways in non-conventional hostile situations categorised above. Various aspects of Grey Zone operations need to be deliberated from the point of view of air power involvement. A certain amount of reorientation would be required in the application of air power in these Grey Zone situations supported by capability enhancement in certain fields.

Space-based Capabilities: The term Air Power has changed to aerospace power with the aerial warfare envelope expanding to the domain of space. Space-based systems and applications are embedded in every aspect of aerial warfare. In Grey Zone Warfare, the involvement of space-based equipment and systems is on an even larger scale. Space-based systems are becoming increasingly important in air warfare, providing capabilities such as navigation, targeting, communication, early warning of missile launches, and space-based surveillance. The integration of these systems with air assets is expected to continue, providing new opportunities for offensive and defensive operations.

Defence Diplomacy: Defence Diplomacy is conducted utilising several defence activities like defence cooperation, exchange visits, joint exercises, training, and loan or gift of equipment, etc. Air Force has a big role in Defence Diplomacy. It is an effective tool for political signalling and strategic coercion. The escalation matrix can be developed by a combination of the number and extent of these defence activities. Multi-lateral, multi-service and multi-domain exercises are essential for defence cooperation, not only during hostilities, but even for Grey Zone operations during peace. Even without a military alliance, a certain degree of interoperability with friendly foreign forces is desirable.

Self-Reliance, Indigenisation, and Make In India: The IAF has always encouraged the development of indigenous defence production capability and it is one of its key result areas. It has played an important role in creating an aerospace ecosystem in India and has been operating indigenously built aircraft and aircraft built in India under licenced production. This has given impetus to indigenous industry in the past and will continue to support it in future. The important thing to remember is that while supporting self-reliance, the minimum level of deterrence capability needs to be always maintained. Also, the balance between quality and quantity needs to be maintained all the time.

Conclusion

The determinants of a successful air campaign are complex and interwoven. There is no one best solution for all cases. Doctrine shows how things should be done, and the strategy dictates how things will be done in the existing circumstances.

The IAF should continue to prioritise modernisation efforts, including the acquisition of advanced aircraft, weapons systems, and sensors. This will enable the IAF to maintain a technological edge over potential adversaries and respond effectively to emerging threats. The IAF should give up capabilities that are duplicated with the other two services like surface-to-surface weapons and the Special Operations Garud Force and instead, concentrate on new areas of capability development, such as Unmanned Aerial Vehicles (UAVs), cyber warfare, and space-based systems. These capabilities will enhance its ability to conduct a wide range of operations, from intelligence gathering to precision strikes. The IAF should work closely with the surface forces to develop joint operations capabilities, with emphasis on joint conceptualisation, planning, command and control systems, and integrated training exercises. The IAF should continue to be proactive in its role of providing humanitarian assistance and disaster relief, both domestically and internationally.

Overall, the IAF should strive to maintain a balance between traditional air power capabilities and emerging areas of strategic importance. This will enable the IAF to meet its primary mission of defending India's air space and national security interests, while also contributing to regional stability and humanitarian efforts.

Air Marshal Anil Khosla, PVSM, AVSM, VM retired as Vice Chief of the Air Staff in April 2019. An expert fighter pilot, he wields his pen with equal adeptness as his joy stick. He has clocked over 4,000 hours of flying on different aircraft like SEPECAT Jaguar, MiG-21 and HAL Kiran. He has experience in both ground attack and air defence roles, and specialises in maritime role. He holds two MPhil degrees in Defence and Strategic Studies. An ardent blogger (Air Marshal's Perspective), and Sudoku and puzzle solver, he has pursued the latter 11 times up to the national level.

Endnotes

1. Valuable inputs from Air Chief Marshal S.P. Tyagi PVSM, AVSM, VM (Retd) and Air Marshal Vinod Bhatia, PVSM, AVSM, VrC and Bar (Retd).
2. https://www.orfonline.org/expert-speak/closing-gap-doctrinal-capability-appraisal-iaf-plaaf/
3. https://airpowerasia.com/2020/06/15/air-power-transformational-challenges-india/
4. *Aerospace Strategy: An Idea Whose Time Has Come.* Air Mshl D, Choudhury, AVSM, VM, VSM (Retd).
5. https://www.airuniversity.af.edu/Portals/10/JIPA/journals/Volume-01_Issue-1/04-F-Goulter-Pant.pdf
6. https://indianairforce.nic.in/wp-content/uploads/2023/01/2MB.pdf
7. https://theprint.in/opinion/iaf-doctrine-leverages-air-power-it-also-has-the-first-no-war-no-peace-strategy/1379156/
8. https://capsindia.org/wp-content/uploads/2022/10/Bhashyam-Kasturi.pdf
9. https://55nda.com/blogs/anil-khosla/

4

Indian Strategic Thought in the 1950s and 1960s

Major General P.J.S. Sandhu

India emerged as an independent country on 15 August 1947 after nearly 200 years of British rule. This period was marked by a few landmark events, such as the First War of Independence (1857), the two World Wars, and a freedom struggle that lasted for nearly half a century before the British felt compelled to leave India. The events of the last decade of the freedom struggle, which coincided with WWII, had a profound effect on the thinking of the Indian political elite. This thinking governed the strategic thought during the initial years of independent India. The analyses and introspection of this thought process brings an understanding of the decisions and the events of that period from the correct perspective. This article aims to critically analyse the evolution of Indian strategic thought during the first two decades after Independence, its impact on national security, and draws lessons for the future.

The End of WWII and India's Independence

Though India had, by and large, supported the British during WWII, it was marred by the Quit India Movement that was launched in 1942, which necessitated the use of the British Indian Army against the protesting Indian masses. This movement, to a great extent, shook the foundation of the British Empire, not only in India but in South Asia as a whole.

At the end of WWII, the strength of the Indian Army (excluding British troops), as on 1 October 1945, was estimated at 23,43,000 and that of the Royal Indian Air Force at about 26,100.[1] The highest rank achieved by Indians at that time was that of an acting Brigadier (substantive Major) and their numbers could be counted on fingertips. There were hardly any Indian officers posted in the GHQ India or as senior staff officers in the field formations. Indian officers mostly functioned at tactical levels and were deliberately kept away by the British from strategic issues. Indian political leaders who were leading the freedom struggle had deliberately, and rightly so, kept the Indian officers and men away from the freedom movement.

The Indian political leadership, as well as a handful of Indian military officers who had attained higher ranks, were not involved in strategic issues. This was the exclusive preserve of British officers in GHQ India and the War Office in London. For instance, in 1946, a position paper had been prepared by the War Office titled, *The Strategic Value of India to the British Empire,* which analysed the strategic value of India purely from the British perspective. One of the recommendations in this paper was that 'the British ought not to give up the Andaman and Nicobar group of islands, but to hold and develop these as outposts to Burma and Malaya'.[2] Thus, there was no thinking from the Indian point of view about the future strategic and military implications of the Independence and partition of the Indian sub-continent and the creation of an independent Pakistan comprising two wings separated from each other by about 2,000 km. In a note to Lord Mountbatten titled, *The Military Implication of Pakistan*, dated 24 April 1947, Field Marshal Auchinleck, C-in-C India, wrote, 'From the purely military and strategic aspect, which is the only angle from which the problem has been viewed in this paper, it must be concluded that the provision of adequate insurance in the shape of reasonably good defensive arrangements for Pakistan would be a most difficult and expensive business and that no guarantee of success could be given.'[3] The 'good defensive arrangements,' in all probability, were in the context of its western borders where the Russian threat existed.

Indian Military at Independence

Soon after WWII ended, the process of demobilisation of the Armed Forces was put into motion by the British. Under Plan 287, the strength of the Indian Army was to be reduced over a period of 18 months to a lower limit of 2,87,000. In the case of the Indian Air Force (IAF), it was to be reduced to 850 officers and 6,000 airmen.[4] The main reason for large-scale demobilisation was the economic difficulties that the British were facing at the end of the Great War. This lower limit did not correlate with the security requirements of undivided India.

Any plan for the Partition of India would have involved the division of the Indian Army, even though Mountbatten, on 8 April 1947, told Liaquat Ali that there would be no splitting of the Indian Army.[5] The British had toyed with the idea of having a common Armed Force, possibly commanded by British officers in senior ranks, at least for a few years for both the dominions. However, as events turned out, the Armed Forces and their assets were to be divided in a ratio of 2:1 between India and Pakistan. In August 1947, the undivided Army was a little above 4,00,000—India's share was 2,80,000 and that of Pakistan was about 1,50,000.

To get a good sense of the thinking amongst the top political leadership of independent India in 1947, it would be worthwhile to quote an incident from the book, *Major General A.A. Rudra* by Major General D.K. Palit, VrC. Shortly after Independence, General Sir Rob Lockhart, C-in-C Army (India) convened a high-powered meeting to discuss defence strategy and to prepare a policy paper for the Government. The draft policy paper was duly prepared, and the C-in-C Army wrote a minute to PM Pandit Nehru asking for a Government Directive on Defence Policy. The C-in-C went to see Pandit Nehru with this draft policy paper. On returning from the PM's office, General Lockhart summoned Major General Rudra who was then the Military Secretary at GHQ India and recounted his meeting with the PM thus:[6]

> 'What happened, Sir?' Rudra asked.
>
> 'What happened? What happened? You may well ask. I was thrown out of the PM's office; that is what happened. The PM took one look at my paper and blew his top. "Rubbish! Rubbish!" He shouted. We don't need a defence plan. Our policy is *ahimsa* (non-violence). We foresee no military threats. Scrap the Army. The police are good enough to meet our security needs.'

Indian Security Strategy During the Initial Years

The tribal invasion of Kashmir engineered by Pakistan with the connivance of some British officers took place on 24 October 1947. Following the signing of the Instrument of Accession by the then Maharaja of J&K, the Indian Armed Forces intervened on 27 October 1947, and the rest is history. Taking the Kashmir dispute to the UN, and accepting a ceasefire, while Indian territory was still under the occupation of Pakistan, was a strategic blunder, the results of which continue to haunt us today.

The merger of the princely states was handled by the then Home Minister, Sardar Patel with great alacrity and strategic acumen. The Hyderabad Police Action, code named Operation Polo, was another event which was brilliantly planned and executed by the Indian Army. However, the liberation of Portuguese territories was allowed to drag on unnecessarily till 1961.

Communist China emerged on the world stage on 1 October 1949. They annexed Xinjiang by 30 November 1949, and soon announced their intention to 'liberate' (occupy) Tibet. The PLA launched a well-planned politico-military offensive into Tibet from four directions in April 1950 and completed the occupation of Tibet by the end of 1951. With the Chinese occupation of Tibet, the security situation on India's northern borders had undergone a paradigm shift. India now had a new neighbour in the north in China.

Let us now turn to India's thought process on strategic issues during this period. India was projecting itself as a state without any military ambitions, the emphasis being on curtailing the defence expenditure and limiting the strength of the Armed Forces which had no relationship with the security needs of the country. The defence capital expenditure was to be kept constant at an annual ₹35 crores a year and the revenue expenditure was to be progressively reduced from ₹165 crores in 1951–52 to ₹140 crores by the year 1953–54. Based on the PM's directive of 16 September 1947 (Plan 200), the strength of the Indian Army was to be further reduced by 50,000 personnel in the financial year 1950–51.

This was also the time that two power blocks had emerged at the international level, led by the USA and the USSR. India decided not to join any of the power blocks and opted for a policy of non-alignment, which has continued, albeit with some variations in its nuances, to date. In recent times, it has taken the form of 'strategic autonomy'. By and large, it has served India's interests well.

Events Leading to the Sino-Indian War of 1962

India had gained Independence, mainly through non-violent means, whereas China emerged on the world scene on 1 October 1949 after a bitter and prolonged civil war. The Chinese paramount leader, Mao Zedong, believed that the power flowed from the barrel of a gun. The two political systems and strategic thinking were also vastly different. The problem was further compounded by the fact that the two neighbours had a nearly 4,000 km long border, which was neither delineated nor mutually defined.

India was quick to recognise Chinese sovereignty over Tibet and hoped that the two countries would have friendly relations (moralistic approach). The Agreement on Trade and Intercourse Between the Tibet Region of China and India, commonly known as the Panchsheel Agreement, signed on 29 April 1954, was the high point of friendly relations. Through this agreement, India gave up all its special rights and privileges in Tibet, inherited from British India, without negotiating anything substantial in return. There was no reference to the unsettled boundary. India presumed that the absence of the same meant Chinese acceptance of India's perception of the boundary. That it was a fallacy was to be proved soon thereafter.

India did not have to wait for long as the first Chinese incursion into Barahoti in the Central Sector occurred in June 1954. It was also around this time that China started the construction of the Aksai Chin highway through Indian territory, which was completed and inaugurated on 2 September 1957. The Indian reaction to this Chinese action came by way of an informal note by the Foreign Secretary to the Chinese Ambassador in India on 18 October 1958, which complained, 'It is a matter of surprise and regret that the Chinese Government should have constructed a road through indisputably Indian territory without first obtaining permission of the Government of India and without informing the Government of India.'[7]

The above just goes to show how naive India was during the 1950s as far as strategic or national security issues were concerned! Over the next ten years, from 1954 onwards, more than 1,000 memoranda, notes and letters were exchanged between the two Governments. These have been published by the Government of India in a series of white papers. Gradually, these diplomatic exchanges became shriller and accusatory.

The first bloodshed occurred at Longju in the erstwhile Northeast Frontier Agency (NEFA; now Arunachal Pradesh) on 25 August 1959. While the fall-out of this incident was still being resolved, another incident, which was far more serious, took place on 20–21 October 1959 in the area of Kongka Pass in Ladakh wherein an Indian police (now CRPF) patrol was ambushed by the Chinese border guards. Ten Indian policemen were killed, and nine were taken as prisoners. Pandit Nehru admitted that India and China had fallen out, and that even if some kind of peace could prevail in the frontier regions, it would be 'an armed peace and that the future appeared to be one of continuing tension'.[8] The net result of these incidents was that the defence of India's northern borders, which until then was the responsibility of the Indian Police under the Ministry of Home Affairs, and Assam Rifles under the Ministry of External Affairs, was handed over to the Indian Army in 1959, but without consulting the COAS, or a commensurate increase in force levels.

At the beginning of 1960, Nehru decided to make one more effort to resolve the boundary dispute through talks. On 5 February 1960, he invited Zhou, the Chinese Premier to visit Delhi to explore avenues that might lead to a peaceful settlement. The Nehru-Zhou talks, held in Delhi from 19–25 April 1960, were not only a failure but a diplomatic disaster.

After the failure of these talks, China started to establish additional posts on the Indian territory inside their Claim Line. To check this unrelenting forward movement by Chinese troops, Nehru issued instructions on 2 November 1961 for certain measures to be adopted in what came to be known as the Forward Policy.[9] In essence, it involved the establishment of forward posts close to the Chinese posts, previously established, to prevent any further encroachment on the Indian territory. The Chinese responded by establishing their own posts, at times encircling Indian posts. Mao termed this policy as 'armed co-existence'. Thus, Indian and Chinese posts, especially in Ladakh, came to be interlocked with each other.

By the end of 1961, China had concluded that its objective to prevent any further Indian advances without bloodshed was not being met. They began to consider whether a sudden blow might force India to the negotiating table.[10] On 26 July 1962, the Government of India offered to send a ministerial-level delegation to Beijing to discuss, without preconditions, all bilateral problems, and disputes. The Chinese Premier, Zhou Enlai, in a midnight meeting with the Indian *charge d'affaires*, Dr P.K. Banerjee, on 4 August 1962, responded that China was willing to hold talks but only on Chinese terms. By early September 1962, Beijing was warning New Delhi that if India played with fire, it would be consumed by fire.[11] The stage was now set for the events that were to unfold—a full-scale Chinese offensive on 20 October 1962.

Chinese War Aim and Indian Response

The overall aim set by the Central Military Commission (CMC) for the PLA was to inflict a crushing military defeat on the Indian troops deployed on the border. While the real strategic aim of the Chinese lay in the Western Sector, the main military effort was to be directed in the Eastern Sector, and that too, specifically against the Kameng Frontier Division because the terrain there facilitated the employment of large forces. Further, the operations in the Western Sector were directed at securing the 1960 Claim Line, while the aim set for the PLA in Kameng Frontier Division was to annihilate the Indian forces deployed there.[12]

Yet, India continued to believe that China was unlikely to initiate any large-scale military action, notwithstanding the signals emerging to the contrary. In a conference held in the MoD on 15 September 1962, which was chaired by Krishna Menon and attended by the Army Chief, Eastern Army Commander, and Director, IB, amongst others, a decision was taken to evict the Chinese from Thagla Ridge, a task well-nigh impossible under the circumstances. However, this decision set into motion a chain of events, which saw Lieutenant General B.M. Kaul emerge on the scene as the GOC of the newly raised IV Corps on 5 October 1962, and the 7 Infantry Brigade strung along the Namka Chu waiting for the Chinese to strike. To make matters worse, the Indian Prime Minister, Pandit Nehru, while on his way to Colombo at the Chennai airport, talking to the reporters announced that the Indian Army had been ordered 'to throw the Chinese out'.

India just failed to recognise the ground realities and continued to neglect defence preparedness. There was no cohesive military strategy or a defence plan to counter a Chinese military onslaught, which was ready to be launched. There was over-reliance on diplomacy which had run its course by July 1962. The Indian response and decisions were being overly influenced by B.N. Mallick, the then Director, IB. As a result, India was taken by complete surprise and the Indian Army was hustled into a war for which it was not prepared, trained, or equipped. The war itself was an unmitigated disaster for the Indian State and the Indian Army. Three issues can be highlighted for the defeat in 1962, namely, civil-military relations, the failure of intelligence and the structural defects existing in the higher defence decision-making process. Defence reforms were initiated to rectify these issues.

The most high-profile decisions to initiate a defence planning process were—first, the first defence plan envisaged the build-up and maintenance of a well-equipped Army with a strength of 8,25,000 men. Second, a 45-squadron Air Force, improvement of air defence radar, and communication facilities. Last, a phased programme for replacement of overage ships in the Indian Navy, thus, strengthening the defence production base, and improving the organisational base.[13]

Post 1962 and the Indo-Pak War of 1965

India was shocked and its policy of non-alignment lay in tatters. Soon after the second phase of the Chinese offensive, on 18 November 1962, Pandit Nehru turned to the USA for military assistance and wanted the US Air Force to intervene on India's behalf, but the US refused as India had not even committed its own Air Force. However, after the unilateral ceasefire by China on 21 November 1962, the US sent a delegation to India to assess India's requirement for military assistance. India projected for equipping and training 22 Army Divisions, an unusually large demand! However, after discussions, the US agreed to equip six divisions in phase one, but on the condition that India would immediately start a dialogue with Pakistan to resolve the Kashmir dispute.

Six rounds of talks were held at the foreign ministers' level between Sardar Swaran Singh and Zulfikar Ali Bhutto from December 1962 to May 1963. In the meantime, Pakistan signed a boundary agreement with China on 2 March 1963, ceding Shaksgam Valley to China.[14] Thereafter, India lost interest even though it continued with the talks for the sake of them. The talks yielded no results.

Another result of the failure of these talks was that the US went back on its agreement to equip and train six divisions for India. India-US relations took a downturn and India had to turn to the erstwhile Soviet Union for military equipment. At the same time, the US started providing military assistance to Pakistan which had been a member of the Central Treaty Organisation (CENTO) since 1959. Under this programme, the US provided military assistance to Pakistan to equip and train four infantry divisions and one-and-a-half-armoured divisions. This emboldened Pakistan to initiate the Indo-Pak War of 1965.

1965 War and Thereafter

The period of the mid-1960s was a time of great uncertainty for India. With the demise of Pandit Nehru in 1964, there was a change in the political ethos that had prevailed since Independence. Before Lal Bahadur Shastri could really settle down as the PM, India was overtaken by the events leading to a war in September 1965. Though the political and military leadership were greatly surprised, yet, there was a sense of pragmatism in coping with these events. This period also saw a degree of synergy emerge in politico-military-diplomatic fields and our response to the war was swift and determined. Our military, still emerging from the debacle of 1962, managed to not only thwart Pakistan's attempt to annex J&K by force but also ended the war from a position of comparative strength. However, these were initial steps, and hence, faltering. The Tashkent Agreement was to demonstrate the lack of strategic sense, which was evident in returning areas like the Haji Pir Pass, which were part of the territory under illegal occupation of Pakistan.

In terms of strategic thought, we emerged a lot wiser and stronger from the 1965 experience. Our politico-military response to the events of 1965 was pragmatic and strategically sound. The military had the requisite freedom of action to prosecute the war. Soon after that, a new era began, with PM Indira Gandhi taking over the reins of power and guiding the destiny of the nation from January 1966, till her death in 1984, except for a brief period from 1977–1980. During this period, India began to look at the world the way it was, and not the way India wanted or hoped it to be! We shaped our policies with powers, big and small, friendly and not-so-friendly, friends and rivals, in a pragmatic manner, keeping our national interests in mind. The events of 1971, which culminated in the creation of Bangladesh, and Pakistan being cut to size, were a manifestation of this transformation in strategic thinking. The Indo-Soviet Friendship Treaty, signed in 1971, is another case in point. There was a rare synergy between the political, military and diplomatic fields. The military leadership also played a vital role in guiding the strategic discourse of that period.

Conclusion

In retrospect, one may say that the Indian strategic thought during the 1950s and 1960s lacked pragmatism and bordered on a utopian view of the world. It is the political leadership and the strategic community who drive the strategic discourse of a nation. There is a requirement to evolve a vision and work out priorities to achieve that vision. This vision ought to be translated into achievable objectives in different fields, such as economic, industrial, agriculture, social sector, health, education, infrastructure development, and above all, national security.

National security is highly dependent on Comprehensive National Power (CNP) and military strength is an important component of CNP. During the '50s and '60s, our political leadership tended to exclude the military from their strategic discourse. It tended to rely heavily on bureaucratic, diplomatic, and intelligence agencies to evolve policies, and called the military only once a crisis had developed and other instruments had failed. The debacle of 1962 may be attributed to such a flawed way of functioning at the apex level. Since then, much has changed—hopefully for the better. To state the obvious, the military, too, is an important stakeholder in evolving a National Security Strategy which is a *sine qua non* in today's world. It is equally important to identify all the stakeholders and put them to work to evolve a grand strategy.

Major General P.J.S. Sandhu, a 1971 Cavalry War Veteran, rose to be the COS of a Strike Corps, having commanded an Armoured Brigade and an Armoured Division. A graduate of the NDC and Mechanised Commanders Course in former USSR, he has also been the DDG MO. He has been the Deputy Director and Editor at United Service Institution of India. He also revived Gyan Chakra, a Western Command think tank, and served as its first Director. His insights into military history led to critical appraisals of the Indo-Pak and the Sino-Indian Wars. He has been studying China closely, which led him to attend the PLA's Academy of Military Sciences Forum, and later, to lead a USI delegation to Beijing for bilateral discussions with the China Institute for Strategic Studies. His research on the Sino-India boundary and the 1962 War culminated in a widely received published work on the subject. He continues to write for military journals.

Endnotes

1. Khera, P. N., et al. *Official History of the Indian Armed Forces in the Second World War, 1939-45/ Edited by Bisheshwar Prasad, General War Administration and Organisation: Policy and Plans; Bisheshwar Prasad. Defense of India.* Combined Inter-services Historical Section, India & Pakistan, 1962, p 209.
2. Menezes, S. L. *Fidelity & Honour: The Indian Army from the Seventeenth to the Twenty-First Century.* 1993, *pp*. 418-419.
3. Hamid, S. Shahid. *Disastrous Twilight: A Personal Record of the Partition of India.* Secker & Warburg, 1986.
4. *Op. Cit. 1.*
5. *Op. Cit. 2.*
6. Palit, D. K. *Major General A.A. Rudra: His Service in Three Armies and Two World Wars.* 1997, *pp*. 317-319.
7. Government of India, Ministry of External Affairs, White Paper 1, *p* 26.
8. Maxwell, Neville. *India's China War.* 2011, p 221.
9. Nehru, Jawaharlal, and G. Parthasarathi. *Letters to Chief Ministers, 1947-1964 Volume 5.* Oxford University Press, USA, 1985, *p* 285.
10. Kissinger, Henry. *On China.* Penguin UK, 2011, p 189
11. Garver, John W. *China's Decision for War with India in 1962,* http://chinaindiaborderdispute.files.files.worldpress.com/2010/07/garver.pdf, accessed on 30 March 2023.
12. *A History of the Counterattack War in Self Defence Along the Sino-Indian Border,* Military Science Publications, Beijing, 1994, Chapter 4, Section 2. An English translation of the original book in Mandarin is available with the Centre for Armed Forces Historical Research (CAFHR) in United Service Institution (USI) of India (archives).
13. Government of India, Ministry of Defence Annual Report, 1964–65, New Delhi: Government of India Press, 1965, pp 1–2.
14. People's Republic Of China-Pakistan. Agreement on the Boundary between China's Sinkiang and the Contiguous Areas." *American Journal of International Law,* vol. 57, no. 3, July 1963, pp. 713–16, doi:10.2307/2196119.

5

India's Military Strategy for the 1971 Indo-Pak War

Lieutenant General (Dr) J.S. Cheema

General Rupert Smith, in his seminal book titled, *The Utility of Force: The Art of War in the Modern World,* defined the typical sequential paradigm of war as 'Confrontation-Crisis-Conflict-War-Resolution.'[1] The 1971 India-Pakistan War as a whole unfolded in this pattern. The confrontation between the two countries is well-known to be recounted here. The crisis erupted when the Pakistan Army launched a ruthless military crackdown, Operation Searchlight, on 25 March 1971, to suppress East Pakistan's population. This triggered a massive refugee influx into India, posing a severe socio-economic crisis. It was sort of an indirect aggression to destabilise India's northeastern states. Not only did the refugee deluge continue unabated, but a continuous shift in the demographic profile of refugees, from Muslims to Bengali Hindus, was taking place. The higher proportion of Bengali Hindu refugees made India apprehensive of their non-return even after a political settlement.

To resolve the unfolding crisis, India formulated the return of refugees as the political objective. Ruling out immediate military intervention despite public pressure, India strategised to achieve the political objective through diplomacy. Concurrently, it calibrated indirect military support to the Mukti Bahini, keeping the option open to militarily intervene at an appropriate time as a last resort. India's diplomatic campaign—to impress upon the world community to persuade Pakistan to seek a political settlement—did not elicit the desired response. In the first week of August 1971, Pakistan's official refugee list claimed 20 per cent refugees as Muslims and 80 per cent as Bengali Hindus. This, coupled with the unwillingness of foreign powers to persuade Pakistan to a political settlement, catalysed India's propensity towards military intervention. The possibility of war became a distinct probability.

India's Military Strategy

The Eastern Theatre was the logical centre of gravity for India, however, Pakistan and China along the Western and the Northern Theatres, respectively, posed significant threats. India, accordingly, strategised a 'swift offensive in the east, offensive-defensive in the west, and defensive along the northern border'[2] and evolved the following military objectives:[3]

Eastern Theatre: To assist the Mukti Bahini in liberating a part of East Pakistan, where the refugees could return, and live under their government.

Western Theatre: To prevent Pakistan from capturing any Indian territory of consequence in Jammu and Kashmir, Punjab, Rajasthan, or Gujarat.

Northern Borders: To defend the country from a possible attack by China along the Northern borders.

The Indian Army had a distinct quantitative advantage over the Pakistan Army in the Eastern Theatre having eleven infantry and mountain divisions to Pakistan's four divisions. The Mukti Bahini, with a strength of more than 1,00,000, was the force multiplier. There was parity in the Western Theatre with 13 infantry divisions to Pakistan's 10. India had one armoured division and four independent armoured brigades to Pakistan's two and three respectively. The IAF enjoyed a qualitative and quantitative advantage over the PAF, having 350 and 160 combat aircraft to Pakistan's 254 and 19 aircraft in the Western and Eastern Theatres respectively. The IN was considerably more robust, having an aircraft carrier and a larger fleet of cruisers, destroyers, and frigates.

The terrain of East Pakistan, now Bangladesh, is interspersed with numerous rivers and *nullahs*. The Ganges, Brahmaputra, and Meghna rivers bifurcate Bangladesh into four distinct sectors—Western, Northwestern, Northern, and Southeastern. The Army's strategy in the Eastern Theatre was to capture maximum territory bordering the Brahmaputra and Meghna river lines with Khulna and Chittagong being the principal objectives.[4] Thereafter, it was to establish a provisional Bangladesh Government. Subsequently, the strategy was modified to liberate the whole of East Pakistan.[5] Pakistan Army's strategy was to hold firmly the cities and garrisons located along the major roads, and deploy a division in each sector to deny ingress.

India continued to deploy four divisions along the northern borders against China. In the Eastern Theatre, the plan was a multi-pronged offensive along each of the four sectors as follows:

Western Sector: 2 Corps planned to capture Jessore and Jhenida, and subsequently secure Khulna and Faridpur.

Northwestern Sector: 33 Corps planned to capture Bogra and Rangpur.

Northern Sector: 101 Communications Zone was to capture Jamalpur and Mymensingh, and secure Tangail with airborne forces.

Southeastern Sector: 4 Corps was to capture the Meghna Bulge between Chandpur and Ashuganj, Sylhet, Daudkandi-Mynamati, and Chittagong.

The Western Theatre adopted a holding strategy with plans to execute limited offensive operations. Western Command's 15 and 11 Corps defended J&K and Punjab, respectively, deploying ten divisions, while the Southern Command held the desertic Rajasthan Sector with two divisions. 15 Corps planned limited offensive operations in Shyok Valley, Kargil, Lipa Valley, and Chicken's Neck area, while 11 Corps planned to capture the tactically important enclaves along the Ravi River. Southern Command planned an offensive in Jaisalmer and Barmer Sectors. The Strike 1 Corps, with three infantry divisions, was responsible for the Samba-Pathankot area's defence, and launching of the main offensive in the Shakargarh Sector. 1 Armoured Division was the Army Headquarters reserve—positioned near Ferozepore to execute the offensive on orders. The Pakistan Army had three corps (1, 2, and 4) with ten infantry, two armoured divisions, and three independent armoured brigades deployed on the Western Front.

The IAF planned to support the Army and Navy operations, besides attacking the enemy's strategic targets. The transport fleet was considerably enhanced in the East to accelerate the tempo of operations. The IN had deployed an aircraft carrier INS *Vikrant* in the east to secure a complete blockade and bomb the enemy's naval assets. It was to be the Navy's first significant operation since Independence.

Conflict Stage – Escalation

Considering war to be the last resort, India decided to execute the military strategy in a carefully calibrated manner. As the possibility of war became a distinct possibility, India deftly initiated the conflict stage to launch the war at a time and place of its choosing, exploiting geography and weather as deterrence against the Chinese threat. With effect from September 1971, India stepped up military activities along the border with regular troops, and in the hinterland by Mukti Bahini. Commando troops were stealthily embedded to fight alongside the Mukti Bahini within the East Pakistan territory. Pakistan responded to India's intensified activities by strengthening the borders in the east, and mobilising its Army in the west. President Yahya created a war psychosis by stating in an interview, 'War with India is very near, and Pakistan would not be alone in case of war.'[6] It was intended to deter India from the war in the east by posing a threat from its allies—the USA and China.

India was undeterred. Instead, from the second week of October, it further intensified the scale of operations within East Pakistan, and after 21 November, Indian troops began to position themselves within East Pakistan to improve their defensive posture, and secure suitable launch pads for subsequent offensive operations. Both sides employed tanks and their respective Air Force in these border skirmishes. By the end of November, the conflict between the two sides was in full force.

The War and the Ceasefire

India had initiated the conflict stage to compel Pakistan to initiate an open, and declare war—Pakistan was set to be declared an aggressor. It obliged by launching preemptive airstrikes, on 3 December 1971, on several Indian airfields in the Western Theatre, marking the commencement of the 1971 India-Pakistan War. India declared hostilities and recognised Bangladesh. The Armed Forces, concurrently, launched attacks, as planned, in the Eastern, and Western Theatres.

Eastern Theatre

The Army's multi-pronged offensive made rapid progress capturing Jessore, Jhenida, Jamalpur, Mymensingh, and Daudkandi-Chandpur, and securing the eastern bank of the Meghna River by 10 December. The IAF neutralised the PAF effectively, and achieved total air superiority by 7 December, paving the way for uninterrupted close-air support and heliborne or airborne operations. PNS *Ghazi* was sunk outside the Vizag harbour. The IN established a naval blockade to prevent any Pakistani build-up in the region.

To exploit the rapidly-deteriorating situation of the enemy, the Indian Army modified its plans. Between 6–12 December, 4 Corps, employing a combination of helicopters and river crafts, built up almost a division-sized strength across the Meghna River. The IAF flew around 350 sorties, including 100 by night, to lift 4,000 troops, ammunition, and supplies.[7] On 8 December, two brigades were pulled out from the Chinese border to strengthen the Northern Sector.[8] A parachute battalion was airdropped on the eastern bank of the Jamuna River at Tangail on 11 December. On 13 December 1971, the US Seventh Fleet entered the Bay of Bengal. This was a direct conventional and nuclear threat to India. India carried out intensive bombings on naval assets in East Pakistan to render them unusable for the Seventh Fleet. The IAF launched a successful airstrike at the Governor's house on 14 December that caused a huge psychological blow to Pakistan. The Army build-up continued, and by 16 December, nearly five brigades had encircled Dhaka, with four infantry battalions, and an independent armoured squadron entering the city by the afternoon. The Naval air operations mounted 291 sorties from INS *Vikrant* causing extensive damage to the enemy's naval assets.[9]

While India intensified psychological pressure on the Pakistan Army to surrender, the Pakistan Government was desperately looking for a UN-sponsored ceasefire as a face-saving mechanism to avoid the ignominy of surrender. Time was of the utmost essence. Poland submitted a resolution to the UN Security Council on 15 December, calling on India and Pakistan to accept an immediate ceasefire, withdraw forces from each other's territory, renounce claims to any occupied territories, and transfer power in East Pakistan to the representatives elected in December 1970. A ceasefire followed by troops' withdrawal before the capture of Dhaka would have deprived India of Pakistani forces' surrender and substantially curtailed its capacity to ensure the smooth return of refugees and

Bangladesh's liberation—the desired end-state. The resolution failed due to Bhutto's ulterior motive.[10] With the Indian Army closing in on Dhaka, the Pakistan Army had no option but to surrender on 16 December 1971.

Western Theatre

15 Corps captured Turtok in the Partapur sub-sector, and several vital posts in Kargil. It secured significant success in Lipa Valley, and the Chicken's Neck area. Pakistan's offensive, as appreciated, materialised in Punch and Chhamb sub-sectors. The Army defended Punch resolutely but suffered a significant reversal in Chhamb. 11 Corps captured Jassar Enclave in the Dera Baba Nanak, and Sehjra Bulge in the Khem-Karan sub-sectors. Pakistan achieved meaningful success in the Ferozepur and Fazilka sub-sectors. 1 Corps launched an attack on Shakargarh Bulge on 5 December when the likely Pakistan offensive did not materialise. It achieved limited success, and could not fully exploit battle opportunities. The Southern Command captured Parbat Ali overlooking the Naya-Chor defences in the Barmer sub-sector. It tenaciously defended the Longewala post in the Jaisalmer sub-sector, with the IAF playing a significant role. However, it could not carry out a successful pursuit towards Rahim Yar Khan, despite Pakistan troops in total disarray. The IN conducted a well-planned missile attack on Karachi harbour, causing substantial damage. India announced a unilateral ceasefire on the Western Front after Pakistan Army's surrender in the east. Pakistan accepted, and the 14-day war ended on 17 December 1971.

Analyses of India's Military Strategy

India, flawlessly, executed the military campaign with great aplomb to achieve a decisive victory over Pakistan. More than 92,000 Pakistani soldiers, paramilitary, police personnel, and civilians surrendered. It captured 5,620 square miles of territory against the loss of 120 square miles on the Western Front. However, a critical analyses is imperative to draw meaningful lessons.

War-Avoidance – Compellence and Deterrence Strategies

The purpose of deterrence in statecraft is to discourage an adversary from waging war to achieve political objectives. From September onwards,

India applied a compellence strategy by intensifying military activities within East Pakistan to coerce Pakistan to seek a political settlement with its eastern part and avert war, failing which, to set the stage for military intervention. To counter the same, Pakistan applied a deterrence strategy by mobilising in the west to deter India from waging war in the east. According to S. Kalyanaraman, a research scholar, compellence and deterrence are two major subsets of strategic coercion.[11] Compellence is active and attempts to alter the status quo, while deterrence is passive, seeking to maintain the status quo. The strategies rely on threats to persuade each other's hostile behaviour. In this case, both strategies failed. Pakistan could not deter India from the war in the east by mobilising in the west and overplaying the threat of its perceived alliances with the US and China. India had credible intelligence about Chinese strategic calculations not to intervene militarily, and had not given any specific commitment to help protect Pakistan's territorial integrity.[12] The US, too, had not made any commitment to Pakistan. Likewise, India could not compel Pakistan to seek a political settlement with its eastern wing. For the compellence strategy to succeed, the coercing power's threat must be credible enough to convince the adversary of its military capacity. The Indian Armed Forces had a favourable force ratio of 1.4:1 over Pakistan, but not adequate to compel Pakistan to accede to India's demand for a political settlement. However, its provocative escalation matrix succeeded in strategic dislocation, and deception, of Pakistani forces. The synchronisation intensified activities along the border and in the interior, made Pakistan apprehensive of India's possible politico-military objectives in East Pakistan. It was in a dilemma. Would India capture limited territory close to the border to install a puppet Bangladesh Government, and recognise the same internationally, or launch a well-planned military offensive to defeat and secure its Army's surrender? Appreciating the former option, the Pakistan Army relocated its forces from the interior to build up strong defences around major towns, leaving the geographical space denuded by Pakistan open for the Mukti Bahini to dominate.

India's occupation of East Pakistan territory since 21 November incensed the Pakistani officers, who felt that their leadership was not doing anything except giving empty statements. They strongly felt that declaring war on India was a matter of pride, prudence, and necessity.[13] Adding fuel to the fire, Bhutto warned the President that if he did not react forcefully to India's aggression, he would be 'lynched by the people'.[14] Yahya ordered preemptive air strikes on 3 December 1971. India, naturally, welcomed the development. When informed, D.P. Dhar, the member of PM's core group, succinctly remarked, 'The fool has done exactly what one had expected.'[15] Pakistan was trapped to initiate the war, though western analysts believed that India started the war in November 1971 when its Army occupied chunks of East Pakistan territory in more realistic terms.[16] From India's viewpoint, these were preliminary operations.

Military Strategy – War-fighting

Considering East Pakistan to be the centre of gravity where the war was to be won or lost, the overall Indian military strategy of 'a swift offensive in the east, offensive-defensive in the west, and defensive along the northern borders' was eminently logical, sound, and prudent. A quick offensive in East Pakistan was imperative to achieve a decisive victory before the international community could intervene. It was exactly opposite to that of Pakistan, which had planned to defend East Pakistan, by waging war in the west to draw the Indian forces away from the East, thereby gaining enough time for the international community to intervene. Considering the vast geographical separation between the two Pakistans, its strategy for defending the east by war in the west was sound and correct, however, it could not aggressively execute its offensive plans.

Eastern Theatre – Dhaka, not a Military Objective

The Indian Army did not earmark Dhaka—the capital and the geopolitical centre of power in East Pakistan as a military objective, not even a contingency task. The planners considered its capture an ambitious proposition. According to Raghavan, Major General K.K. Singh, the Director of Military Operations felt that 'the Indian Army with its inherent inhibitions against anything unorthodox and a more speedy type of manoeuvre was ill-suited for attempting the capture of Dhaka'.[17] It considered crossing one of the three rivers—Padma, Jamuna, and Meghna—in the face of enemy opposition to attack Dhaka a tall order. In August 1971, the Eastern Command had proposed to keep Dhaka as the final objective, but the COAS overruled it. According to Lieutenant General Jacob, the COAS felt that by capturing Khulna and Chittagong, Dhaka would automatically fall, and that there was no need to take it.[18] Both Khulna and Chittagong did not fall until 16 December—the day the Pakistani forces surrendered.

The Army, learning from the 1965 War experience, factored in the likely international pressure for a ceasefire. It was apprehensive that an early ceasefire might end the war without capturing vast territory or Dhaka. It opted to secure a vast area, appreciating that the military's rapid progress would lead to the eventual collapse of the Pakistani resistance and make Dhaka untenable before a ceasefire. Therefore, the task assigned to Eastern Command was 'limited to occupying the major portion of Bangladesh instead of the entire country.'[19] India did not expand its strategic aim to secure Dhaka even after achieving significant success in the first week of the war. Instead, it needlessly captured some tactical objectives that did not contribute to the strategic aim of a swift offensive to occupy vast territory. The advance to Khulna after the fall of Jessore, the capture of Hilli, Jhenida, Rangpur, and the attack on Mynamati are few such examples. Attrition battles were fought instead of manoeuvre. General Rao, the former Army Chief, rightly lamented, 'If forces employed on these strategically unimportant and infructuous missions could be utilised for developing thrust towards Dhaka, perhaps its capture would have been further speeded up, and the number of casualties reduced.'[20] The Army justified capturing these tactical objectives to have substantial territory in its control before the imposition of any UN-sponsored ceasefire. However, in the final analysis, it was the threat posed to Dhaka by more than five brigades across the Meghna River that made the Pakistani position militarily untenable. Lieutenant General Sagat Singh's boldness to execute a brilliant manoeuvre, to transport more than a division-size force across the Meghna River, made a crucial difference.

The Army allotted the least amount of troops to the Northern Sector, which did not have any river obstacle, negating the DGMO's assertion that Dhaka's capture was not attempted due to the operations' difficulties that would arise out of crossing the river. The lack of an adequate logistic axis in the Northern Sector curtailed the quantum of troops employed. However, it could have been built up in the preparatory period. Despite India having credible intelligence about Chinese non-military intervention and the Indo-Soviet Treaty's deterrence, it remained unduly worried about the Chinese threat. The Army did not pull out any forces from the Chinese border till 8 December 1971 and employed only a brigade of its strategic reserves for an offensive. India could have hastened the operations had Dhaka been kept as a strategic military objective, and thrust lines developed along the Western, Northern, and Southeastern Sectors to converge on Dhaka. One of the formations could have been tasked *ab-initio* to attack earliest in conjunction with securing territory. 2 Corps were in a good position to execute a manoeuvre similar to the one by 4 Corps.

River Meghna's crossing demonstrated the highest degree of close synergy between the Army and the IAF. Lieutenant General Sagat Singh and Group Captain Chandan Singh meticulously planned and brilliantly executed the heliborne lift of almost three brigades in over 350 sorties. This build-up rendered Dhaka's position untenable. The synergy assumed greater significance as it was not preplanned, but the Pakistan Army's rapid collapse offered the opportunity that was optimally exploited. The pressure exerted by the IN on Chittagong and Cox's Bazar, the interdiction of Pakistani shipping, added to Pakistan's psychological pressure to surrender. Mukti Bahini played a useful role in providing intelligence and harassing Pakistani forces by raiding isolated and lightly held posts and static installations.

Western Theatre – Cautious Approach

The Western Theatre, adhering to its strategy to hold ground, considerably succeeded not only in thwarting Pakistani designs but also capturing significant territory. India took a significant risk in deploying its defensive formations quite late to provoke any Pakistani offensive. The Pakistan Army was battle-ready by mid-October, and the Indian Army achieved operational readiness by mid-November. Had Pakistan mounted a surprise attack, the situation would have become precarious for the Army. The decision not to launch a 1 Corps offensive till Pakistan mounted its offensive led to the loss of initiative and surprise. 1 Corps could not secure Zaffarwal or Shakargarh. Excessive caution in its employment limited its potential, however, its initial deployment in a defensive role ensured the Pathankot corridor's security. In the Chhamb Sector, the Field Commander's obsession with offensive operations despite impending enemy attack inputs led to the neglect of defensive preparations. In Rajasthan, the Barmer Sector's offensive achieved significant success and set the stage for further exploitation, but the lack of adequate logistic support inhibited it. 1 Armoured Division remained unemployed throughout the war, catering to a Pakistani threat which did not materialise. Nor it posed any threat to Pakistan, despite its offensive in Shakargarh, and Rajasthan had drawn in additional Pakistan forces. Arjun Subramaniam commented very aptly, 'The anticipated mother of all battles between the two armoured divisions remained in the realm of fiction.'[21] General Rao was right in asserting that India could have made substantial gains in the Western Theatre had the strategy been implemented more vigorously.[22] India could have continued military operations in West Pakistan after the surrender in the east. However, the Government considered the political advantages of international prestige and goodwill accruing out of a unilateral cease-fire of far greater significance than inflicting additional attrition and capturing crucial territory. It overlooked the long-term strategic deterrence on any futuristic Pakistani misadventure and did not invoke the Clausewitzian theory of suppressing the enemy's will.

Conclusion

India comprehensively achieved its political objective through a decisive military victory. The establishment of lasting peace after the war is an essential ingredient of the paradigm of war, but it has rarely happened. If we go by the Clausewitzian dictum that the object of war is not victory but enduring peace, most wars would fall short of the standards.[23] The 1971 Indo-Pakistan War partially exemplifies the same. India comprehensively attained the national interest of maintaining its socio-cultural identity. India orchestrated the refugee crisis through a deft calibration of politico-diplomatic-military strategy. India's decision to intervene militarily after exhausting other alternatives proved eminently right.

Lieutenant General (Dr) J.S. Cheema, PVSM, AVSM, VSM superannuated as the Deputy Chief of the Army Staff in November 2017. After retirement, he acquired a PhD from Panjab University, and is presently the Vice Chancellor at the Maharaja Bhupinder Singh Punjab Sports University.

Endnotes

1. Smith, Rupert. *The Utility of Force: The Art of War in the Modern World.* Penguin UK, 2012, p 183.
2. Rao, K. V. Krishna. *Prepare Or Perish: A Study of National Security.* Lancer Publishers, 1991, p. 170 and, Prasad, Sri Nandan, and Uma Prasad Thapliyal. *The India-Pakistan War of 1971: A History.* 2014, pp. 105-106.
3. Prasad and Thapliyal, op cit, p. 105.
4. Jacob, Lt. Gen J. F. R. *An Odyssey In War And Peace.* Roli Books Private Limited, 2011, pp.79-80. Also see Raghavan, Srinath. 1971 *A Global History of the Creation of Bangladesh.* Permanent Black, 2013, p. 238.
5. Rao, op cit, p. 171.
6. Rao, op cit, p. 158.
7. Subramaniam, Arjun. *India's Wars: A Military History, 1947-1971.* Harper Collins, 2016, pp. 382-83, quoting Air Vice Marshal Chandan Singh, *The Meghna Crossing* in Katoch, Dhruv C., and Quazi Sajjad Ali Zahir. *Liberation: Bangladesh* - 1971. Bloomsbury, 2015) pp. 218-22.
8. Jacob, op cit, p. 84.
9. Prasad and Thapliyal, op cit, p. 395.
10. While speaking in the Security Council, Bhutto lambasted the UN for not acting on time, tore up a copy of the resolution, and walked out of the session. No further discussion took place, and the resolution was dead. Bhutto calculated that only an ignominious surrender of the Pakistan Army would lead to his political ascendancy. He was proved right. Five days later, on 20 December 1971, he took over as President and Chief Martial Law Administrator of Pakistan. The previous day, when President Yahya seeing an opportunity to avoid the surrender rang up Bhutto in New York to accept the Polish resolution, the latter pretended not to hear despite repeated calls and even admonished the operator, who intervened to state that the telephone connection was good. See Raghavan, op cit, p. 261, quoting 1614th Meeting of the UN Security Council, 14/15 December 1971, S/PV.1614, UN Archives
11. Kalyanaraman, S. "Operation Parakram: An Indian Exercise in Coercive Diplomacy." *Strategic Analysis,* vol. 26, no. 4, Oct. 2002, p. 479, doi:10.1080/09700160208450063.
12. Raghavan, op cit, pp. 186-88.
13. Sisson, Richard, and Leo E. Rose. *War and Secession: Pakistan, India, and the Creation of Bangladesh.* Univ of California Press, 1990, p. 228.
14. Ibid, p. 230 quoting Interviews Pakistan and USA, 1979.
15. Raghavan, op cit. p. 234 , quoting Dixit, Jyotindra Nath. *Liberation and Beyond: Indo-Bangladesh Relations.* Konark Publishers Pvt. Limited, 1999, p. 89.
16. Sisson and Rose, op cit, n. 1, p. 214.
17. Raghavan, op cit, p. 236.
18. Jacob, op cit. p. 80.
19. Raghavan, op cit, p. 236, quoting Sukhwant Singh. *India's Wars Since*

Independence: The Liberation of Bangladesh. Lancer, 1980, pp. 68-69, 72, 90-91. Major General Sukhwant Singh was the deputy director of military operations in 1971.

20. Rao, op cit, p. 200
21. Subramaniam, op cit, p. 418
22. Rao, op cit, p. 244
23. Raghavan, V.R. *Wars Old and New: Structural Changes,* adapted from the Field Marshal Memorial Lecture delivered on Infantry Day, 27 October 2015 and published in USI Journal, vol. CLXV, no. 602, October- December 2-15, p. 463

6

Rose and Thorn Siachen: The Frozen Wedge

Colonel Amit Vig

Geographical and Climatic Setting

Balti herdsmen and traders revelled at the 'abundance of Sia' (wild rose) after the winter thawed and snow-melted as they travelled the few Silk Road feeder routes for trade, pilgrimage, and settlement. Centuries later, a British adventurer and explorer would name it Siachen – Gardens of Rose. Lying in the Eastern Karakorams (Turkic for black gravel – as they appeared), at an average altitude of 18,000 ft, the Siachen Glacier is 76 km in length, one to eight km wide and frozen the whole year round. Bounded by the Saltoro Ridge (sub-range of Karakorams) on the west and the main Karakoram Range on its east, the Glacier slopes downwards from Indira Col (20,000 ft) in the northwest to its snout (11,000 ft) in the southeast. Several small glaciers join it from the western and eastern flanks, providing routes into and out of it. Blizzard, avalanche, crevasse, white-out, sunburn, light blinding, low oxygen, wind-chill, rarefied atmosphere and extremely low temperature are the constant characteristics of Siachen. The Karakorams lie between the Shaksgam, Indus and Shyok river systems. Several tributaries emanating from the glaciers flow into them, and extend from the Mintaka Pass in the west to the Karakoram Pass in the east. Karakorams lie in the border zone between Xinjiang (China), Hunza-Baltistan (Pakistan-occupied), and Ladakh (India) and contain such peaks that offer dangerously attractive challenge to mountaineers. Major routes skirt the ranges following river valleys as the Karakorams are a substantial natural barrier.

The region of Ladakh is a cold, high altitude desert. Vegetation is sparse for grazing animals, requiring pastoral families to often live a nomadic life. River valleys support some farming. Mountains are barren and rivers make deep and steep gorges and sudden wind gusts are dangerous to driving and flying. Siachen Glacier gives rise to the Nubra River that merges with River Shyok that eventually joins the Indus which flows from Tibet (China) through Ladakh and Gilgit-Baltistan to Pakistan and the Arabian Sea. The topography, climate, and weather are a consequence of the northward abutment of the Indian Plate into the Eurasian Plate. Climate change seems to be affecting the rate of recession of glaciers in the summer months and flooding is more frequent. The region also offers mineral wealth, besides fresh water for living, farming, and hydro-power generation. Wind and solar power can also be fruitfully harnessed. Being remote and isolated, connectivity by land and air needs massive resources but are vital for administration and defence. Population density is low and life is simple and slow. Buddhism and Islam are the major religions followed since centuries.

Historical Setting

Till the conquests of Maharaja Ranjit Singh in this region and its incorporation into the Sikh Empire, the region was mostly under Tibetan dynastic rule or tutelage, or semi-independent under the major tribes that inhabited the region. Ladakh consisted of the Dards, Kampas, Mons, Brokpas, and others (Indo-Aryans). Tibetan, Indo-Greek immigrants and immigrants from Skardo had also settled down in Ladakh, as had Baltis and some Hunza. It also came under Kushan rule when Buddhism took hold in the region and beyond. Bon religion was introduced by Tibetan dynasts and the mixed population became Tibetanised in culture (Kang culture – Kangri, Kangra and so on). Lalitaditya (Ruler of Kashmir) had also captured Ladakh, extending his influence up to Central Asia. Later, Islam entered Ladakh from Central Asia. The Chinese, Tibetans, and Arabs frequently fought in the area for control. Shey and later, Leh, have been the capitals of independent Ladakh since the tenth century. For a time, Ladakh extended from Mansarover to Swat (including Himachal). Sultanate rule began in the mid-fifteenth century, followed again by Tibetan rule (Namgyal dynasty). Mughal rule extended up to the borders with Ladakh and even helped Ladakh's ruler Gyatso to fight back Tibeto-Mongol forces. Subsequently, the Sikh empire overran Ladakh and parts of Tibet. The British, in the nineteenth century, took over the region from the descendants of Ranjit Singh and installed a Dogra King in J&K, but without much authority over Ladakh.

Political Setting

The issue of settling the frontiers in Ladakh had been considered since Curzon's Viceroyalty. But the Dogra ruler's claims, Chinese tactics of ambivalence, and British strategic interests in Central Asia led to indecisiveness as to where the boundary should run. With British withdrawal, the Partition plan gave the right to the Dogra ruler to decide on merger, but he took the path of a standstill agreement. The regions under his control were Jammu, Kashmir, Gilgit-Baltistan, and Ladakh – the state's boundaries had been delineated by the British and finalised at the time of delineating the Durand Line. Coinciding with the Partition, Pakistan's attacks across borders of J&K and Ladakh, aided 'very timely' by the British, led the 'rebellion' against the King in Skardu-Gilgit and resulted in the merger of the state with India on the one hand and the creation of Pakistan-occupied Jammu & Kashmir (PoJK) across the Cease Fire Line (CFL) and 'Northern Areas' (Pakistan-occupied Gilit Baltistan [PoGB]) excluding Ladakh. J&K became a UN issue. In the 1960s, Eastern Ladakh (Aksai Chin) was claimed and occupied by China, which

A map of J&K highlighting the area of Siachen.

also took over the Shaksgam Valley from Pakistan in the Balti-Hunza area, north of the Karakorams. In 1971–72 the CFL became the LOC up to map grid point NJ9842 (since the Karachi Agreement of 1949). The Indian J&K state assembly keeps 24 seats reserved for the representatives of PoJK and PoGB, which for obvious reasons, have to be left vacant.

Strategic Setting

In 2019, India redrew the map of the J&K state vide which the Union Territory (UT) of Ladakh includes PoGB. This is the region where there is physical collusion between Pakistan-China, being of strategic interest to both. Previously, from 1947–84, the Karakorams were never contested during any of the Indo-Pakistan wars. The LOC delineation and demarcation, officially agreed by both, stated that the non-delineated area north of grid point NJ9842 would be defined by a notional line 'Running North' from that point along the Saltoro ridges up to the Shaksgam border in the north.

The implication being that the uninhabited glaciated region was expected to remain unoccupied by either side. China, in occupation of Aksai Chin up to the Karakoram (KK) Pass in the east and of Shaksgam Valley north of Karakorams, and Pakistan, in areas across Turtok and in Balti-Hunza in the west, meant that the Siachen Glacier and surrounding ridges were a wedge between the west (Pakistan) and east (China). The River Shyok runs close to the KK Pass east of the Karakorams, descends southwards, somewhat parallel to China's 1959 Claim Line but within Indian control, till it reaches the Ladakh range and turns northwestwards, skirting the Karakorams from the south and entering PoGB across the Chorbatla-Turtok LOC to join the Indus. The Nubra River merges with the Shyok as it runs southwards from Siachen Glacier's snout. While the river runs mostly in Indian controlled territory from Turtok to Daulat Beg Oldi (DBO) and KK Pass, the river has strategic value for all three.

But for the glaciers and altitude, any student of military geography can see that occupation of the Siachen wedge would be to the strategic advantage of the occupier providing dominance over the areas to the north, west, and east. Logistics is critical to force sustenance on the glaciers and lines of communications are but one or two. Only in good weather are low altitude air supply drops feasible. High altitude drops are wasteful. Stocking on the Glacier is limited and is mostly at base camp and other maintenance bases in the rear.

The Play

Pakistan had used the Karakorams for running coveted mountaineering expeditions for foreign enthusiasts from Europe and Japan. It was a money-earner and Pakistan enjoyed international acceptance of the region as being nominally under its control. As international airlines need identification lines when flying overhead across nations, Pakistan had provided maps showing a straight line running from NJ9842 to the KK Pass in the Northeast, thereby including the Saltoro and eastern Karakoram ridges within territory under its control. In 1978, a US expedition for the Siachen from Indian side, being escorted by Colonel Narendra 'Bull' Kumar, PVSM, KC, of the Indian Army, a brilliant and tough mountaineer with Everest and other peaks under his belt, was seen carrying maps of the region showing the 'Hodgson Line', as had been surveyed by the US. 'Thence northwards' was thus exploited by Pakistan as to run to the KK Pass. This was reported to Corps Commander and to the Army HQ as 'cartographic aggression' by Pakistan. Pakistan could not be allowed joining up with China through the southeastern Karakorams. Colonel Narendra, then Director HAWS, began more frequent expeditions with Army's mountaineering teams up to Indira Col, reconnoitring and mapping the glaciers and the ridges and the environment, looking for signs

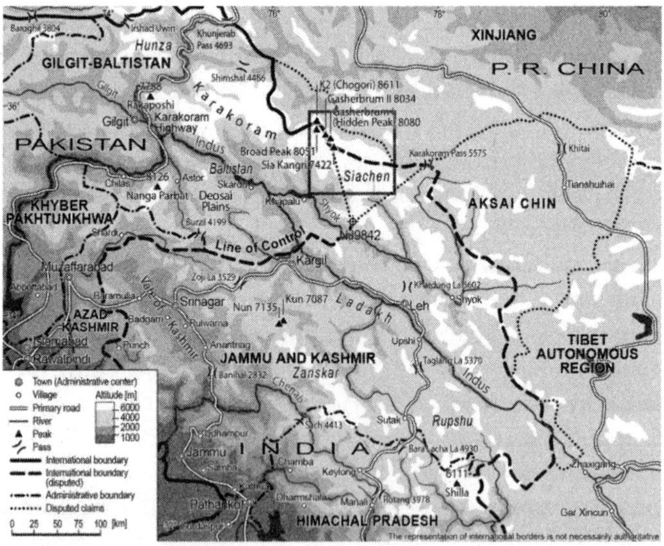

The location of the Siachen glacier showing the physical terrain, overlapping boundary claims, and de facto borders of India, Pakistan, and China.

of Pakistan Army escorted expeditions. The pattern continued during the summer months in subsequent years. In 1982, Pakistan began objections to India's forays onto the Glacier and ridges without its permission. Indian Army had launched Exercise Ibex on the Glacier followed by Exercise Polar Bear I and II in 1983. Between these two, the Pakistan Army also ran an exercise to the Glacier but deinducted, leaving behind a note reminding the Indian Army that the Glacier was theirs. Apparently, an innocent 'demarche'.

The Challenge

The challenge was huge. If the Pakistan army had to do the improbable, the Indian Army had to do the impossible—occupy the Glacier and heights before the Pakistan Army could and stay there. After all, it is the mountain logic: the first on it, takes all. It was to be a zero-sum game. Since 1979, General Zia, the Chief Martial Law Administrator (CMLA) Pakistan, was in a sweet spot with US and international diplomatic support, and aid was pouring in to fight the Soviet Army in Afghanistan. His plan for Punjab and J&K was yet be fulfilled, especially with increasing Islamisation of the Armed Forces and the progress on the Bomb that he had hastened by 1983-84. The plan for Siachen was largely left to the COS, the DGMO, 10 Corps and Northern Light Infantry (NLI) Commanders, who decided to move onto the Glacier's southern half – Bilafond La – starting 1 May 1984. They were confident since access from Pakistan to Bilafond La and Siala and other Saltoro peaks was relatively easier and faster, but Indian intelligence had done a better job than Pakistan's.

Strategy

Lieutenant General M.L. Chhiber was the DGMO in 1978, to whom Colonel 'Bull' Kumar showed the commercial/civil map. The Chief, General Raina, was informed and permission was taken to run yearly summertime expeditions on the Glacier's peaks. MoD and the MEA were also informed of the 'aberration'. Pakistan sent no expeditions in 1981 and 1982. In 1983, a Pakistani patrol left a protest note from from the Pakistani Sector Commander at Bilafond La for 26 Sector Commander, Brigadier Vijay Channa, which was replied with a counter-protest note. Thereafter, notes on claims of intrusions across LOC by Indian patrols continued with warnings and threats. Their helicopter (heptr) patrols would fly over Indian patrols. In 1983, General A.S. Vaidya was the COAS, and

Lieutenant General Hoon took over 15 Corps. A prefabricated hut and some troops were sent by chopper as a trial to establish living conditions. Lieutenant Genera Chhiber took over as the Northern Army Commander.

In 1983, Pakistan Army mounted a two-company mission of NLI and Special Service Group (SSG) troops from its base in Skardu, to occupy Siala and Bilafond La, but failed due to poor logistical planning. In January '84 Pakistan began lifting arctic clothing for the 'Burzil Force'. Their DGMO, GOC 10 Corps, Brigadier T.M. Shaheen, 62 Brigade and SSG under Major Khan, planned Operation Ababeel in March 1984, which was postponed to 1 May 1984, on considerations of weather and preparations required. Incidentally, Musharraf was with the SSG then, but later, as Brigadier in the sector, he mounted several assaults in 1986 and 1987, each of which failed.

The Directive from the Government and the Chief to Northern Army was 'Pakistan Army was to be prevented from occupying Siachen, but in a way as to prevent a larger war.' Lieutenant General Chhiber, Lieutenant General Hoon, Major General Shiv Sharma (3 Division), Brigadier Channa, Colonel Narendra and other officers (Captain S. Kulkarni, Colonel Pushkar Chand, Majar Bahuguna, Major Sandhu) who had trained and participated in patrols under him, began planning Operation Meghdoot in late 1983. Whether the name came from Kalidasa's poem and/or after the Meghdoot Force of 1965 War under Major Megh Singh (who raised and commanded 9 Para Commando, the first Special Forces unit in the Army), we do not know. Air Headquarter (HQ) and Air Officer Commanding (AOC) J&K was part of the planning process. In March 1984, 4 Kumaon and Ladakh Scouts began staging up from Leh towards the Siachen Base.

The strategic and operational issues that were considered were:

Surprise: Surprise was key and preemption was the only and logical choice. Hence, a platoon-size force for each pass – Bila and Sia – was planned to be inducted by heptr to retain surprise. The date decided was 15 April, before Pakistan's Ababeel date. There were risks, but dealing with weather was considered better than dealing later with an enemy occupying the heights.

Sustenance: Sustenance of the operation for permanency meant that trained reserves and reinforcements had to be in proximity and a logistics chain that had to function in all-weather with quick turn-round timings. Living had to be provided for year-round survivability. Staying power needed infrastructure and fighting wherewithal. The road connectivity had to eventually provide for two-way traffic, and while helicopter lift (helilift) was planned, it was vulnerable to weather.

Logistics: The logistics plan included Chandigarh Air Base, Srinagar, Kargil, Leh, and Partapur-Thoise. Logic dictated that the chain further up to Siachen Base had to be staged at two points to prevent enemy bombers or artillery from destroying the single largest base. In the mountains, it is a war of logistics, and Pakistan's patrols and missions had been failing for this very reason. Lessons from 1962 were also clear. On the Glacier, six-way camps, a mission HQ camp, and base camps for Sia and Bilafond were necessary to provide for staging up and down of troops and storage of stores. Drop Zones were earmarked. Helipads at the passes Kumar HQ and Nubra (Glacier) Base were also planned.

Unique Fighting Techniques: This unique and unprecedented military mission involved surviving extreme weather realities and an enemy. Speed of operations would be very slow and the defender had all the advantage. Attacking was not a viable option. This implied acclimatisation, proximal medical support and casualty evacuation, special clothing, tentage, heating, equipment and weapon, and munitions had to be functional in adverse weather.

Diplomacy: Several conversations at the MEA level and by military commanders across the LOC were held to size up each other's intent and prevent a conflict. The MEA had to dissuade Pakistan from precipitation of the issue while preventing support to Pakistan by foreign powers. Military officers' visits to Europe were kept low profile, engaging in the assurance of clothing and equipment while picking up the scent of Pakistan's preparation levels. Pakistan, under Zia, was to be kept in the dark about our intent. Hence the wording and tenor of the conversations made them sound like standard practice. Besides, noise on Pakistan's interference in Punjab using Afghan (anti-Soviet) related funds and armament was kept at a high pitch, and Pakistan 'saw' Indian Army's focus only on Punjab. The UN Mission for India and Pakistan, monitoring the LOC since 1949, had no access to Siachen on the Indian side since LOC ended at NJ9842. They were kept in good humour by some cross-border firing notifications or complaints in the LOC sector outside Ladakh. Diplomacy helped in the cover for the achievement of surprise. In fact, Meghdoot's success emboldened democratic forces in Pakistan against Army rule.

The Preemptive Insertion

Operation Meghdoot began on 13 April 1984, when India and Pakistan celebrate Baisakhi, a day of harvest and merry making – an auspicious day. The Task Force was organised into two parties – the trekking and the heliborne parties. A pair of Allouttes dropped the first team from 4 Kumaon, consisting of an officer and three men, on Bilafond base in the early morning of 13 April. Lacking firm ground to land on, the first team jumped with their loads and radio, prepared a firm landing for both heptrs to land, off-load, and take off to base to ferry up the next group. Flying is hazardous in the best of times, with heptr flight ceiling of 18,500 ft or so, and it needs to keep the rotors running due to low oxygen to fire its engines in cold temperatures. Soft snow is unsuited for landing, and take-off or landing throws up so much loose snow that the heptr may not even be seen for a short while! The ground party snaked up the Nubra snout to set up Camp I. Camp sites are chosen on tactical, administrative and weather considerations, and for safety from possible avalanches and crevasses. But the clear day suddenly turned sour, blizzards would not allow flying, and so the second Kumaon team and the Siala Team of Ladakh Scouts were held up. The four men of the stranded Kumaon team and Meghdoot now had their first altitude sickness death. Radios were silent for secrecy and for two days, the hapless team dragged itself towards Bila pass on a luckily functional compass. When the weather lifted on day three, heptr sorties were made to Bila base and it was only on 17 April that it became possible for Ladakhis to be heli-dropped on Siala base. They reached Siala the same day. The Corps Commander flew in with Indian Flag, which was promptly hoisted! The team at Siala later did the same. In the meantime, a recce heptr (Lama) of the Pakistan Army, flying to Bila on the 16 April, was challenged by Kumaonis, which then turned quickly back to debrief its perplexed seniors. The race had earnestly begun.

Trudging uphill through 3 ft snow, slowly (due to low oxygen) but steadily, trekking parties established Camps I to VI at Bila and Sila bases and the 'Kumar' Camp, the controlling HQ of the Mission Commander over about ten days, along the 75 km length of the Glacier up to Indira Col base. Ski Troopers blazed ahead, pitching in coloured rods for direction and Signallers rolled out lines through short time blizzards, anchoring and aligning lines over rocks and holes. Heptr drops continued with troops, man-pack armament and stores. IAF's modified Packet aircraft airdropped supplies of food, tentage, duckboards, medicine, etc. Porters fetched kerosene and ammo. Heavier weaponry, dismantled, was flown in under slung. On 27 April, a Pakistan patrol that went up the Alibrangza Glacier to approach Bilafond La was fired upon. The strategic surprise was complete both for Pakistan and China. That put Pakistani commanders in a huddle. There was now nearly a battalion strength of armed troops of all arms on Siachen with secure logistics lines. In spite of bad weather, the Indian Army had pre-empted them. They were there to stay it seemed.

Dilemmas Unfold

The Saltoro ridge line was under control, in spite of the daily weather or terrain casualties. Flanking ridges and glaciers were under observation as was Shaksgam to the north. Indian Commanders were elated by possibilities and the PM was pleased. Zia was bewildered. A Pakistani heptr recce on Siala was fouled; an SSG team sent up the Burzil pass in late April to probe Bila was shot at. The first shots were exchanged. The Pakistan Army moved up its troops towards Saltoro to establish bases or camps along the Bila, Siala and Gyongla axes, to try and recce heights overlooking the passes. Pakistan and Indian forces on the other LOC sectors were brought to 'stand to' status. Indian Commanders, the MO, COSC, MEA, RAW, IB and PMO were also in heads-in mode. What military or diplomatically options did Pakistan have? Would the USA, China, and UNSC pressurise? Certainly, it was a morale booster for the Armed Forces and Balti roses had become a large thorn for the Pakistan establishment. Several of these questions had been war gamed, of course, yet the situational dynamics required a continuous monitoring and decision making.

The Game Was On

There was no surprise for Pakistan after 27 April. The month of May was mostly clear except for the 10 days when the weather unexpectedly remained packed-up, causing serious supply hardships, affecting the morale of some of the superstitious Ladakhis. Continuous snow and then an avalanche buried most the camp down! It was rumoured that a sacred bird had probably been killed causing its spirit to bring punishing weather. Even the Ski Troopers using navigation rods and compass found it difficult to go to Siala Base to fetch rations and kerosene, but they finally managed. Siala had been nearly fasting! It took the officers multiple rounds of talking to the Ladakhi troops to calm them down! Control HQ at 'Kumar' was also anxiously concerned!

In the meantime, Indian Army was reinforcing itself with artillery Grad-P, 23 mm AD guns, and Strela missiles, wrapped up in snow bedding for protection against moisture and cold. Engineers' teams laid out mines on access routes, anchoring them to prevent sinking in snow. SOPs for patrolling, 'stand to', personal hygiene (snow bath), and so on, were laid down. Special food items such as chocolates, energy drinks, biscuits, toffees, nuts, etc., were flown in, and mail sent out. To maintain morale, the wives of the Army Chief, the Army and Corps Commanders, gathered a team to write letters (the red field letter) to each officer and soldier on Meghdoot, for their bravery against odds and for serving the nation. The ladies signed each letter personally. The touch was warming and worked very well. The DRDO came up with ready-to-eat-meals which were sent up on trials. There were small arctic tents (or igloos) and larger ones. Troops moving subsequently in small groups carried two-man small tents. A Dutch-made wax tin was used for warmth, and to heat and warm food. Sigris came up for the bigger tents. Troop rotation was planned on a six-to-eight-week basis. Airdropped supplies would be damaged, even lost deep in snow or in inaccessible areas. Medicines in liquid form would freeze. Firing of weapons would be sluggish but achieve greater range than prescribed. The trajectory of the round or shell, in the weapon's close proximity, would be physically visible because the surrounding air would quickly freeze, leaving a white wake of ice. Gun and mortar emplacements had to be restrengthened regularly and often their positions shifted. The pressure of the base plate would melt the snow, necessitating improvisation. Rather clever solutions were found too. Trenches and machine guns were continuously re-dug and re-positioned. Parachute fabric had to keep all weapons and stores covered at all times.

In the month of May, crevasses began to open making loud sounds akin to a detonation, shaking the ground. Moraines ran down the edges as snow melted. Crossing over crevasses is risky and a team skill that requires practice. Additional challenges had, thus, to be faced and overcome. Reinforcements moved up and casualties moved down. In the 'good' month of June, Pakistan Army made its first assault on Bilafond La on the 22–23 June. Op Ababeel, which was to begin on 1 May, but attempted a preponement in vain between 15 and 27 April, finally found its feet in June '84. The Bilafond force, called 'Zorawar' by us, was to be removed by the Pakistan Army's 'Burzil force' and occupy the pass. The assault began with mortars, troops moved up on skis and firing, followed by troops on foot. The Kumaonis took a couple of casualties, but retaliated strongly, picking off about a dozen of the enemy. Pakistan's move as a tactic was doomed. At dawn, against a white background, spotting was easy and targeting easier. The Kumaonis were alert and not hunkered down by snow, as was perhaps assumed by the Burzil commander. The assault broke. Their casualties were allowed to be taken back. It was a slow-motion battle as can be expected on the glacier.

Aftermath

Over the next two to three years, while India strengthened and expanded its hold on Siachen and reorganised its forces, a brigade-sized force held the Glacier with Pakistan mirroring it. The Pakistan Army made several attempts to move up as close as possible to find opportunity targets and heights to occupy. Repeated attempts were made, but each attempt failed. The Indian Army began testing its new doctrine on the western borders, simultaneously overcoming the trouble in Punjab (after having cleansed the Golden Temple of terrorists), with manoeuvre forces, through a number of exercises from 1984 to 1987. The Pakistan Army had little inclination now towards Siachen. It was uncertain about the east while its west was still hot. India had also raised its 28 Division in Kupwara-Gurez and had moved its HQ with some troops in 1984–85 to Nimu in Ladakh. By 1987, the Division responsible for the LOC sector from Zojila to the KK Pass was well acquainted with 'battlefield' Siachen. The Pakistan Army's SSG had occupied the Qaid Post, on Gyongla Glacier, in the southern sub-sector of Siachen, which dominated the Bilafond deployment by observation and fire. To dislodge them, Op Rajiv was launched under 28 Division, with teams of JAK Rifles, in June '87. Indian Army's Amar and Sonam posts came routinely under fire, interfering with the movement of supplies and causing casualties. A dangerously sheer cliff climb with a two-abreast formation was only possible on the approach ridge. Repeated attacks were repulsed by Qaid Post that had led to severe casualties till it was finally crushed and renamed Bana Post, after the then Havildar Bana Singh, PVC. The approach march, and the ice wall climb in the snow and the wind had all to be stealthily undertaken. Fire support was attempted, but it took four days to finish the task, teetering literally on the edge. A herculean task by any standard, yet it was accomplished.

In September 1987, Pakistan Army launched another attack towards Bilafond La, to recapture the Bana Post with SSG troops, this time with better determination. Operation Vajr Shakti dealt another fatal blow to the attempt, while also improving the Bilafond position. Thereafter, the battle shifted to the southwestern parts of the Glacier with attempts from 1989

(28 Div had moved to Kupwara) to 1999, on lower peaks and passes, but were thwarted. Pakistan Army could not regain the honour it so wanted. By now, there was artillery support available, Igla missiles, snow scooters and much better wherewithal.

In 1989, the Soviets left Afghanistan and Pakistan moved the battle-hardened terrorists into J&K. India reinforced the Valley and fought back. Finding Kargil thinned out, their Chief planned the Kargil War in 1999, to cut Siachen off. Incidentally, General Musharaf was the Battalion Commander in the Northern Areas in 1984.

The Cost

India spends about ₹4 crore every day to hold Siachen. About ₹3,000 crore have been spent thus far. The human cost in terms of lives lost (about 800) and wounded by enemy action, and by weather and terrain (mostly), is difficult to measure. In military terms, soldiers lay down lives for the nation's security and are honoured for it. Yet, the morale has remained high and units feel proud to be part of it—of doing the tough thing, and carry back stories. Cost of equipment damage and re-supplies are absorbed into the overall cost. The entire sector is now transformed into a regular military garrison suited to Glacier conditions. Human losses on the Pakistan side have been higher and its overall costs are severe, given its economic condition.

Opening up the Glacier to regular tourism could bring in good amount of funds and forex. Books and media coverage could also bring in some funds from royalties and sponsors.

What Next

Siachen has gone into public consciousness, especially after Kargil, and thereafter, due to the social media. Since the ceasefire in 2003, the Glacier has been quiet, but since 2019, alert levels have again been raised. More than 4,500 troops now secure it.

Strategically, India cannot accept Pakistan's offer of demilitarisation since only Indian troops will have to move out. Demilitarisation was seriously discussed by Indian leadership mostly due to diplomatic compulsions but was negated by the COAS and the NSA. Besides, any vacation will promptly be used to occupy the Glacier by the Pakistan Army. It is a ruse and Pakistan cannot be trusted. What they could not achieve through force and with Kargil, they wish to achieve through overtures. No military will ever give up the height advantage.

Secondly, the security of Ladakh and Leh is inherent in the security and control of Siachen. Pakistan's occupation of Siachen would threaten Ladakh across the Khardungla, right up to the Ladakh Range. Due to the physical hand-shake with China, the entire sub-sector north of eastern Ladakh up to KK Pass would be jeapordised.

Thirdly, Pakistan gaining advantage over the Shyok Valley to the west and the east threatens Turtok and DBO respectively. It also gains control of the waters of rivers Nubra and Shyok.

Fourthly, any advantage to Pakistan is likely to bring China strategically into Ladakh. Its China Pakistan Economic Corridor (CPEC) is already looking for connectivity in PoGB.

Fifthly, Siachen is a strategic leverage for India to deal with Pakistan's Kashmir policy, to influence the population of POGB in its own favour, and to dominate and threaten Shaksgam, if the need ever arises.

Lastly, the glaciers and the Shyok Valley provide India the very strategic connection into PoGB and DBO-KK Pass in the area of Sub Sector North which is under tension because of the Chinese incursions in Galwan and Dipsang plains.

Any adversarial security situation in Ladakh is likely to negatively affect Tibetans in Himachal and Arunachal. China will gain immense strategic advantage. In any case, India has reclaimed its own legal territory. International community has accepted the fact. India has not gone further into PoGB.

Thus, the advantages far outweigh the costs. Till such time that the overall relations with Pakistan and China are settled and Indian interests are secured, Siachen, the frozen wedge, must remain in Indian hands. Incidentally, after Indira Gandhi in 1984, Dr Manmohan Singh as the PM, visited the Siachen. And since then, only the present PM, Mr Modi has visited Siachen on Diwali, in support of the troops.

'Juley', as the Ladakhis would greet.

Colonel Amit Vig, an Army Air Defence Veteran, was an Instructor at the National Defence Academy and Army Air Defence School. He has also served in Operation Meghdoot, Operation Vijay (and subsequently, recce of Ladakh and After-Action Report compilation), and CI operations in J&K. He holds Masters degrees in Defence and Strategic Studies (Gold Medalist), Public Administration, Mass Communication, and Personnel Management. He trained in AD Missile Systems in the USSR, and in Disaster Management at the National Civil Defence College. He compiled a book on the history of AD Arty in 2004, and has also served with Defence R&D in AD missile systems, and sensitive zone security.

Endnotes

1. Raikar, Sanat Pai. "Siachen Glacier." *Encyclopedia Britannica,* 20 July 1998, https://www.britannica.com/place/Siachen-Glacier.
2. Wilkinson, Freddie. "Nepali Mountaineers Achieve Historic Winter First on K2." *National Geographic,* 18 Jan. 2021, https://www.nationalgeographic.co.uk/adventure/2021/01/nepali-mountaineers-achieve-historic-winter-first-on-k2.
3. Francke, August Hermann. *A History of Ladakh.* Sterling Publishers, 1977.
4. Baghel, Ravi, and Marcus Nüsser. "Securing the Heights: The Vertical Dimension of the Siachen Conflict between India and Pakistan in the Eastern Karakoram." *Political Geography,* vol. 48, Sept. 2015, pp. 24–36, doi:10.1016/j.polgeo.2015.05.001.
5. Varghese, B. G. "Siachen Follies: Defining Facts and Objectives." *Centre for Policy Research,* May 2012.
6. The Tribune India. "Ladakh's Long Wait for More." *The Tribune India,* 30 Oct. 2018, https://www.tribuneindia.com/news/archive/comment/ladakh-s-long-wait-for-more-675649.
7. Gokhale, Nitin A. *Beyond NJ 9842: The SIACHEN Saga.* Bloomsbury Publishing, 2015.

8. Paul, Amit K. *Meghdoot: The Beginning of the Coldest War.* Notion Press, 2022.
9. Raghavan, V. R. *Siachen: Conflict Without End.* Viking Adult, 2002.
10. Kulkarni, Ramesh, and Anjali Karpe. *SIACHEN*, 1987: *Battle for the Frozen Frontier.* HarperCollins India, 2022.
11. "Siachen Glacier: Battling on the Roof of the World." I*ndian Defence Review (IDR), Quarterly Journal,* 18 Dec. 2018, http://www.indiandefencereview.com/spotlights/siachen-glacier-battling-on-the-roof-of-the-world/. Gen P Musharraf: In the Line of Fire, published by Simon & Schuster, Mar 2008
12. News, ANI. "EP-5." *YouTube,* 12 Apr. 2023, https://www.youtube.com/watch?v=wSYQRJWld0c.
13. Discovery, Veer by. "Operation Meghdoot." *YouTube*, 2 Feb. 2018, https://www.youtube.com/watch?v=3Q7AC66O8nU.
14. "Operation Meghdoot." Wikipedia, 16 Apr. 2023, https://en.wikipedia.org/wiki/Operation_Meghdoot.
15. "ResearchGate." *Research Gate*, http://15. www.researchgate.com. Publications related to Siachen conflict.
16. Author notes from personal diary, Siala 1984

7

A Critical Analysis of Operation Parakram

Lieutenant General Vijay Oberoi

Casus Belli

On the morning of 13 December 2001, a terrorist cell of five armed men attacked the Parliament of India by breaching the security cordon at Gate 12. The five men killed seven people before being shot dead by the Indian security forces.

World leaders and leaders in nearby countries strongly condemned the attack on the Parliament; Pakistan did the same too. On 14 December, the ruling NDA blamed Pakistan-based terrorist organisations, Lashkar-e-Taiba (LeT) and Jaish-e-Mohamad (JeM), for the attack. Indian Home Minister L.K. Advani indirectly referenced Pakistan and these militant groups by stating, 'We have received some clues about yesterday's incident, which shows that a neighbouring country, and some terrorist organisations active there are behind it.'

The same day, in a *démarche* to Pakistan's High Commissioner to India, Ashraf Jehangir Qazi, India demanded that Pakistan stop the activities of LeT and JeM, apprehend the organisation's leaders, and curb their access to all financial assets. Following the Indian Government's statements, Pakistan immediately put its military into full combat readiness.

The spokesman for the Pakistani military's public media wing, Inter-Services Public Relations (ISPR), Major General Rashid Qureshi, said that the attack on the Indian Parliament was a result of India's efforts to start a conflict with Pakistan, claiming that 'those [Indians] who can kill thousands of defenceless people in Kashmir can resort to such tactics to gain international sympathy. We demand the international community probe this attack independently to know the truth'. Another senior official maintained that India's failure to solve internal problems pushed them to blame Pakistan for everything without cause, stating, 'Why have the Indians rejected the US Government's offer to send an FBI team to investigate the attack on the parliament?'

Amid calls from the United States, Russia, and United Nations to exercise restraint, India mobilised and deployed its troops on the border, including in Kashmir, in what was India's largest military mobilisation since the 1971 War. The Indian codename for this mobilisation was Operation Parakram.

Planning

The three Service Chiefs were directed to commence the complete mobilisation of the Armed Forces. However, no directive defining the task or mission was issued, despite questioning by the Chiefs. The reply given was that the tasks would be given later. It was expected that the deployment of troops on India's Western border would take three to four weeks.

In the following days, while the troops and equipment were on the move, military actions involving a limited offensive against the terrorists' training camps in PoK were planned by India's Cabinet Committee on Security (CCS) for the second week of January 2002. 14 January 2002 was decided as the tentative D-Day.

According to the Indian strategy, a limited strike in PoK was preferred to convey the Indian resolve to Pakistan and keep the international retribution manageable. Indian actions would be comparable to the then ongoing US offensive in Afghanistan against Al Qaida terrorists.

Intelligence assessment suggested that the Pakistani Army was not well prepared. This further minimised the chances of Pakistan launching a full-scale war. A strong economy strengthened the Indian plans with low inflation and high petroleum and forex reserves. Finance Minister Yashwant Sinha further announced that the Indian economy was prepared for war, despite it being the final option. The build-up of troops signalled India's seriousness to the international community. If Pakistan's strategy did not change, India would have no other option but to obtain a decision through war.

Military Confrontations

In late December, both countries moved ballistic missiles closer to the border, and mortar and artillery fire was stepped up along the LoC in Kashmir. By January 2002, India had mobilised around 5,00,000 troops and three armoured divisions to the border with Pakistan, including along the LoC. Pakistan responded similarly, deploying approximately 3,00,000 troops.

The rising tensions between the two countries were partially diffused after Musharraf's speech on 12 January 2002, when he promised action on terror emanating from Pakistan.

Diplomatic Talks

India initiated its diplomatic offensive by recalling India's High Commissioner in Pakistan and banning civilian flights from Pakistan.

Pakistan initiated diplomatic talks with US President George W. Bush. US Secretary of State, Colin Powell, engaged with India and Pakistan to reduce tensions. In the first week of January, British Prime Minister Tony Blair visited India with a message that he was pressurising Pakistan's President Musharraf. The USA also declared LeT and JeM as foreign terrorist groups.

Musharraf's Speech

On 8 January 2002, India's Home Minister L.K. Advani visited the US, where he was informed about the contents of the upcoming landmark speech by Musharraf. On 12 January 2002, President Parvez Musharraf gave a speech intended to reduce tensions with India. For the first time, he condemned the attack on Parliament as a terrorist attack and compared it with the 9/11 attacks in the US. He declared in his speech that terrorism was unjustified in the name of Kashmir and that Pakistan would combat extremism on its own soil. Pakistan would resolve Kashmir with dialogue, and no organisation would be allowed to carry out terrorism under the pretext of Kashmir. As demanded by India, he also announced plans for the regulation of *madrasas* and banning known terrorist groups that were operating out of Pakistan. In addition, he formally banned five *jehadi* organisations, including JeM and LeT, engaged in militancy in Kashmir.

The Indian Decision

Indian Prime Minister Atal B. Vajpayee, though sceptic of the seriousness of Musharraf's pledges, decided not to carry out the military attack planned for 14 January.

Subsequently, for nearly four months, Indian policymakers took no decisions, although, after Musharraf's assurances, a decision to de-escalate could have been taken. As far as the Armed Forces were concerned, they continued their plans for conducting active operations. The tempo was, in fact, scaled up as the general feeling was that of euphoria amongst the troops because the victory seemed inevitable. However, such high levels of readiness could not be sustained for long as no decision was coming from the policymakers. In addition, fatalities, especially in the Indian Army, due to battle accidents as a result of faulty or outdated munitions, particularly land mines, did affect morale.

The Kaluchak Massacre

Tensions escalated significantly in May 2002. On 14 May, three suicide terrorists attacked an Army camp at Kaluchak near Jammu. They killed 34 people and injured 50 more before being killed themselves. Most victims were the wives and children of Indian soldiers serving in Kashmir. This terrorist incident again revived the chance of a full-blown war.

On 15 May, PM Vajpayee was quoted in the Indian Parliament saying, '*Hamein pratikar karna hoga.*' (We will have to counter it.) The US Deputy Secretary of State, Richard Armitage, quoted the incident as a trigger for further deterioration of the situation.

The Indian Cabinet had little faith that diplomatic pressure could stop Pakistan's support for the militants in Kashmir. India accused Pakistan of failing to keep its promise to end cross-border terrorism. India observed Musharraf's follow-up to his speech on 12 January as weak and disingenuous. Pakistan did not extradite the terrorist leaders demanded by India, and Lashkar was allowed to continue its operations in Pakistan as a charity with a new name. During the spring, *jehadi* militants started crossing the LoC again.

Review and Planning

On 18 May, Vajpayee reviewed the preparedness for war with Defence Minister Fernandes and senior military officers. The CCS met and favoured taking military action against terrorists in Pakistan. However, a limited military action like the one planned in January was now ruled out as Pakistan had strengthened its forces on the LoC, and any action in PoK alone would not have significant military gains. Therefore, the Indian military favoured an offensive along the Indo-Pak border, which would stretch the Pakistani troops and provide India access to PoK.

Accordingly, the Indian Armed Forces prepared the plan to target the war-waging capabilities of Pakistan and destroy terrorist camps. The battle canvas planned for June was larger than the one planned in January. The Indian Air Force and a strike corps would launch an attack in the Shakargarh Bulge against Pakistan's Army Reserve North (ARN) that was spread from Muzaffarabad to Lahore. Simultaneously, dual-tasked forces from the Eastern Command would carry out the offensive across the LoC and capture the strategic positions used by the terrorists for infiltrations. The period being considered was between 23 May and 10 June.

Military Confrontations

Towards the end of May 2002, the Indian and Pakistani Armed Forces continued to be fully mobilised. The tenor of statements published in the media and intelligence information collected pointed to an imminent invasion by India. An SOS sent to Israel by India's MoD for defence supplies during the month of June confirmed the intelligence.

On 18 May, India expelled the Pakistani High Commissioner. That same day, thousands of villagers had to flee due to Pakistani artillery fire in Jammu. On 21 May, clashes killed six Pakistani soldiers and one Indian soldier, as well as civilians from both sides. On 22 May, Indian Prime Minister Vajpayee announced to his troops to prepare for a 'decisive battle'.

Between 25 and 28 May, Pakistan conducted three missile tests. India reviewed its nuclear capability to strike back. On 07 June, the Indian Air Force lost an unmanned aerial vehicle near Lahore, which Pakistan claimed to have shot down.

The Threat of Nuclear War

As both India and Pakistan are armed with nuclear weapons, the possibility of a conventional war escalating into a nuclear one was raised several times during the standoff. Various statements on this subject were made by Indian and Pakistani officials during the conflict, mainly concerning a 'No First Use' policy. Indian Minister of External Affairs, Jaswant Singh, stated on 05 June that India would not use nuclear weapons first, while Musharraf stated on the same date that he would not renounce Pakistan's right to use nuclear weapons first.

Diplomacy

Vajpayee contacted the leaders of the global community, including Bush, Blair, Putin, and Jacques Chirac, and informed them that since Musharraf could not deliver on his 12 January speech, the patience of India was running out. In the diplomacy that followed, Bush, Putin, Blair, and Japanese Prime Minister Junichiro Koizumi requested Vajpayee to avoid taking the extreme step. The global community informed India that it would negotiate with Musharraf to clarify his position on stopping the cross-border infiltration.

Restraint was urged by the global community, as there were fears that Pakistan would proceed to use its nuclear weapons to counter its conventional asymmetry as compared to the Indian armed forces. Pakistan's nuclear threats led to US Secretary of State Powell contacting Musharraf on five occasions in the last week of May and reading the 'riot act' to him.

On 05 June 2002, American Deputy Secretary of State, Richard Armitage, visited Pakistan. He asked Musharraf if he would 'permanently' end cross-border infiltration and help to dismantle the infrastructure used for terrorism. On 06 June 2002, Musharraf's commitment was conveyed to Powell and India after his arrival. On 10 June 2002, Powell announced Musharraf's promise to the global community, after which India called off its strike plans.

Political logic implied it was better to give another chance to Musharraf. The military build-up on the border by India in January and June had forced both the international community and Pakistan into action. However, the Indian Armed Forces were disappointed with the political decision.

July-August Strikes

On 29 July 2002, for the first time after the end of the Kargil War, India used air power to attack positions held by the Pakistani forces at Londa Post on the Indian side of the LoC in the Machil Sector. Eight IAF Mirage 2000 H aircraft dropped precision-guided bombs weighing 1,000 pounds each to destroy four bunkers that were occupied by Pakistan. In addition,

155-millimetre Bofors guns were also used. The air assault was conducted in daylight, and it demonstrated India's willingness to escalate the conflict in response to provocations.

Pakistani troops stationed near the post in the Kupwara sector's Kel area of the LoC had been shelling the Indian positions across the LoC. India suspected a troop build-up situation near the border post that was similar to Kargil. The Indian Army launched an attack on the Pakistani post. The initial ground attack to retake the post failed, with the Indian army suffering 11 casualties. Later, the plan was modified, and instead of only a ground assault, it was decided first to attack Pakistani positions using the IAF jets, followed by a ground assault. At 1330 hours on 02 August, IAF's Mirage 2000 H fighter aircraft, loaded with laser-guided weapons, bombed the Pakistani bunkers, and the ground attack followed.

Easing of Tension

While tensions remained high throughout the next few months, both governments began easing the situation in Kashmir. By October 2002, India had begun to demobilise their troops along her border, and later Pakistan did the same, and in November 2003, a cease-fire between the two nations was signed.

Casualties

The Indian casualties were up to 1,874, including 798 fatal. Pakistani casualties were not divulged.

Cost of Standoff

The Indian cost for the build-up was $3 to $4 billion, while Pakistan's was $1.4 billion. The standoff led to a total of 155,000 Indians and 45,000 Pakistanis displaced, as per Pakistani media estimates.

One of the reasons for the failure of Operation Parakram was the slow mobilisation of 500,000 troops. It took nearly three weeks for India to move these troops, including three armoured divisions and other supporting units, to their Forward Concentration/Assembly Areas. The delay allowed Pakistan to move its own 300,000 troops, along with the supporting units, to the border. Lacking strategic surprise, operations could not be launched in accordance with initial plans.

Comments and Major Lessons Learnt

The attack on the Parliament of India in Dec 2001 was a major intelligence and internal security failure. It could be surmised that many individuals and agencies were responsible for this failure, but since no details of the investigation are available in the public domain, one can only speculate about the involvement of Indians. The government's post-incident actions were a mix of action and restraint for two reasons. Firstly, the highest policy-making body being the target, severe action was called for, and secondly, the government felt that the serious nature of the incident would invite severe blame. Hence, the military option became the preferred option from the very first day.

The actions of the government were later informally referred to as 'Coercive Diplomacy', but the chain of events and decisions did not have any ingredients of the latter. The definition of 'Coercive Diplomacy' states: 'Attempt to get a target, a state, a group (or groups) within a state, or non-state actors, to change their objectionable behaviour through either the threat to use force or the actual use of limited force.' The reality was that there was hardly any diplomacy in the early days; India ordered its military to mobilise the next day after the incident and commenced deployment, both on the international border (IB) and the LoC in J&K. Within days, mortar and artillery fire duels commenced on the LoC.

For clarity, the timelines are listed below.

> Terrorist attack on Parliament on 13 December 2001; 12 persons were killed, including the five who had attacked.
>
> On 14 December, Indian Government formally blamed Pakistan-based LeT and JeM for the attack.
>
> On the same day, in a demarche to Pakistan, India demanded that Pakistan stop the activities of LeT and JeM, apprehend their leaders, and stop supporting these groups.
>
> Pakistan responded by placing its military on high alert the same day (14 December 2001).
>
> India commenced mobilisation, but no surprise was left!

> By January 2002, India had mobilised around 500,000 troops, including its three Strike Corps, and Pakistan had responded in a similar fashion, deploying around 300,000 troops.

On account of no existing National Security Strategy, the Indian Armed Forces were planning various military strategies in a vacuum. The policymakers were actually making political decisions without really knowing what the armed forces should aim for. Despite this, while mobilisation was going ahead, military and political plans kept changing. Even today, India does not have a formal National Security Strategy.

Although the Indian Military had a considerable edge over the Pakistani Military, it appeared that the political and military leadership were not on the same page, as could be discerned from statements of the Prime Minister and other political leaders.

The nuclear factor did play a role in the final decision not to adopt the military option. The Indian Military was ready to take the calculated risk, but apparently, the civil leadership backed out. The nuclear factor did prompt the global players to act fast, and in the final analysis, it was the danger of escalation from the conventional to the nuclear level that prompted the protagonists to de-escalate. India needs to re-visit its nuclear policies for the future, and the political leadership needs to 'bite the bullet' at the appropriate time in future.

The mismatch between political and military thinking, especially in nuclear issues, needs to be bridged and 'political will' must be exhibited at crucial junctures. This will happen only when the armed forces hierarchy becomes part of the policy-making loop on a permanent basis.

Lieutenant General Vijay Oberoi, PVSM, AVSM, VSM, commissioned into the Maratha Light Infantry, rose to be the VCOAS. Wounded in battle in 1965, he is a rare Infantry Officer to command an Armoured Division successfully, laying down new concepts, which he continued with as the DGMO, and as Western Army Commander. He later shaped it into a doctrine as GOC-in-C ARTRAC and VCOAS. An International Fellow at the US Army War College, Founder-Director of CLAWS and Founder-President of War Wounded Federation, his experience includes tenures as Defence Attache in Malaysia and UN Observer Group in Gaza. A frequent contributor to books, and a speaker on security strategy, international relations and doctrine, he was on the goodwill mission to Pakistan in 2003 and is sought for his views on national security and power dynamics.

8

A Cold Start Doctrine for a Hot War (2004–14)

Major General Amarjit Singh

All men can see these tactics whereby I conquer, but what none can see is the strategy out of which victory is evolved.

—Sun Tzu

The victory of 1971 in the Eastern Sector was spectacular. Historically, it is the only morally justifiable war post WWII, which created a new state, and liberated a brutally suppressed population. The rightful fruit of the victory was tribute, homage and respect and not an annexation. It reignited the belief of Indian troops in their war-fighting abilities and their quest for victory. An offensive spirit with a psychological ascendancy was born in both the military war strategists and the troops.

In the Western Sector, the war ended in a relative stalemate, but that was India's war aim of the war in the West. Strategically, the threat from East Pakistan was exterminated and the Indian Army could now, in the next war, concentrate its combat power on West Pakistan. There was a revolutionary change in the security environment. Political and diplomatic initiatives held out in favour of India, and the threat from China seemed to be under diplomatic control. The Indian war planners, after a hangover of success, soon realised that the war strategy of 1971 was obsolete for the future security scenario. Many war planners, like Lieutenant General K.K. Hazari, had written about the need for a new armoured strategy to decisively defeat Pakistan instead of continually being forced to accept a virtual stalemate. Indian Defence Policy was dominated by an orthodox offensive doctrine with a defensive mindset. The new-found confidence resulted in a thought process of a decisive battle deep in the enemy's territory. In 1975, a study group under General Krishna Rao took forward the process of creating a new strategy in organisational and material terms. General Rao stated, 'Our enemy—the people who hurt us—is Pakistan.'[1] The doctrine that was developed called for the massing of offensive army formations to strike deep towards politically important objectives with aid from the Indian Air Force and Navy. The doctrine's theory of victory relies on the logic of deterrence by punitive punishment. The concept relied on the fact that India's military threat of a prohibitively costly retaliation would convince its enemy to refrain from aggression and initiating another attempt to regain Kashmir.

The doctrine of a decisive battle deep in the enemy's territory resulted in the reorganisation of the Indian Army into Strike and Defensive Corps. The Army raised new Infantry Divisions specialised for a deep offensive. They comprised mechanised Infantry Units equipped with armoured personnel, suitably supported by Armoured Regiments.[2] The Strike Corps were assigned the wartime task of penetrating deep into Pakistan—not only to capture borderlands but also to threaten key strategic centres and lines of communication. This concept was tested out in Exercise Digvijay. The Commander for this exercise was General Krishnaswamy Sundarji. This concept reached its maturity when Sundarji became the Chief and is, at times, also referred to as the 'Sundarji Doctrine'. Exercise Brass Tacks was the culmination of testing the decisive battle strategy. Three Strike Corps were exercised in offensive operations with objectives having a depth measuring well into the political heartland of Pakistan. So profound was the effect of this exercise that Pakistan felt the reverberations of the strength of the Indian Army both in numbers and in the strategy that was exercised on its borders. Pakistan decided to mobilise as a defensive measure, and the Indian Army retaliated by fully deploying its power in the offensive mode. War was avoided by some deft political and diplomatic moves both on the Indian and Pakistani sides. This strategy forced Pakistan to commit more forces in defence at the cost of its offensive formations. Pakistan's strategy, for the first time, indicated a defensive side to its otherwise offensive strategy against India. The 1989 Pakistan Army's exercise, Zarb-e-Momin, was largely based on a defensive offensive, which catered for the decisive battle design by the Indian Strike Corps. If a strategic estimate is to be made, it would not be wrong to say that Pakistan's offensive designs in the plains sector of Punjab and Rajasthan were foreclosed. This is the time Pakistan re-evolved the British concept of 'Strategic Depth'[3] for itself; seeking depth against India's offensive inside of Afghanistan. Evidence to this effect can be found in our deterrence threat of 1999, in the opening of the plains sector, if Pakistan opted for an attack in the mountains of J&K. There was relative peace for nearly two decades on the conventional front. To somehow retain parity in dominance in the strategic sphere, Pakistan switched from its competition in the conventional sphere into the unconventional proxy war by directly abetting and guiding insurgency in J&K, and Punjab. In 1998, Pakistan acquired nuclear capability and devised a nuclear doctrine to deter India's conventional might. Pakistan attempted to squeeze out the space of conventional war by the pressure of nuclear threats on one end and a proxy war on the other.

Pakistan's attempt to stay within the unconventional sphere in the 1999 Kargil War was suitably responded to by the Indian Army by bringing its conventional power to bear on Pakistan's strategy despite the nuclear saber rattling by Pakistan's leadership. The terror attack orchestrated by Pakistan on the Parliament in 2001 resulted in Operation Parakram. It was the lessons learnt from Operation Parakram that generated the requirement of a new strategy formulation to cater to Pakistan's growing aspirations because of a bonanza of military aide from the United States under the garb of the 'Global War on Terror'.[4] The new thought process was loosely termed as the 'Cold Start Strategy' but was never formally promulgated as such. The Army preferred to call it a pro-active strategy. This strategy was primarily developed for the western front with Pakistan in mind. The battlefield indicators and experiences of Operation Parakram were the basis that generated a new thought process to create dominance over Pakistan. Some of the major experiences that caused a change in our strategic thinking were:

Decision-making: Given the strategic culture of our political decision-making leaders and the established procedures, it was surprising that the decision to mobilise and go to war was taken within a day of the terror attack on the Parliament. But this capacity to take a quick strategic decision was again seen in Surgical Strikes after the Pulwama incident. To interpret this, in military terms, would be that the military had to be ready at all times and fully organised to go to battle in a very short time. The strategic surprise created by a quick decision must not be lost by a sluggish and slow mobilisation to war by the military.

Pakistan's Dilemma: In the 'Global War on Terror,' Pakistan promised to provide an adequate number of troops on the Afghanistan frontier in return for modern military equipment and financial aid. Operation Al-Mizan was conducted by the United States and Pakistan to combat Al-Qaeda, Taliban, and other foreign terrorist organisations who were carrying out their activities in Waziristan after the United States' invasion of Afghanistan. These terrorists from Afghanistan fled into the safe havens of Pakistan's western borders.[5] At one point of time, a large part of active offensive and defensive formations were in this operation and were not available *ab initio* for operations against India.[6] There would be a serious time penalty to get these troops to their battle locations against India. This time penalty gave Indian Army a window of two to three days of freedom for a strategic manoeuvre into Pakistan's defences. Pakistan had two unstable fronts and a disturbed internal situation. Its forces were dissipated with no capability of a quick offensive.

Delayed Mobilisation: In 2001, the Indian Army was still organised into defensive and offensive corps. The Defensive Corps were located close to the borders and mobilised in a short duration but were incapable of offensive action. The Strike Corps were located in the hinterland and they required heavy resources and extended time to mobilise. The overall time to mobilise the Army for war was estimated to be three to four weeks. The D-Day for an offensive could only be after this time lapse to which the time for battlefield procedure of field formations preparation for an assault was also needed to be factored in. A study was carried out by the College of Defence Management on the mobilisation of a few formations of command, and concluded that the first attack by the strike formations could not be conducted till four to five weeks the decision was given. In five weeks' time, Pakistan prepared its defences, laid out its minefields and even carried out rehearsals for counterattacks. The initial Indian troops of the defensive formations to be mobilised for Operation Parakram reported that they could see no activity on the Pakistan side and even requested to occupy Pakistani defences as there was no one there. However, this window closed within seven days. An attack after five weeks would culminate in an attrition battle.

The Indian Force Structure: There was a sharp differentiation between defensive and offensive forces. Defence forces mobilised faster but could not launch an offensive and the offensive forces could not avail the window of opportunity because of delayed mobilisation. The Army was configured for mass application for objectives in-depth, well beyond the red lines laid down by Pakistan in its nuclear banter. Command and control were centralised at the Corps and there were visualisations of fighting a Corps-coordinated battle at the decisive stage. All this enforced a slow calculated launch with little scope to exploit opportunities at lower formations.

The Political Initiative: The decision to go to war is based on a political initiative and the diplomatic strength to retain this initiative. The Indian doctrine of a massed decisive warfare indicated dismemberment of Pakistan, which the international community did not favour. The military operational window of action was related to this political initiative, which would be lost rapidly with the involvement of international pressure.

The Nuclear Threshold: Pakistan's nuclear doctrine deterred a decisive battle. It kept lowering its threshold as it perceived threats, in order to reduce the gap between conventional and nuclear war. The nuclear overhang would also increase international pressure to cease hostilities. However, operations in Kargil clearly indicated that even though the gap between conventional and nuclear war was small, there was a window where India could exploit its strengths in the conventional sphere. This window was small and it required agile, small and prepared forces to exploit it.

The Cold Start Strategy

The Cold Start Strategy is a Pakistan-centric strategy. It was developed by the Indian Army in 2004 to facilitate small-scale, rapid, and decisive conventional offensive operations into Pakistani territory in the event of a Pakistan-sponsored asymmetrical attack on Indian soil before the international community could actively intervene, and before Pakistan would feel compelled to launch nuclear retaliatory strikes to repel an Indian invasion. I am unable to trace the original discussions of the Cold Start Strategy and therefore, unable to prescribe the credit to any single general. However, there are strong indicators that its origins were in Western Command. It seems there is no ownership to this doctrine. Chief of Army Staff General V.K. Singh's public announcement that the Cold Start Doctrine did not exist further adds to the ambiguity of this doctrine. However, General V.K. Singh did acknowledge that the Indian Army possessed a 'pro-active strategy' for war with Pakistan, which probably is a derivative of the Cold Start Strategy. The strategy has not been discussed in the open and the Indian Army has deliberately been ambiguous about it in order to keep the subtle details as a secret.

The Cold Start shifted the overall pattern of warfighting from a total decisive war to a limited war. The doctrine, *per se,* is for conventional total war, but embedded in it are the tenets of limited war. The understanding is that whether a war is 'limited' or 'total' would depend on political aims of the conflict and their strategic and operational translation. Since political aims can reasonably only be limited in the nuclear age, the doctrine can be taken as being a limited war doctrine. To achieve political and military aims, 'compellence' was the chosen theoretical concept. The first part of the basic essence of the strategy was a quick political and military decision on the action to be taken in response to an attack like that of the one on the Parliament or the Mumbai attacks of 26 September 2008. Any delay in decision-making gives Pakistan time to prepare internally and on the international stage, which closes both the political and military window of operation.

Strategically, the first part was to gain a surprise in terms of the time of launch of the offensive. The war aims would be limited to tactical or operational depth but the offensive would have a large width in multiple thrusts, to keep within the red line of Pakistan's nuclear policy. The second part was that once the decision was made, the Indian Army and the Air Force would extract full advantage of the strategic surprise and cross the border without delay and occupy the unheld or light Pakistani defences with offensive capability generated from the holding formations while the rest of the strike formations commenced mobilising. The strike formations would then exploit the success of the holding formations as and when they arrived on the battlefield to capture multiple objectives at tactical and intermediate depths. This was called the 'Hit, Mobilise and Hit Harder'[7] concept.

Thereafter, any one of the tactical objectives could be exploited further based on the military aims and the political time and depth available. It was anticipated that there would not be enough time available to destroy Pakistan's military in detail before cease fire was imposed. Military victory was described in terms of the territory captured, which would set the stage for conflict termination at a position of strength with enough value territory to bargain with. The war was expected to be intensely fought for a short duration. The implication of this was the application of maximum force capability at the onset, over wide areas, keeping little in reserve.

The execution of this strategy required total organisational change and a change in mindset. The institutional and doctrinal changes that became necessary were:[8]

Restructuring of Defensive Corps: The Defensive Corps were renamed as Pivot Corps removing the defensive mindset and orientation of these Corps. Reserves were created by reorganising the defences and these reserves constituted the offensive content. They were the 'Hit' portion of the 'Hit, Mobilise and Hit Harder' concept. These reserves were located close to the border and were prepared to launch in a given time frame as was given in the operations plans. They exploited the strategic surprise.

Restructuring the Strike Corps: The Strike Corps were organised into Integrated Battle Groups (IBGs) which were division-sized. All the IBGs would be capable of launching limited strikes up to intermediate depth, along different axes of advance, into enemy territory. They were the 'Hit Harder' part of the concept of 'Hit, Mobilise and Hit Harder.'[9] The Indian Army is purportedly planning to turn each of the three brigades of a division-sized IBG into an autonomous unit capable of independent military operations now.

Shifting Military Stations: The mobilisation time of strike formations was unacceptable for this strategy. To reduce the time for the mobilisation, military stations were relocated near the borders of Pakistan. New military stations would be established, which would conform to the mobilisation time, to execute this strategy.

Integration of Fire Power: The firepower of the Pivot Corps and the Strike Corps was integrated to provide adequate fire support to all assaulting troops. An unofficial concept of 100 guns for a thrust line was devised to provide adequate fire support to assaulting troops.

Integrated Logistics: Logistics would be based on areas and sub-areas. All transiting formations would hook up to the logistics of the area. Integral logistics elements of formations would move into enemy territory. The logistic area would also move forward based on the rate and depth of advance of the IBGs.

The problems that were encountered were, firstly, the civil-military relations at the top were not streamlined and the military was out of the institutional framework of decision-making, and so India's higher decision-making needed reforms to execute this strategy. There was an absence of a National Security Directive and, therefore, decisions would have a very strong personality bias. Secondly, the initial offensive by the

Pivot Corps would not be strong enough to sustain itself, and moreover, no immediate reserves were available to the Pivot Corps. Thirdly, operations got decentralised to divisions, and each division generated its own plan, often outstretching itself in its aims, which created an imbalance in the defences, making them vulnerable. There would be little in reserve to protect against a counter-offensive. Fourthly, the time differential in the mobilisation of Pivot formations and the strike IBGs was large and on the edges of the staying power of the Pivot Corps. Fifthly, there were major differences in understanding between the Army, Navy, and Air Force in executing the strategy. The Air Force required a finite time for suppression of enemy air before it could support ground operations, by which time the IBGs would have reached their objectives. The Navy had their own time constraints to move and deploy their assets. Sixthly, there was a strong psychological effect of nuclear weapons, especially on the civilian leadership, which precluded them from any hasty actions.

There has been no official confirmation of the adoption of this strategy and it could well be an exercise of alternative options. The Army seemed content with this strategy and kept modifying to suit changing conditions. The Air Force and Navy have never acknowledged this doctrine. The Army reviewed this doctrine in 2012 and was still found suitable. In January 2019, Chief of Army Staff, General Bipin Rawat, for the first time, publicly acknowledged the doctrine in an interview, 'The Cold Start doctrine exists for conventional military operations. Whether we have to conduct conventional operations for such strikes is a decision well thought through, involving the government and the cabinet committee on security.'[10]

Pakistan was caught on the back foot with this strategy and became very vulnerable in the conventional sphere. The rhetoric of nuclear weapons grew and the claimed acquisition of tactical nuclear weapons came into the limelight. The nuclear capable NASR with a tactical nuclear warhead was considered the answer to India's Cold Start Strategy. In the conventional sphere, Pakistan's responded to the Cold Start Strategy by adopting a New Concept of War Fighting (NCWF),[11] and further with the enunciation of Triple R (Rearticulation-Reorganisation-Relocation) coupled with merging of the nuclear warfighting with conventional conflict. The resolving of the Afghanistan issue and the US withdrawal has given Pakistan time to redeploy its forces. These factors have imposed a degree of caution and recalibration in this strategy.[12] This is always the case as every strategy has a life span before it is checkmated by the enemy and the environment. For a military strategy to mature and be fielded, it needs at least a minimum of three to four years of deliberations and war-gaming.

The Cold Start Strategy inherently suggests a short swift war, and the force and logistics were structures for such an engagement. The current war in Ukraine has shown that if global powers want the war to be extended, the duration could last for years. The need for balance between aggression and defence, and the power to sustain, has become an important factor for which the Indian Military needs to recalibrate.

Conclusion

The Cold Start Strategy has lost most of its premises for its conception. It is high time that the Indian military come out with a new doctrine to maintain its dominance over Pakistan. China has emerged as an expansionist power with its demonstrated designs in Ladakh and Arunachal Pradesh. It is recommended that new theories of victory must be thought of to make coercion and territorial revisionism prohibitively costly or unfeasible for the enemy rather than relying on *ex post facto* punishment. We need to consider how to synergise the elements of a joint force. Indian forces will, increasingly, be compelled to deter and fight in multiple domains and different theatres, and the army should, therefore, consider how to play a productive role in new missions where it supports a main effort in a different domain. We must consider new niche capabilities in the field of intelligence, surveillance and reconnaissance capabilities, long-range precision strike, and making use of non-kinetic weapons to get decisions in battle.

Major General Amarjit Singh, VSM (Retd) was commissioned into the Armoured Corps. He was posted as MGGS REDFOR ARTRAC, where he was part of Command War games during the evolution of the Cold Start Strategy of the Indian Army. A post graduate from Defence Services Staff College, Willington, College of Defence Management, Osmania University and an MPhil from Panjab University (Gold Medalist), Singh is presently a Visiting Professor in Panjab University and the Director of Gyan Chakra Think Tank, a Western Command intiative.

Endnotes

1. Bhatt, Sheela. 'The Rediff Interview Gen K V Krishna Rao (Retd).' *Rediff.com,* October 15, 2001, https://www.rediff.com/news/2001/oct/15inter.htm
2. Reorganised Army Plains Infantry Divisions (RAPIDs).
3. "Some Pakistani military strategists retain a military understanding of the term and appear to believe that Afghan's territory could provide a strategic rallying point in the case of an Indian attack. They are concerned about the fact that Pakistan geographically is a narrow country and an indian attack can cut through the country and divide it into two halves. In such a case, they believe, Afghan territory could provide a suitable "Strategic Depth" to which the Pakistan army can retreat and regroup in order to launch a counter attack". Aziz Hakimi, Af-Pak: what strategic depth? 4 February 2010. http://www.opendemocracy.net/opensecurity/aziz-hakimi/af-pak-what-strategic-depth
4. The war on terror, officially called the Global War on Terrorism (GWOT), was a global counterterrorism military campaign initiated by the United States following the 11 September attacks and spanned multiple wars in Iraq, Afghanistan, and the Middle East. The main targets of the campaign were militant Islamist and Salafi jihadist armed organisations such as Al-Qaeda, the Islamic State, and their international affiliates, which were waging military insurgencies to overthrow governments of various Muslim-majority countries. Pakistan was an official partner of the United States in its war in Afghanistan.

5. Dodaro, Gene L. (March 10, 2010). *Securing, Stabilizing, and Developing Pakistan's Border Area with Afghanistan: Key Issues for Congressional Oversight.* DIANE Publishing. ISBN 9781437914092
6. According to data obtained, somewhat fewer than 120,000 regular army, Frontier Corps, and Frontier Constabulary troops were located in FATA and NWFP between March 2008 and March 2009. These troops accounted for between four and five infantry divisions drawn from headquarters (HQ) 9 Division, HQ 7 Division, HQ 14 Division, and HQ 17/23 Division. These divisions draw, in turn, from XI Corps (Peshawar), X Corps (Rawalpindi), II Corps (Multan), and I Corps (Mangla). Organisationally, there were approximately 17 infantry brigades, 45 infantry battalions, and some 58 Frontier Corps wings. Seth G. Jones and C. Christine Fair, Counterinsurgency in Pakistan, Rand Corporation. https://www.jstor.org/stable/10.7249/mg982rc.11
7. Gady, Franz-Stefan. *Is the Indian Military Capable of Executing the Cold Start Doctrine?* 20 January 2019. https://thediplomat.com/2019/01/is-the-indian-military-capable-of-executing-the-cold-start-doctrine/.
8. It is very interesting to read the Pakistan authors and their analysis of how they viewed the Cold Start Strategy. See Hafeez Ullah Khan, Ijaz Khalid; Indian Cold Start Doctrine: Pakistan's Policy Response, *Journal of the Research Society of Pakistan* vol 55, Issue No. 1(January - June, 2018)
9. Saba Hanif a Pakistani scholar in his analysis has stated "India raised eight IBGs to launch an offensive inside Pakistan and hold territory later to use as a bargaining chip. Furthermore, during the Cold Start, the Indian army's time was reduced from three weeks to 72 hours at most. Under this doctrine, India aimed to keep Pakistan's response under the latter's nuclear threshold."
10. Ibid
11. Meenakshi Sood, Pakistan's (Non-Nuclear) Plan to Counter 'Cold Start'. *The Diplomat* (25 March 2017). https://thediplomat.com/2017/03/pakistans-non-nuclear-plan-to-counter-cold-start/
12. Singh, Colonel Harsh Vardhan, Evolution of Warfighting Strategy in India, October 22, 2020. https://www.claws.in/evolution-of-warfighting-strategy-in-india/

9

India's Military Strategy During the Surgical Strikes

Lieutenant General D.S. Hooda

On 29 September 2016, the Indian Army's DGMO stated in a hastily-called press conference, 'Based on very credible and specific information, which we received yesterday, that some terrorist teams had positioned themselves at launch pads along the LoC with an aim to carry out infiltration and terrorist strikes in J&K, and in various other metros in our country, the Indian Army conducted Surgical Strikes last night at these launch pads.' Although not clearly stated by the DGMO, the operation was also a response to a terrorist attack in Uri, J&K, on 18 September 2016 that claimed the lives of 19 Indian soldiers.

This article outlines the military strategy adopted for the Surgical Strikes, looks at the impact of the operation, and important lessons that could be drawn.

Objectives

Any military strategy is drawn based on the objectives. Some of these objectives were specified by the political leadership and are based on these directions—the military leadership further refined the objectives.

Retribution: 19 lives were lost in the terrorist attack at Uri and Army was criticised for not being able to protect even its garrisons. One of the objectives was to seek retribution for the loss of lives and to demonstrate India's commitment to defending its territorial integrity, and the safety of its soldiers and citizens.

Deterrence: One of the main objectives was to send a strong message to terrorist groups and their sponsors in Pakistan that India would not tolerate cross-border terrorism. The strike aimed to deter future attacks by showcasing India's resolve and capability to respond effectively to terrorism.

Target Terrorist Infrastructure: The Surgical Strikes aimed to target terrorist launch pads and infrastructure used for planning, training, and launching attacks against India. By eliminating these facilities, the Indian Army sought to disrupt the operational capabilities of the terrorist groups operating in the region.

Asserting India's Right to Self-defence: The Surgical Strikes was intended to assert India's right to self-defence under international law. By conducting a limited, targeted operation against terrorist infrastructure, the Indian Government aimed to signal that it reserved the right to respond to cross-border terrorism in a manner consistent with its obligations under international law and its obligation to protect its citizens.

The Strategy of the Surgical Strikes

Once the objectives were clear, preparation commenced for the Surgical Strikes. Some of the strategic considerations that went into the planning are outlined below:

Selection of Targets: The aim was to target multiple terrorist launch pads and infrastructure used by militants to infiltrate into Indian territory, with minimal collateral damage. The targets also had to be at such distances that they could be struck, and soldiers return to our side of the LoC within one night. An important consideration for selecting the targets was the routes for infiltration and extraction that provided the least risk from Pakistani posts. Very precise intelligence had to be obtained about the targets and this was done through a mix of technical and human intelligence.

Timing: The date for the Surgical Strikes had to be chosen with care. We were conscious that too much delay in launching the operation could dilute the impact of the message that India would respond strongly to a major terrorist attack on its soil. At the same time, we did not want to send in soldiers across the LoC with inadequate preparation and intelligence. The Special Forces had been training for cross-border strikes for some time, and this preparation enabled the launch of the Surgical Strikes within 10 days of the Uri attack.

Scope of the Operation: There was a need to respond strongly, and therefore, a small-scale single strike would not have the desired impact. At the same time, there was a need to keep the operation controlled to limit the risk of escalation. This was also conveyed by the DGMO, when he stated, 'The operations aimed at neutralising the terrorists have since ceased. We do not have any plans for the continuation of further operations. However, the Indian Armed Forces are fully prepared for any contingency that may arise.'

Operational Security: Information about the Surgical Strikes was very tightly controlled and given out strictly on a need-to-know basis. It was also for this reason that the operation was not given any code name.

Contingency Planning: Multiple targets had to be hit on the same night at different times (due to the distance to be traversed). There was almost a six-hour gap between attacking the first and last target, sufficient time for the Pakistan Army to come to a higher level of alertness. Numerous contingencies were planned, mainly on how to extract soldiers, if they got into a firefight with Pakistani soldiers. Plans were also made to respond to any escalation that Pakistan could plan after the operation was completed.

Post-Strike Diplomacy: After the Surgical Strikes, the Indian Government engaged in a diplomatic campaign to inform the international community of the reasons behind the operation and to garner support for its actions. The aim was to convey that the strike was a targeted response to cross-border terrorism and not an act of aggression against Pakistan.

Differences from Earlier Operations

It is often stated that the Indian Army had been conducting cross-border operations in the past and that the Surgical Strikes of 2016 were no different. It is true that the Army has been proactive on the LoC, and achieving moral domination over the adversary requires that it not feel completely safe even in its own territory. Indian soldiers have certainly conducted cross-border operations against Pakistani soldiers deployed along the LoC. However, there were certain key differences in the 2016 strikes:

Scale of the Operation: The scale of the operation was larger than what had been attempted in the past. Hitting multiple targets that were located behind the Forward Line of Pakistan's defences and at different times, increased the complexity of the operation. The total number of soldiers employed was also larger than had been attempted in the past.

Public Acknowledgement: Unlike some previous cross-border operations, the Indian Government publicly acknowledged the Surgical Strikes shortly after its completion. This decision was made to convey a strong message of deterrence to terrorist groups and their Pakistan sponsors, and to assert India's right to respond to terrorist strikes.

Shift in Strategic Approach: The Surgical Strikes marked a change in India's approach to dealing with cross-border terrorism. It signalled a willingness to use military force in a more proactive manner as opposed to relying solely on diplomatic efforts to address the issue. This shift also forced the military to look at a range of options, including cross-border strikes, to respond to terror emanating from Pakistan.

Widespread Support: The Surgical Strikes received widespread domestic and international support, reflecting the perception that India's actions were a measured and appropriate response to cross-border terrorism. This level of support may not have been present for all previous cross-border operations.

Pakistan's Response

Pakistan's response to the Surgical Strikes was a combination of denial, criticism, and enhancing their readiness levels along the LoC.

Denial: Pakistan initially denied that the Surgical Strikes had occurred, claiming that it was a fabrication by the Indian Government. Pakistani military officials stated that there had only been an exchange of gunfire across the LoC, not a targeted operation by Indian Special Forces. This denial can be attributed to a desire to downplay the incident and avoid admitting that the Indian Forces were able to infiltrate Pakistani-controlled territory successfully.

Criticism: Pakistani authorities criticised the Indian Government's claims of a Surgical Strikes, accusing it of creating a false narrative to score political points domestically and to divert attention from alleged human rights violations in J&K. They also portrayed the Indian actions as aggression and a violation of the ceasefire agreement between the two countries.

Enhanced Readiness: The Surgical Strikes came as a big shock to the Pakistan Army, not only because of the scale of the Indian operation but also because the response of their Army had been extremely sluggish and poor. Communication intercepts of the Pakistan Army after the Surgical Strikes indicated a level of panic and attempts to enhance readiness levels to ensure that there was no repeat.

Pakistan's response to the Surgical Strikes can be attributed to various factors, including its desire to maintain a strong public image, the need to deny any breach of its territorial integrity, and the inclination to counter India's narrative. Additionally, acknowledging the Surgical Strikes could have been seen as admitting to the presence of terrorist infrastructure on its soil which would have been detrimental to Pakistan's international standing.

Lessons Learned

The 2016 Surgical Strikes offer many lessons and insights that can be valuable for future military operations, strategic planning, and diplomatic efforts.

Importance of Planning and Preparation: Planning for the operation, intelligence gathering, and training of the Special Forces for cross-border operations had been going on for almost one year. That provided a lot of confidence to the soldiers and officers who spearheaded the Surgical Strikes, and on whose shoulders the success of the operation rested.

Value of Covert, Targeted Operations: The strike demonstrated the effectiveness of covert, targeted operations in achieving specific objectives with minimal collateral damage and reduced risk of escalation. This approach can be considered in future operations to address security threats while minimising the potential for broader military confrontation.

Deterrence and Messaging: The Surgical Strikes sent a strong message that India would not tolerate cross-border terrorism. The Surgical Strikes marked a shift in India's strategic approach to dealing with terrorism, signalling a willingness to use military force when necessary. This action showcased the value of deterrence and signalling in shaping an adversary's behaviour, and managing security threats.

Managing Escalation: While the Surgical Strikes achieved their immediate objectives, they also led to increased tensions along the LoC. This serves as a reminder that military actions can have unintended consequences and that managing escalation and de-escalation is a critical aspect of any military operation. The Balakot Strikes of 2019, and the response by the Pakistani Air Force, have reinforced the lesson that management of the escalation matrix is no simple matter.

Need for a Long-term Strategy: The operation was a success, but there was never a sense among the military that the Surgical Strikes would entirely eliminate the threat of cross-border terrorism. The hype around the strikes could have been tempered down and a consistent strategy adopted at the national level on how the Surgical Strikes tie into a strategic approach combining diplomacy, international pressure, and military force to deter Pakistan from using terrorism as a state policy. Premature victory must not be declared for short-term optics.

Lieutenant General D.S. Hooda, PVSM, UYSM, AVSM, VSM & Bar, Gurkha Veteran, a graduate from Command and Staff College, Canada, has commanded a Corps in Jammu and, later, the Northern Army. He has been an instructor at the Military College of Telecommunication Engineering, Mhow, and Colonel General Staff of a Strike Corps. He has also had tenures in the Military Operations Directorate and the Quarter Master General's Branch at the Army Headquarters. He has also served on the United Nations Mission in Ethiopia and Eritrea, for which he was awarded the UNMEE Medal. His vast experience guided the uniquely successful, retaliatory, and policy-shifting Surgical Strikes across the LOC. As a Co-Founder of the Council for Strategic and Defence Research, New Delhi, and an Advisor in Cyber Research and Security to PEC, Chandigarh, he is a regular contributor to press and online media portals and professional journals on security affairs.

2

The Strategic Future

10

India's Strategy for Grey Zone Warfare

Lieutenant General Praveen Bakshi

Understanding Grey Zone Warfare

The genre of asymmetric conflict has gradually morphed in recent times to a reconfigured form of warfare, which stays below the conventional spectrum, largely avoids kinetic contact, offers deniability, and targets the social space away from the frontline rather than military objectives in contact. It comprises of a series of campaigns seemingly unconnected, which transform and refine over a period, to ultimately achieve the political objective. Heather Bothwell defines *Grey Zone conflicts* as security challenges initiated through purposeful aggression that exceed the bounds of normal competition, but remains below the threshold of conventional warfare. Grey Zone conflicts result from adversarial attempts to change the status quo for benefit through gradual belligerence that might be difficult to publicly attribute to the aggressor. Adversaries that initiate Grey Zone conflicts avoid the costs associated with conventional warfare while miring their opponents in questions involving international law, policy, and trade, thereby, effectively preventing decisive responses.

Grey Zone Warfare is not a new phenomenon – it has been employed throughout history in various forms. In ancient times, states would use espionage and subversion to undermine their adversaries. In the modern era, the use of propaganda, covert operations, and economic sanctions became popular tactics in the Grey Zone. During the Cold War, the US and the Soviet Union employed Grey Zone Warfare through proxy wars, such as the Korean War and the Vietnam War. These wars were fought through third-party actors. The allegation of some Indian politicians being on the payroll of the Central Intelligence Agency (CIA) or the KGB in the '50s and '60s can also be attributed to Grey Zone actions on part of these nations.

The current use of the term dates back to the mid-2010s when 'Grey-Zone' started appearing in briefings and articles about using Special Operations Forces. The term applied then to conflicts ranging from Russia's seizure of Crimea and interventions in the Donbass, to Boko Haram in Nigeria, and to the rise of the Islamic State. Further debate about these conflicts that fell between traditional war or peace led to 'Grey Zone' becoming more precisely defined, thus narrowing its scope and characteristics. In recent years, major powers such as China, Russia, and the US have increasingly employed Grey Zone tactics in their foreign policies. They have used this approach to advance their strategic objectives while avoiding open conflict. Grey Zone Warfare can take many forms, including cyber-attacks, disinformation campaigns, economic coercion, and military coercion through proxies. Use of technology and cyber space has in recent times given an exponential fillip to Grey Zone Warfare in its scope, reach, spread, and effects.

Grey Zone Warfare had not officially entered the lexicon of the Indian Army at least till 2017. To date, in the public domain, there has been no official articulation of this concept, no doctrinal research initiated, and no resultant defensive or offensive strategy articulated. Post the Galwan conflict, which unintendedly breached the barriers of Grey Zone conflict resulting in application of hard power by both India and China, the Indian Armed Forces may have undertaken a classified study on this subject. But it is important for strategists to note that Grey Zone conflicts transcend mere Armed Forces canvass and need a whole of Government or people approach.

Dr Micheal J. Mazzar, in his seminal essay in 2016 on *Mastering the Grey Zone: Understanding a Changing Era of Conflict*, has comprehensively examined the idea of Grey Zone conflict. He categorised Grey Zone conflicts according to four approaches—involving purposefully pursuing of political objectives through carefully designed operations; moving carefully towards the objectives rather than seeking decisive results within a specified time period; acting to remain below key escalatory thresholds to avoid war; and using all instruments of national power, particularly non-military and non-kinetic tools. The seven hypotheses of future Grey Zone conflicts espoused by Mazzarare are particularly instructive.

Amongst others, he states that Grey Zone conflicts are likely to constitute the default mode of conflict in the coming decades, which will demand new strategies to deal with them. Interestingly, he avers that Grey Zone campaigns undermine deterrence, which is premised on kinetic tools of war. Of greater value is the strategy to engage in the Grey Zone to deal with campaigns.

There is infinite manoeuvre space in the Grey Zone with complete deniability; security measures against such actions must include both people-centric and military-centric strategies. Cyber-attacks will affect people distant from the battlefield, thus, offering the potential for displacing the adversary psychologically. Adding a characteristic to this framework, Barno and Bensahel argue that the defining feature of Grey Zone activities is their ambiguity, regarding either 'the ultimate objectives, the participants, whether international treaties and norms have been violated or the role that military forces should play in response'. Reinforcing this characteristic, Grey Zone activities are often hidden, undeclared and combined with active deception measures aimed to obscure and confuse. For example, Russian Grey Zone actions in Ukraine occurred simultaneously with carefully targeted cyber-attacks across the Ukrainian Government in Kiev, Poland, European Parliament, and the European Commission.

Grey Zone activities are, thus, clearly complex strategic-level endeavours, wherein the main effort is not a single line of operation or entity; rather it is the orchestration of all elements and effects of the campaign. This is necessary to achieve the greatest gains with the least resistance. The campaign is flexible and will exploit opportunities as they arise and reduce or avoid obstacles as required. Grey Zone activities actively try to avoid starting a war but they are not intended to reinforce a state of peace either. Grey Zone activities are, instead, specifically intended to push the limits of others tolerance to just short of the breaking point. The existing peace needs to be able to absorb the Grey Zone activities and bounce back, not shatter. A core aspect of the Grey Zone is that for its activities to succeed, aggressors rely on the existing peace being sufficiently resilient. Such operational artistry requires an effective strategic command. Moreover, given the protracted nature of the Grey Zone approach, this strategic command needs to be in place for an extended period.

Hybrid and Grey Zone Warfare are often used in an interchangeable manner. Hoffman popularised 'Hybrid Warfare' in 2007 defining it as 'waged by states or political groups, and incorporating a range of different modes of warfare including conventional capabilities, irregular tactics and formations, terrorist acts including indiscriminate violence and coercion, and criminal disorder'. The concept has since expanded somewhat and the major distinguishing feature of Hybrid Warfare is now considered the integrated combination of conventional and irregular military forces, psychological operations, and information warfare. The Russian campaigns in Georgia and Ukraine, and the forces Hezbollah developed to fight Israel, and now used in Syria, are considered examples of Hybrid Warfare. Hybrid Warfare seeks to conclusively win a campaign through using or threatening with force, in sharp contrast to Grey Zone's strategic incremental-ism. Mazarr argues that the Hybrid Warfare concept clearly imagines a far more violent clash that involves direct use of many military instruments. In this sense, Hybrid War is truly 'war' in a Clausewitzian sense, whereas Grey Zone strategies are a less violent, and looser form of conflict.

The annexation of Crimea by Russia in 2014, the alleged Russian manipulation of the US elections, or the multiple transgressions in recent times by China at Doklam, Arunachal Pradesh and Eastern Ladakh, are all evidence of established powers seeking to drive low-cost asymmetric outcomes that have the potential of creating disproportionate strategic effects. However, the deterrence value of hard power is in no way undermined by the existence of the Grey Zone, as witnessed in the recent conflict situation in Eastern Ladakh.

China's Enduring Grey Zone Challenge

Today's China is an interesting case in having a long tradition of strategic thinking that is in some respects quite different to contemporary Western strategic notions. Arguably, this difference is most evident in the early Chinese notion that strategies effectively have no endpoint. Time is a river that flows ever onwards; its path may be deflected but it cannot be made solely by our own actions into the tomorrow we want. If European strategic thinkers placed great emphasis on using one's agency to shape the world, early Chinese strategic thinkers stressed exploiting the course the world was already on. Gaining strategic advantage, or *shi*, deemed by some as the foundation of most Chinese actions in the international system, involves working mainly with the flow. China simply needs to manipulate what are seen as favourable trends to succeed.

The most important perceived trend is that 'the East is rising, the West is in decline and the tide of history is flowing in China's favour'. Given such a foundation, several characteristics of the international system are apparent to Chinese strategists. The international system is becoming multi-polar so providing abundant space for China to strategically manoeuvre within; China's strongest card, economics, is the dominant force shaping the world today, not military might. There is a resilient peacemaking effort making major power war improbable, and modern Chinese culture is morally superior to others given its continually restated, long-standing pre-disposition towards peaceful interaction with all. China's Grey Zone activities are both made possible by these discerned trends and designed to reinforce them. The Party's strategists accordingly have created a Grey Zone approach that leverages the trends to give China a persistent permanent strategic advantage over all others.

Their Grey Zone strategy is consequently incremental, slowly nibbling at the edges, making use of diverse military and non-military measures, being careful not to drive others into a major war, controlled at the highest Party levels, and enduring. China's particular Grey Zone model is an approach that is a forever drain on the other, smaller country's resources. China's Grey Zone activities grind remorselessly on, but in doing so, educate all about Grey Zone characteristics and create an opposing pushback. As is customary, the paradoxical nature of war applies in that those impacted by a damaging strategy will over time devise optimised counter-moves. Over the last few years, there has been a steadily deepening concern about Chinese Grey Zone activities. International attention is now focused on them, and they have become of great global media interest. Countries are starting to take actions in response, reorient their defence force structures accordingly, and most worryingly for China, beginning to come together to act collectively.

Dr Peter Layton has written a forward-looking paper on the threat from China for the Australian *Defence Strategic Update 2020*. Commencing with a review of pertinent traditional Chinese strategic thinking, the paper discusses present PLA Grey Zone guidance and advice, and examines three topical Grey Zone cases, including Eastern Ladakh. The paper then moves into the future in considering how today's Chinese Grey Zone activities might change, hopefully for the better, but possibly for the worse. As per Layton, decades-old planning assumptions about a long warning time before possible military actions have now been deemed invalid. This calls for better defence preparedness, which involves both being able to employ the force-in-being today against Grey Zone activities, and to develop the future force to be more able to meet tomorrow's Grey Zone challenges.

Undertaking Chinese Grey Zone activities focus principally on the PLA. There could be many other Chinese Government agencies, state-owned enterprises, and sub-state groups involved in major and minor Chinese Grey Zone activities. However, these non-military entities ultimately rely for their effectiveness on the sometimes concealed, hard military power wielded by the PLA. Without the PLA, providing backup and acting as the ultimate guarantor of the non-military entities survival, Chinese Grey Zone activities would be very different and probably be much less effective.

China has employed Grey Zone Warfare tactics against India in several ways, particularly along the disputed border region between the two countries. China has been accused of using its military forces to conduct border incursions into Indian territory. These incursions are often carried out by Chinese troops disguised as civilians or border patrols. China has also constructed roads and infrastructure in disputed areas, which India sees as a violation of its territorial integrity. China has also used economic coercion as a form of Grey Zone Warfare against India. For example, China has been accused of blocking India's entry into the Nuclear Suppliers Group, a group of countries that regulate global nuclear commerce. China has also been accused of blocking India's attempts to designate Masood Azhar, the leader of the Pakistan-based terrorist group Jaish-e-Mohammed, as a global terrorist by the United Nations. China has been accused of carrying out cyber attacks against India to gain access to sensitive information. In 2012, a Chinese state-sponsored hacking group was accused of carrying out a cyber attack on India's national security database. China has also been accused of using social media platforms to spread false information and influence public opinion in India. China has been using diplomatic pressure as a form of Grey Zone Warfare against India. For example, China has blocked India's attempts to join the United Nations Security Council. China has also been accused of using its influence in the region to isolate India diplomatically. Overall, China's use of Grey Zone Warfare against India reflects a broader strategy of expanding its influence in the region and challenging India's rise as a regional power. These tactics have increased tensions between the two countries, and raised concerns about the potential for escalation and conflict.

The case study on the use of PLA units in the Ladakh area on the Indian-Chinese border is of particular relevance to us. This is the most recent Grey Zone case involving the PLA violently assaulting Indian troops, killing 20 Indian soldiers. Chinese deaths are disputed, with the PLA conceding four killed, including Battalion Commander, Chen Hongjun. Qi Fabao, the Regimental Commander from the Xinjiang Military Command, was also acknowledged to have been seriously injured. India claimed at least 45

PLA soldiers died. This level of violence marks a worrying new phase in Chinese Grey Zone activities that could be repeated in other Grey Zone areas in the future.

The border dispute between India and China is too well-known to be enumerated. In recent years, China has ramped up its Grey Zone activities along the so-called LAC, which separates the two nations. What began at Doklam in June 2017 manifested in a more overt campaign in early May 2020, in the eastern Ladakh part of the border, which continues to fester. Menon, ex Foreign Secretary and NSA, opined what China did by changing the situation on the ground, shifting the LAC, and preventing Indian patrols on territory hitherto controlled by India, was a fundamental and consequential shift in behaviour, a successful salami-slicing manoeuvre. Because India's initial response was non-strategic, we were forced to cede ground, and now face a *fait accompli.* Indian deterrence and strategy had apparently failed, and by occupying territory and establishing buffer zones on the Indian side, China put the onus of escalation on India if it wished to restore the status quo.

In response, India imposed economic sanctions on Chinese firms operating within India, and moved closer to the USA and its allies, including Japan and Australia. In terms of military reaction, horizontal escalation in other parts of the border or at sea was ruled out in favour of vertical escalation. However, after 18 talks at Corps Commander level, complete disengagement remains a chimera, especially in the strategically important Depsang Plains, and bilateral relations have nose-dived.

Eastern Ladakh marked a new chapter in China's evolving Grey Zone tactics. Previously, such actions did not intentionally aim to kill others. With the PLA's initial crossing of the LAC in April-May significant in scale and intent, it seems reasonable to assume that the decision to then move to deadly violence was both deliberate and made at the highest levels, and not inadvertently by some low-level tactical commander. Future Chinese Grey Zone activities, hereafter, may also be violent. In some respects, one of the more impressive aspects of Chinese Grey Zone activities is the Party's tenacity. Quite costly actions involving numerous militia units, many state-owned enterprises, the Chinese Coast Guard, and three branches of the PLA have been undertaken and then sustained, sometimes for more than a decade. While the Party's objective of gaining and then maintaining strategic advantage over others has probably been achieved, this is an intrinsically expensive strategy. Moreover, with the design of the strategy being never-ending, the Party's Grey Zone activities will remain a permanent burden on Chinese society and the economy. India needs to take serious note of this persistence by the Chinese and be prepared for the long haul.

India's Response Options

There are no quick-fix solutions to India's Grey Zone challenges, and as such, should be preparing itself for the long haul. India faces several challenges from China and Pakistan, which employ Grey Zone tactics to achieve their strategic objectives. China has been expanding its influence in the region through its Belt and Road Initiative (BRI), which involves the development of infrastructure projects in countries across Asia, Africa, and Europe. The BRI is seen as a way for China to expand its economic and political influence in the region, and it has been criticised for its lack of transparency and environmental impact.

China has also been using Grey Zone tactics in its territorial disputes with India. China claims large parts of the Indian states of Arunachal Pradesh and Ladakh, and has been increasing its military presence in the region. It has also been using economic coercion to try to undermine India's influence in the region. For example, China has been supporting Pakistan's development of the CPEC, which passes through PoK, a region claimed by India.

Pakistan has also been using Grey Zone tactics against India, particularly in the context of the long-standing dispute over Kashmir. Pakistan has been supporting terrorist groups operating in the region, such as LeT and JeM, which have carried out attacks on Indian security forces and civilians. Pakistan denies any involvement in these attacks, but India maintains that they are supported by the Pakistani military and intelligence agencies.

India's overall strategy should be guided by the principles of deterrence, defence, and diplomacy. India's strategy should focus on a combination of defensive and offensive measures, including improving its intelligence, economic, technological, and military capabilities. By adopting a multi-dimensional approach, India can effectively counter Grey Zone Warfare, and safeguard its security and interests. Lieutenant General Ton van Loon and Susan Verstegen opine that in order to operate successfully in a Grey Zone environment, a fundamental change of thinking from one focused on military options to one that incorporates the whole context must take place. For an effective military contribution to a comprehensive approach, close cooperation with the civilian and private sectors is indispensable. This new paradigm of cross-national and cross-domain interdependency requires a change in administrative culture, one where the key military leaders must understand that their effectiveness depends heavily on cooperation with other actors, both in the military and non-military domains. In the famous words of former US Secretary of Defence James Mattis, 'If you cannot create harmony across service lines, across coalition and national lines, and across civilian-military lines... your leadership in today's age is obsolete'. Militaries should, therefore, aim at being an effective partner in cross-national and cross-domain cooperation, and identify the value of actions applicable therein. In this role, the military can act as enabler for other indispensable actors and, emphatically, should not be in the lead. It can act as a coordinator, which aims at creating effective interaction between governmental, non-governmental and military organisations. It is this ability to synchronise combat effects with other actions seeking to outmanoeuvre the adversary that should be the pivotal contribution of the military to the comprehensive approach.

The challenges posed by Grey Zone Warfare from China and Pakistan require a comprehensive and coordinated response from India. India needs to adopt a whole-of-nation (peoples) approach, where all instruments of national power – diplomatic, economic, military, and informational – are integrated to counter the threats. Diplomacy is an essential tool in India's arsenal to counter Grey Zone Warfare. India should focus on strengthening its relationships with other countries in the region, including those that have traditionally been close to China and Pakistan. India should also work towards building international alliances to counter China's growing assertiveness and its attempts to change the status quo in the region. India should also make use of multilateral forums like the UN and ASEAN to raise its concerns over China's activities in the region. India should use these forums to highlight the need for rules-based order in the region, and to promote peaceful resolution of disputes.

Economic instruments can also be used to counter Grey Zone Warfare. India should work towards diversifying its economy and reducing its dependence on China. India should also explore new trade and investment opportunities with other countries in the region, especially those that are not aligned with China. India can also use economic tools to counter China's BRI, which has been used as a tool to expand China's influence in the region. India should work with other countries to develop alternative connectivity projects that are transparent, financially sustainable, and respect the sovereignty of participating countries.

The military is an essential element of India's response to Grey Zone Warfare. India should continue to modernise and strengthen its Armed

Forces to counter the emerging threats. India needs to develop its Ballistic Missile Defence System, and should also focus on developing its Special Operations Forces to conduct operations in the Grey Zone. These forces should be trained to operate in non-permissive environments and conduct operations to counter the unconventional tactics of China and Pakistan. Additionally, India can explore innovative strategies, such as the use of drones and unmanned vehicles, to counter Grey Zone threats effectively. India should invest in developing new capabilities, such as cyber and space capabilities to counter China's asymmetric warfare. India should also work towards developing a comprehensive maritime security strategy to protect its interests in the IOR. India should invest in developing its naval capabilities to counter China's growing presence in the region. India can also improve its intelligence gathering, and sharing capabilities to quickly identify and respond to Grey Zone threats. India needs to establish a strong information-sharing network between all intelligence and security agencies, including state and local police. Additionally, India can explore partnerships with other countries, such as the United States, Japan, Australia, and Israel, to strengthen its intelligence capabilities. Most importantly, India should strive for self-sufficiency in manufacture of modern weapon platforms and cutting-edge military technologies.

Robbin Laird states that how we shape information dominance is a key part of the evolving approach to Grey Zone Warfare. Accelerated warfare means owning the speed of initiative to outpace, out-manoeuvre and out-think conventional and unconventional threats. It requires excellence in the art and science of decision making. A key element of shaping such a capability revolves around the kind of Command and Control which the force can exercise in multi-domain operations. The ability of our forces to dynamically adapt and respond in a contested environment to achieve the desired effect through multiple redundant paths could form the best defence against Grey Zone offensive. India should work towards building a strong information ecosystem that can counter the propaganda and disinformation spread by China and Pakistan. India should work towards developing a strong cyber security framework to protect its critical infrastructure and information networks. India should also work towards building its soft power by promoting its culture and values in the region. India should leverage its diaspora and its vibrant cultural heritage to build relationships with other countries in the region.

One area where Grey Zone activities have been most prominent is the cyber and information arena – another branch of the comprehensive approach. Open societies are almost by definition vulnerable to fake or exaggerated news. Countering cyber attacks necessitates not only defensive tools, but also offensive tools that allow for a proportional response in this domain. These tools employed by a specially created organisation are needed to manoeuvre in the cyber and information domains. The German Cyber and Information Domain Command and the UK 77 Brigade are two examples of capability development in this area, but notably the two initiatives differ substantially. The German initiative unites the various units and agencies working in the cyber domain under one roof, thus, placing the cyber domain next to the land, air, and maritime domains. The British approach is more effect-centric, as it aims to bring together influencing capabilities. The creation of a People's Liberation Army Strategic Support Force (PLASSF) by China in December 2015 was aimed at providing the PLA with the capacity of undertaking integrated joint operations, and fighting and winning informationised, if not intelligentised, wars of the future. Creation of the PLASSF is rated by some analysts as the most potent reform undertaken by China in its transformational theaterisation of the PLA.

India would do well to create an overarching organisation on similar lines but best suited to our own environment. Piecemeal raising of smaller organisations, not connected organically, would not yield the desired strategic effects. Most importantly, we need an organisation at the apex level of the Government to coordinate and direct Grey Zone campaigns, both defensive and offensive, in a sustained and enduring manner. Since Armed Forces, Internal Security Agencies, diplomacy, economy, infrastructure, and technology would play a prominent role, amongst others, this organisation could be created under the NSA with overriding clout over all players involved. But to do so, we need to bring the appointment and office of the NSA under the ambit of the Constitution and answerable to the Parliament. The DMA could take on the responsibility of coordinator, being part of the government. This issue needs to be debated, refined and implemented with right earnest.

Future Trends

The future trends in Grey Zone Warfare are likely to be shaped by technological advancements and changes in the geopolitical landscape. The following are some of the likely future trends that will affect India's strategy against Grey Zone Warfare:

Firstly, technological advancements are likely to play a significant role in the future of Grey Zone Warfare. China has invested heavily in developing new technologies, such as AI and quantum computing, which it is using to enhance its military capabilities. India, too, needs to invest in developing its own technologies to counter China's emerging capabilities, and work towards developing its AI and quantum computing capabilities to enhance its military and economic power.

Secondly, the geopolitical landscape is also likely to shape the future of Grey Zone Warfare. China's growing assertiveness and its attempts to change the status quo in the region are likely to continue. India will need to continue to work towards building alliances and partnerships to counter China's growing influence in the region. The Armed Forces need to sensitise policy makers on the urgent need to leverage the exponential power of the cyber and information domains to optimise India's capabilities to tackle the emerging multi-domain, Hybrid, and Grey Zone challenges of the twenty-first century. To counter these new threats, India needs to build nimble pre-war capabilities, which are immune to the compartmentalisation of war, NWNP, and peace time categorisations. In conformity with the need to create organisational and doctrinal tools to compete in the Grey Zone, technological innovation, and innovative approaches in defence policy is the route towards creating a war-winning military.

Conclusion

In conclusion, Grey Zone Warfare is a complex and evolving threat that poses significant challenges for India's security and requires a comprehensive and multi-dimensional response. China and Pakistan have been using Grey Zone tactics to undermine India's stability and territorial integrity for a long time. India must take proactive measures to counter these threats by developing its capabilities, building partnerships with like-minded nations, and enhancing its intelligence gathering capabilities. The Indian Government should also focus on enhancing its strategic communication to build public awareness and support for its policies.

India's response options to Grey Zone Warfare should include a range of measures, including diplomatic engagement, economic pressure, and military deterrence. India must also invest in enhancing its cyber capabilities, developing unmanned systems, and deploying advanced surveillance technologies to monitor its borders and coastal areas.

Future trends indicate that Grey Zone Warfare will continue to evolve, becoming more sophisticated and challenging. As technology advances, new opportunities and challenges will emerge, requiring India to remain agile and adaptive in its response. It is essential for India to continue to invest in research and development to develop advanced technologies, build strategic partnerships, and enhance its strategic communication to counter Grey Zone threats. India must remain vigilant and proactive in its approach to counter these threats and safeguard its security and interests. With a strategic approach and a strong resolve, India can effectively counter Grey Zone tactics and maintain its status as a responsible and influential regional power. As the challenges of the twenty-first century continue to emerge, develop, and mature, so must our solutions—for just as the nature of warfare is immutable, so is the conduct of warfare constantly changing.

Lieutenant General Praveen Bakshi was commissioned in Skinner's Horse in December 1977 and retired from the Indian Army on 31 July 2017 as General Officer Commanding-in-Chief, Eastern Army after forty years of service. He was responsible for the border defence with four countries, including the LAC, internal security of the insurgency areas in the Northeastern States, and strategic military engagement with China, Myanmar, Bangladesh and Bhutan. As the Army Commander, he orchestrated the military response to the Doklam incident with China on the Sikkim border in June 2017.

Endnotes

1. Bothwell, Heather M. "Gray Is the New Black: A Framework to Counter Gray Zone Conflicts." *Joint Force Quarterly*, no. 101, Mar. 2021.
2. Bensahel, Nora. David Barno. "Fighting and Winning in the 'Gray Zone.'" *War on the Rocks*, 19 May 2015, https://warontherocks.com/2015/05/fighting-and-winning-in-the-gray-zone/.
3. Mazarr, Michael J. Dr., "Mastering the Gray Zone: Understanding a Changing Era of Conflict" (2015). *Monographs, Books, and Publications.* 428.

4. Hoffman, F.G. *Conflict in the 21st Century: The Rise of Hybrid Wars.* Potomac Institute for Policy Studies, Dec. 2007, p. 58, https://www.potomacinstitute.org/images/stories/publications/potomac_hybridwar_0108.pdf.
5. Thomas Dobbs, Garth Fallon, Sarah Fouhy, Tennille Marsh and Machlan Melville, *Grey-Zone Activities and the ADF: A Perry Group Report*, Canberra: Australian Defence College, 2020, p. 5, https://theforge.defence.gov.au/sites/default/files/2020-10/Grey%20Zone_0.pdf
6. Peter Layton, 'Fighting Artificial Intelligence Battles: Operational Concepts for Future AI-Enabled Wars', *Joint Studies Paper Series,* No. 4 (Canberra: Department of Defence, 2021). https://doi.org/10.51174/JPS.004. pp. 40-43.
7. Tellis, Ashley J. "Hustling in the Himalayas: The Sino-Indian Border Confrontation." *Carnegie Endowment for International Peace*, 4 June 2020, https://carnegieendowment.org/2020/06/04/hustling-in-himalayas-sino-indian-border-confrontation-pub-81979.
8. Clary, Christopher. "Personalities, Organizations, and Doctrine in the Indian Military." *India Review*, vol. 17, no. 1, Jan. 2018, pp. 100–21, doi:10.1080/14736489.2018.1415283.
9. Subramaniam, Arjun. *Full Spectrum: India's Wars, 1972-2020.* Harper Collins, 2020.
10. Tarapore, Arzan. "India's Use of Force: The Missing Indirect Approach." *ORF*, no. 106, Sept. 2015.
11. Gady, Franz-Stefan. "What the Nagorno-Karabakh Conflict Revealed About Future Warfighting." *World Politics Review,* 19 Nov. 2020, https://www.worldpoliticsreview.com/what-the-nagorno-karabakh-conflict-revealed-about-future-warfighting/.
12. Loon, Tom van, and Susan Verstegen. "Manoeuvring in the Hybrid Environment." *Militaire Spectator*, 16 Sept. 2019, https://militairespectator.nl/artikelen/manoeuvring-hybrid-environment.
13. Laird, Robbin. "The Manoeuvrist Approach: Past, Present and Future." *Second Line of Defense*, 3 Nov. 2019, https://sldinfo.com/2019/11/the-manoeuvrist-approach-past-present-and-future/.
14. Gady, Franz-Stefan. "What Does AI Mean for the Future of Manoeuvre Warfare?" *IISS*, 5 May 2020, https://www.iiss.org/online-analysis/online-analysis//2020/05/csfc-ai-manoeuvre-warfare.
15. Menon, Shivshankar, "What China Hopes to Gain From the Present Border Standoff With India" *The Wire*, 3 Dec 2020.
16. Tarapore, Arzan. "Defence without Deterrence: India's Strategy in the 1965 War." *Journal of Strategic Studies,* vol. 46, no. 1, Oct. 2019, pp. 150–79, doi:10.1080/01402390.2019.1668274.
17. Khattak, Masood Ur Rehman. "Implications for Pakistan." *Strategic Studies*, vol. 39, no. 1, 2019, doi:10.2307/48544286.
18. Hawkes, Jon, et al. "The Tank Is Dead. Long Live the Tank." *Wavell Room,* 1 Oct. 2020, https://wavellroom.com/2020/10/01/a-critical-analysis-of-the-future-of-the-tank/

11

Strategy for Defence Innovation in India: Armed Forces as Pivot

Lieutenant General (Dr) R.S. Panwar

Technology has always played a major role in determining war-fighting strategies, and technological dominance is considered a key determinant of military supremacy. Cutting-edge technologies, whose manifestation on the battlefield, real or virtual, is expected to have a significant impact on the character of warfare, are often referred to as disruptive military technologies. Defence innovation in disruptive technologies is becoming increasingly important since technology is impacting warfare in ways never witnessed before, and this trend is expected to accelerate even further in the coming decades.

For India, a focus on the development of disruptive technologies has acquired an even greater urgency consequent to the unexpectedly rapid change of national strategy by China from a peaceful rise to an aggressive, expansionist stance in recent years. A conventional conflict with this daunting adversary has rapidly become an imminent threat which, till recently, was considered unlikely in the near term. Moreover, since China is working vigorously towards equalling and eventually surpassing the US as the dominant military power in the world, its efforts towards developing military technology presently far surpass those of India.

Fortuitously for India, two of the key technology areas which are the prime drivers for the changing character of warfare in the twenty-first century, namely, ICT and AI, are both rooted in computer science disciplines, which enjoy strong moorings in India's academia and industry. This inherent strength has, unfortunately, not been exploited so far by India, particularly by its Armed Forces. In general, India's defence R&D ecosystem and its Defence Science, Technology, and Industry (DSTI) sector have performed poorly so far, earning India the dubious distinction of being the largest importer of arms in the world during the period 2018-22.[1]

This article adopts an introspective approach from the standpoint of the Armed Forces, based on the conviction that to achieve self-reliance in defence, the role of our defence services in the defence R&D process needs to be critically reviewed. It advocates structural changes which deviate significantly from existing practices, premised on the following principles: firstly, the Armed Forces must act as a pivot for driving defence innovation, and be suitably empowered accordingly; and secondly, to perform this role effectively, they must make transformative changes internally for efficiently managing high technology projects, by creating specialist structures and grooming soldier-scientists.

Identifying Key Technologies

Based on the degree of impact on war-fighting methodology, it may be useful to loosely classify disruptive military technologies as either revolutionary or transformative, with the former having the potential of resulting in a Revolution in Military Affairs (RMA).[2]

Revolutionary Technologies

These may be discussed under the framework of two notional RMAs, as under:

Current 'ICT' RMA: Beginning with the Iraq wars and continuing to the present juncture and beyond, ICT is widely believed to have resulted in the ongoing system of systems RMA.[3] This RMA is based on two operational concepts, namely, Network-Centric Warfare (NCW) and Information Operations (IO). NCW leverages its networks and applications for enhancing combat potential by speeding up the Observe-Orient-Decide-Act (OODA) loop. IO, on the other hand, aims to achieve information dominance through war-fighting in the information space, in the process shifting the arena of conflict from the physical to the information and cognitive realms. The technologies which power this RMA and those which enable Cyberspace Operations (CO) and Electronic Warfare (EW) include ICT.

Looming 'AI' RMA: With astonishing breakthroughs occurring in the field of AI, together with the already visible advent of Autonomous Weapon Systems (AWS) on the battlefield, the combination of AI and robotics technologies is widely believed to be the harbinger of the next RMA, which is expected to manifest fully over the next two decades. AI-powered AWS will provide a potent new dimension to non-contact warfare; AI in Intelligence, surveillance, and reconnaissance (ISR) and Decision-Making (AI in DM) will enormously improve the quality of the OODA loop and AI in cyber operations will take IO to a whole new level.

Transformative Technologies

There are several other technologies which are expected to have transformative effects on war fighting over the next few decades. Internet of Things (IoT) and 5G (new additions to the ICT group) are expected to give a further boost to NCW. Hypersonic weapons are expected to lead the changes in operational concepts as well as missile defence systems. Directed Energy (DE) weapons will facilitate the development of new types of missile defence, counter-drone, and Anti-satellite (ASAT) systems. Quantum technologies are expected to create disruptive effects on secure communications and stealth systems. Nanotechnologies might have limited impact in the near and medium terms but may result in transformative or even revolutionary effects in the long term.

Need for Prioritisation

Given the wide spectrum of technologies listed above, it would not be feasible and prudent for India to pursue all with equal vigour. Therefore, prioritisation of our defence R&D efforts must be done based on the following considerations:

> The primary focus must be on technologies that are likely to have an impact on the battlefield in the near term and are not expected to be pursued by the private industry for civilian clientele.

> For dual-use technologies, the strategy must be to adapt commercially available technologies.
>
> Finally, adequate efforts must also be devoted to those technologies, which, though expected to mature over a longer time-frame, have significant implications predominantly in the military domain.

With the above considerations in mind, some of the technologies on which our defence R&D establishments must focus their attention are as follows: ICT, technologies for CO and EW, AWS, AI (DM, CO, ISR), DE weapons, ASAT weapons, hypersonic weapons, and quantum cryptography and sensing.

Fresh Approach to Defence Innovation

Despite having a very large military-industrial enterprise, comprising more than 50 Defence Research and Development Organisation (DRDO) laboratories, nine Defence Public Sector Units (DPSUs) and 41 Ordnance Factories (OFs),[4] the low self-reliance in defence has long been a matter of serious concern for the Government of India (GoI). Several government-sponsored studies have carried out analyses and recommended solutions to boost self-reliance in the defence sector, and some of the recommendations have been implemented. In addition, our defence procurement policy has undergone numerous changes, especially during the last two decades, aimed at boosting indigenous defence R&D.[5]

A scrutiny of past efforts as well as the ongoing *atmanirbharta* initiative shows that these are mostly aimed at improving the defence procurement process by incentivising the industry. While these are welcome steps, there has been no attempt so far on improving and indeed transforming the technology development process *per se*. There is an urgent need, therefore, to evolve and implement a defence innovation strategy which revitalises the R&D processes from concept to fielding of military systems.

Existing Approach

The existing approach to defence research and innovation may be summarised as follows: the DRDO, notwithstanding an uninspiring track record, continues to be the mainstay for defence research; the private industry, despite having been given increasingly attractive incentives to participate in defence manufacturing, has not yet entered the game with enthusiasm; another important stakeholder, the academia, is envisaged only in a supporting role to the DRDO and industry; the role of the Armed Forces is limited to floating requirements, monitoring progress and carrying out trials, and the MoD controls the entire defence R&D ecosystem.

Core Issues

There are several core concerns associated with the above approach which lie at the heart of its limited success, as under:

Creating Synergy Amongst Stakeholders: A review of India's military-industrial landscape shows that there is a lack of synergy amongst its major stakeholders, namely, the MoD, defence services, DRDO, industry, and academia. For the desired level of synergy to manifest itself, a driving force is needed, endowed with three essential features: military domain knowledge, technological expertise, and authority. It is felt that, with suitable policy and structural changes, in the Indian context it is the Armed Forces, and not the MoD, which are best suited to provide this driving force. Therefore, the pivot for defence R&D must shift from the MoD to the Armed Forces.

DRDO to be Accountable to the Armed Forces: The lack of accountability of the DRDO to the Armed Forces is, perhaps, a fundamental structural weakness which has stymied our indigenous efforts at harnessing defence technology, despite a huge number of public resources being allocated to it.

Tapping the Potential of Academia: Efforts, so far, to tap the enormous technological expertise available in our premier academic institutions have been half-hearted and ineffective. The role of academia needs to be upgraded from being mere consultants to becoming mainstream players in developing defence technologies.

Specialisation Within the Armed Forces: The vast potential for indigenous expertise which exists within the private industry, academia, and R&D establishments can be efficiently tapped only by specialists in uniform, both in the fields of military technologies as well as project management. Presently, the lack of adequate focus on specialisation is a critical drawback responsible for our inability to leverage cutting-edge disruptive technologies.

Broad Contours of the Approach

With the above core issues as guiding considerations, this work proposes an approach to defence innovation along several lines of action: the evolution of a national strategy for defence innovation (as opposed to defence procurement), development of concepts and doctrines on modern warfare, reviewing existing organisational structures and creating new ones for promoting indigenous defence technology, and most importantly, carrying out transformative reforms within the Armed Forces, with specialisation as a primary goal. All these aspects are discussed further.

National Strategy for Defence Innovation

A comprehensive national strategy for defence innovation would encompass many facets. In this section, two of these are briefly discussed: a defence innovation model in which the Armed Forces play a pivotal role, and the importance of Civil Military Integration (CMI).

Defence Innovation Model: Armed Forces as the Pivot

Successful indigenisation of defence technologies requires the right blend of war-fighting expertise on the one hand, and proficiency in military technologies on the other. In the Indian context, there is an abject lack of military domain knowledge within the industry, academia, and even the DRDO. Although the defence services have a fair number of technically qualified soldiers on their rolls, their poor management leaves this expertise largely unutilised. In short, the scientists do not understand warfare, and the soldiers in project management assignments do not understand technology well enough. Moreover, the interfaces between the defence services and the industry, academia, and DRDO are structurally unsuited for the desired quality and intensity of interaction.[6]

The MoD, which is manned by generalist bureaucrats, has neither the military nor the technical expertise to contribute fruitfully towards defence R&D processes. Thus, their role is *de facto* limited to exercising executive and financial control.

Under the circumstances, it is felt that the Armed Forces are best placed to act as a pivot for steering the defence innovation process, albeit with important transformational changes.

Civil Military Integration and Dual-use Technologies

The increasing sophistication and costs associated with modern weapon systems are forcing even the most advanced nations to adopt the concept of CMI in some form or the other.[7] The simultaneous digitisation and intelligisation of the battlefield as well as society has expanded the spectrum of dual-use technologies and increased the chances of success for a good CMI strategy. The central idea is to overcome the guns versus butter dilemma to the extent feasible, by ensuring that investments in the commercial sector have spin-offs in the defence industry and vice versa.

China has, perhaps, demonstrated the maximum determination in making its CMI strategy a success. At the same time, other top arms-producing countries including the US, Russia, and France have all focused on the exploitation of dual-use technologies by achieving synergy amongst their military and civil R&D capabilities.

India, so far, has not yet evolved a CMI strategy, much less operationalised it. Such a strategy, suitably tailored to the Indian context, must be evolved and implemented as a national priority.

Strategic Guidance on Future Warfare

Absence of Higher Direction

As per the Defence Acquisition Procedure (DAP) 2020, the Technology Perspective and Capability Roadmap (TPCR), flowing out of the 10 years Integrated Capability Development Plan (ICDP) and the two five years Defence Capital Acquisition Plan (DCAP), is designed to provide necessary guidance to the industry and defence research establishments for developing the requisite defence technologies.[8] The ICDP itself should ideally flow out of a National Security Strategy, defence planning guidelines, and a defence capability strategy or plan, none of which have ever been issued by the Indian establishment.[9]

Thus, while a classified Long Term Integrated Perspective Plan (LTIPP) 2012–27 exists (ICDP in its previous avatar), and two TPCRs have been issued so far (in 2013 and 2018),[10] these documents are not grounded in formally evolved strategic military thought. With the institution of the Defence Planning Committee (DPC)[11] and the Department of Military Affairs (DMA)[12] in April 2018 and December 2020 respectively, national or military security policies will hopefully be issued in the foreseeable future.

Need to Evolve Concept Papers and Doctrines on Modern Warfare

Despite the ICT RMA manifesting in the battle space over the past two decades, there are hardly any concept papers and doctrines which have been issued by our Armed Forces to analyse and operationalise its impact on our war fighting methodologies.[13] Those which do exist are not insightful or comprehensive enough to be able to provide strategic guidance for carrying out innovative R&D. Similarly, the current level of interest in disruptive military technologies is mostly restricted to keynote addresses and paper presentations at various conferences.

There is an urgent need, therefore, to evolve effective joint services and service-specific doctrines on NCW, IO, CO, EW, and cognitive operations. In addition, concept papers must be issued enunciating how the disruptive technologies discussed above would be leveraged by us on the battlefield in the coming decades. Also, open-domain versions of these doctrines should be made available to spread awareness and understanding among all stakeholders.

Harnessing Information Age Technologies – Past Performance

There is a growing school of thought that traditional large weapon platforms such as tanks and aircraft carriers would soon give way to smarter, more agile Lethal Autonomous Weapon Systems (LAWS).[14] Therefore, instead of trying to play catch up on Industrial Age weapon systems, it would be a good strategy for India to focus our R&D efforts on Information Age technologies. Towards this end, our national expertise in ICT disciplines (including its super-specialist sub-domain of AI) can be leveraged to our advantage. Our efforts in this direction so far have been very feeble, as summarised below.

Harnessing ICT: Lacklustre Performance

Establishments within the Armed Forces specifically chartered to develop indigenous defence systems in Information Age technologies include the Army Design Bureau (ADB), the Directorate General of Information Systems (DGIS), various Project Management Organisations (PMOs) for Tactical C3I (Tac C3I) systems and networks, and the Naval Weapons and Electronics Systems Engineering Establishment (WESEE), amongst others. Project managers and senior leadership posted to these organisations lack specialisation in the desired fields and, more importantly, their postings are mostly on a single tenure basis. In other words, almost all these establishments are manned by a floating population of non-specialists.

The performance of the DGIS (including its earlier avatars) over the last three decades is disappointing. Despite long gestation periods, none of its flagship tactical C3I and Command, Control, Communications, Computers, Intelligence, Surveillance and Reconnaissance (C4ISR) projects have reached full operational status, with most of them either still under development or short closed, even though the underlying technologies are being extensively used in commercial environments. With such poor results, it would be futile to expect the DGIS to steer the development of much more sophisticated AI-enabled systems, unless it undergoes major transformation.

In contrast to the DGIS, establishments with a higher degree of specialisation in their ethos have produced better results over the years, most notably the WESEE.

Leveraging AI – Weak Initiatives

Our national as well as military efforts to leverage AI for military operations have also been very tardy. Based on the report submitted in June 2018 by the AI task force for Artificial Intelligence for National Security and Defence set up by the MoD, a High-level Defence AI Council (DAIC) was constituted in 2019 under the chairmanship of the Defence Minister, with the primary charter of providing strategic direction for AI-driven transformation in defence. Simultaneously, a Defence AI Project Agency (DAIPA), with Secretary (Defence Production) as the Chairman, was also instituted.[15] However, there is as yet no evidence of any impactful initiatives undertaken by these apex organisations, although some projects are now being progressed by the three Services under the directions of DAIPA.

The Centre for Artificial Intelligence and Robotics (CAIR), DRDO's main establishment working in AI, has made limited headway in making some prototype systems. However, if India is to keep pace with advancements in the international arena, these efforts are grossly insufficient.[16]

Agile and Responsive Organisational Structures

This section recommends transformative changes to defence innovation organisations to resuscitate their current sluggish performance. However, organisational restructuring related to procurement and production functions is not being analysed here.[17]

DRDO Restructured as Service Laboratories

Since the primary charter of the DRDO is to support our Armed Forces, it must be made accountable to the Defence Services. This requirement can be met by placing the Directorate of Defence Research and Development (DDR&D) under the DMA. The current arrangement of DDR&D and the DMA being peer departments under the *Raksha Mantri* (Defence Minister), with oversight by the Defence Secretary, is felt to be ineffective for steering indigenous defence innovation.

In a rapid follow-up phase, the DRDO is recommended to be restructured into four clusters and placed under the direct control of Headquarters Integrated Defence Staff (HQ IDS) (for tri-services research) and the three Services.

Indian DARPA – High Risk-High Payoff Research

An Indian Defence Advanced Research Project Agency (I-DARPA) with a team of 75-100 project leaders or managers including men in uniform, structured on the lines of the US DARPA[18], needs to be established under the DMA, with the following characteristics: only high-risk high-payoff R&D for potentially transformative technologies to be undertaken, highly specialist profiles of its leaders and managers; unfettered leeway given to project managers, and R&D to be carried out entirely by extramural agencies, primarily the industry as well as academic and research institutions.

Defence Innovation Unit – Furtherance of the CMI Strategy

A Defence Innovation Unit (DIU) with an executive workforce of 30-40 professionals must be set up to efficiently harness emerging civil and commercial technologies for military applications and systems, in furtherance of India's CMI strategy. The DIU models being followed by the US and France may be suitably adapted for setting up the Indian DIU. [19,20]

Military Incubation Centres – Leveraging Entrepreneurship

Military Incubation Centres need to be set up within our premier academic and research institutions, including military ones, as an effective means of encouraging and leveraging entrepreneurship in emerging and niche military technologies.

Apex Committee

It is imperative that defence innovation be steered from the highest level of governance. Presently the Prime Minister chairs several cabinet committees, such as committees on security, economic affairs, and political affairs. Along similar lines, defence innovation must also be provided leadership directly by the Prime Minister through a new cabinet committee constituted for this purpose.[21]

Defence Services – Introspect and Transform, or be Doomed!

The changes envisaged above would effectively shift the fulcrum of the defence innovation process from the MoD to the Armed Forces. However, mere restructuring would not suffice to achieve the desired results, unless complemented by transformative reforms within the defence services, as discussed below.

Transforming the Military Mindset

The CDS and Service Chiefs have often proclaimed the need to modernise the Armed Forces and have stressed the importance of developing military technologies indigenously.[22, 23] However, there has been hardly any effort to introspect and analyse why our military-industrial complex has failed to adequately deliver over so many decades.

It is felt that this indifferent performance is largely rooted in existing mindsets of the military hierarchy on the importance of technology in warfare and the role of the Armed Forces towards leveraging disruptive technologies. As per current convictions, warfighting in info space, AI-based decision-making, and fielding of autonomous weapon systems are regarded as esoteric concepts and not given due attention. Moreover, active participation in defence research is not considered to be within the purview of the uniformed community.

The view that a generalist with a rounded combat profile is best suited to steer projects involving cutting-edge technologies has perhaps been largely responsible for underperformance by our project management establishments. The increasing role of specialist war-fighters in twenty-first century warfare in general, and in the realm of defence innovation in particular, has not yet been fully appreciated. The specialisation referred to does not necessarily imply deep technical expertise, but rather a thorough understanding of modern war-fighting concepts complemented with appropriate grounding in the underlying technologies. A change in mindset, therefore, is necessary for bringing about a transformation in the defence innovation process.

Grooming Soldier-Scientists

It is essential for the Armed Forces to groom soldier-scientists who can be part of R&D teams working within the industry, academia, and the DRDO, as well as in establishments such as the I-DARPA and the DIU. To enable this, HRD policies need to undergo drastic changes, by jettisoning the policy of rounded profiles for all, and ushering in a culture of specialisation. In this regard, Israel's Talpiot program is an interesting case study, worth emulating.[24]

Towards this end, several measures must be taken, as follows: giving ownership of different technologies to specific arms or services; ensuring that a sufficient number of officers undergo formal training in the desired disciplines, providing multiple tenures to specialists in vacancies related to their specialisation, getting the most talented soldiers to opt for specialisation and protecting their careers up to the highest ranks, a life-cycle association of specialists to projects amongst many others.[25]

Participative R&D

Our project management organisations (DGIS, PMOs, etc) need to be revitalised both in terms of numbers and quality, with soldier-scientists as project managers as well as in leadership roles.

Given that our industry, academia and even the DRDO all possess very little domain knowledge about warfighting concepts and procedures, it is imperative for the Armed Forces to adopt a model of participative R&D, where soldier-scientists and civilian scientists work together as teams for conducting cutting edge research.

Strategy and Policy Measures
Strategy for Defence Innovation
Guidance on Future Warfare
Transforming the Military Mindset
Grooming Soldier-Scientists
Participative R&D

Organisational Restructuring
DRDO as Service Laboratories
Indian DARPA
Defence Innovation Unit
Military Incubation Centres
Apex Committee

Transformative Restructuring – Recommended Approach

Our Armed Forces must assume responsibility for steering defence innovation with the same commitment and vigour as all other facets of defence preparedness. This involves, first and foremost, making an attitudinal shift from being requisitioners of defence systems to drivers of indigenous defence R&D. Several measures suggested in the previous two sections are purely internal to the Armed Forces, while others require government approval, as explained below:

Measures Internal to the Armed Forces: These measures include evolving requisite concept papers and doctrine; carrying out substantial modifications to our HRD policies to usher in a culture of super-specialisation, in particular, grooming soldier-scientists with protected career prospects, and revitalising our PMOs.

Measures Requiring Government Approval: These comprise measures such as raising new establishments (DIU, I-DARPA), restructuring the

DRDO, and establishing incubation centres in our academic and research establishments.

A two-pronged approach must therefore be adopted, as follows: resolutely implement the internal measures, and, on a parallel track, prepare and pursue cases requiring government approval vigorously till accepted and implemented.

Conclusion

In this work, a fresh approach to defence innovation in India has been proposed, contingent on two principal ideas: firstly, the Armed Forces must play a pivotal role in the defence innovation process, and secondly, they must carry out internal restructuring to usher in higher levels of specialisation. The approach is transformative in character, quite likely to be vetoed as being impractical, even absurd, by certain sections of the bureaucracy and military hierarchy alike. Yet, each of the measures suggested has been successfully adopted by one or more world leaders in military technology, and adapting them to the Indian ecosystem is felt to be immensely feasible, provided the will to do so exists. With the military might of China growing at an alarming pace, our quest for self-reliance in the defence sector needs to be given an impetus like never before. Incremental steps taken in the past have at best been weak attempts in this direction. The time to take radical but well-thought out action is now!

Lieutenant General (Dr) R.S. Panwar, AVSM, SM, VSM, a Signals Veteran, is a graduate of IIT and the NDC. He has commanded an EW Group, logistics formations in the SW and NE Armies, served in CI environment applying theatre-wide secure network communications and policy. An expert in the field of Cyber security and AI, he has been Commandant MCTE, Mhow, and has several awards and citations to his credit including the unique Distinguished Alumnus Award by IIT, Bombay. He writes for professional journals on technology strategy, ICT and subjects that have been training models for innumerable military students studying communications and spectral policy.

Endnotes

1. Wezeman, Pieter D., et al. *Trends in International Arms Transfers,* 2022. Stockholm International Peace Research Institute, 13 Mar. 2023, http://dx.doi.org/10.55163/cpns8443.
2. Panwar, R. S., Dr. "Disruptive Military Technologies: An Overview – Part I." *Future Wars,* 28 Apr. 2020, https://futurewars.rspanwar.net/disruptive-military-technologies-an-overview-part-i/#disruptive-military-technologies-a-classification.
3. Panwar, R. S., Dr. "Network Centric Warfare Vis-a-Vis Modern Warfighting Concepts." *Future Wars,* 1 Jan. 2018, https://futurewars.rspanwar.net/network-centric-warfare-vis-a-vis-modern-warfighting-concepts/#ncw-vav-rmas.
4. Behera, Laxman Kumar. *Indian Defence Industry: Issues of Self-Reliance.* Institute for Defence Studies and Analyses, no. 21. July 2013. pp 9
5. Panwar, R. S., Dr. "Ideation for Defence R&D in India: Transformative Approach with Armed Forces as Pivot – Part I." *Future Wars,* 1 Sept. 2020, https://futurewars.rspanwar.net/ideation-for-defence-rd-in-india-transformative-approach-with-armed-forces-as-pivot-part-i/#previous-studies-and-policy-initiatives.
6. Panwar, R. S., Dr. "Disruptive Military Technologies: An Overview – Part

III." *Future Wars,* 12 May 2020, https://futurewars.rspanwar.net/disruptive-military-technologies-an-overview-part-iii/#effective-defence-rnd-model.
7. Panwar, R. S., Dr. "Ideation for Defence R&D in India: China's Approach to Defence Innovation – Part I." *Future Wars,* 28 July 2020, https://futurewars.rspanwar.net/ideation-for-defence-rd-in-india-chinas-approach-to-defence-innovation-part-i/#civil-military-integration.
8. Ministry of Defence, Government of India. *Defence Acquisition Procedure 2020.* pp. 6–7.
9. *Make In India Through Indigenous Research and Development by DRDO/Industry.* Vivekananda International Foundation, https://www.vifindia.org/sites/default/files/vif-task-force-report-make-in-india_0.pdf.
10. *Technology Perspective and Capability Roadmap* (TPCR) - 2018, Ministry of Defence, Accessed 7 April 2023, https://mod.gov.in/sites/default/files/tpcr.pdf.
11. "Defence Planning Committee." Wikipedia, 11 Feb. 2023, https://en.wikipedia.org/wiki/Defence_Planning_Committee.
12. "Department of Military Affairs." *Ministry of Defence,* https://www.mod.gov.in/department-military-affairs. Accessed 11 May 2023.
13. Panwar, R. S., Dr. "IW Structures for the Indian Armed Forces – Part IV." *Future Wars*, 21 Apr. 2020, https://futurewars.rspanwar.net/iw-structures-for-the-indian-armed-forces-part-iv/.
14. Panwar, R. S., Dr. "Artificial Intelligence in Military Operations: An Overview – Part I." *Future Wars*, 19 Sept. 2017, http://futurewars.rspanwar.net/artificial-intelligence-in-military-operations-an-overview-part-i/.
15. Government of lndia, Ministry of Defence, and Department of Defence Production. I*mptementation of the Recommendations of the Multi-Stakeholder Task Force Constituted by the Ministry of Defence for "Strategic Lmplementation of Artificial Tntelligence for National Security and Defence".* 8 Feb. 2019, https://www.ddpmod.gov.in/sites/default/files/AI.pdf.
16. Panwar, R. S., Dr. "Artificial Intelligence in Military Operations: An Overview – Part II." *Future Wars,* 29 Sept. 2017, http://futurewars.rspanwar.net/artificial-intelligence-in-military-operations-an-overview-part-ii/.
17. Behera, Laxman Kumar. *Indian Defence Industry: Issues of Self-Reliance. Institute for Defence Studies and Analyses*, no. 21. July 2013. pp 9 pp. 57-70.
18. Gallo, Marcy E. "Defense Advanced Research Projects Agency: Overview and Issues for Congress." *Congressional Research Service (CRS).*, Aug. 2021. pp 1-2.
19. Panwar, R. S., Dr. "Ideation for Defence R&D in India – The US Approach to Defence Innovation." *Future Wars,* 21 July 2020, https://futurewars.rspanwar.net/ideation-for-defence-rnd-in-india-the-us-approach-to-defence-innovation/.
20. Panwar, R. S., Dr. "Ideation for Defence RD in India: Defence Innovation Approaches of Russia, Israel and France – Part II." *Future Wars,* 18 Aug. 2020, http://futurewars.rspanwar.net/ideation-for-defence-rd-in-india-defence-innovation-approaches-of-russia-israel-and-france-part-ii/.
21. Team, The Print. "Here's the Full List of Cabinet Committees after Reshuffle: PM Heads 6, Amit Shah 2." *The Print,* 6 June 2019, https://theprint.in/india/

heres-the-full-list-of-cabinet-committees-after-reshuffle-pm-heads-6-amit-shah-2/246277/.
22. PTI. "Indian Army Chief Bipin Rawat Says Will Fight and Win the next War with Indigenous Weapon Systems." *Financial Express*, 15 Oct. 2019, https://www.financialexpress.com/defence/indian-army-chief-bipin-rawat-says-will-fight-and-win-the-next-war-with-indigenous-weapon-systems/1736204/.
23. PIB. "Indian Army Organises Seminar on Disruptive Technology." *Indian Defence Industries*, 25 Aug. 2020, http://indiandefenceindustries.in/army-disruptive-technology.
24. Gewirtz, Jason. "Inside the IDF's Super-Secret Elite Brain Trust." *The Tower*, Apr. 2016, http://www.thetower.org/article/inside-the-idfs-super-secret-elite-brain-trust-talpiot/.
25. Panwar, R. S., Dr. "Disruptive Military Technologies: An Overview – Part III." *Future Wars*, 12 May 2020, https://futurewars.rspanwar.net/disruptive-military-technologies-an-overview-part-iii/.

12

Approach Towards the Protection of Military Installations

Lieutenant General K.J. Singh

Proxy war manifests in various actions designed to spread terror, in the form of kidnapping, hostage taking, hijacking, attacking and ambushing convoys, planting Improvised Explosive Devices (IEDs), etc. The most audacious form, often involving the application of *fedayeen* (suicide bombers), is the attack on military installations. These nefarious attacks have been occurring as a global trend and India has also witnessed a large number of such attacks. The challenge is in preventing them and, on occurrence, minimising their effect, followed by a credible response.

Scope and Terminologies

Strategy Vis-a-vis Approach

The article attempts to discuss an approach rather than a concrete strategy, as each military base or installation has its own peculiarities and it is difficult to stipulate a universal strategy or even a template like a one-size-fits-all.

However, an approach is more flexible, wherein indicative guidelines can be utilised to evolve a specific action plan or Standard Operating Procedure (SOP), customised to the relevant base.

Base and Installation

The term installation or even base is flexible to cater to small, medium, and large bases or installations, which, in different Armed Forces jargon, are described as Vulnerable Area (VA) and Vulnerable Point (VP). The categorisation of VAs and VPs is customised to targeting parameters, especially for aerial attacks. Consequently, they also help to deduce connected requirements for defenders like air defence cover, size of protection party, and preliminary or reserved demolition plan, in the event of an imminent attack. For the attacker, they help to prioritise targets, and explosive load and other targeting parameters.

Focus

Terrorists choose their target on an entirely different set of factors like possible visibility or Targeted Attack Protection (TRP) or media value of the attack, the chance of success, local support, etc. Repeated attacks in the Samba belt of the Jammu-Pathankot Sector are driven by these visibility factors, the ease of infiltration, proximity to the national highway, and the main communication link to the erstwhile state of Jammu and Kashmir. The focus of this article is tuned to terrorist attacks in the Indian context. However, relevant inferences have been drawn from global and regional scans to devise a recommended approach.

Macro Trends for Protection

Bottom Line Reality

The urge for safety and protection has witnessed the development of fortresses, moats, and barriers in the form of formidable defensive lines and walls. The Great Wall of China, the Berlin Wall, the Maginot Line and the Barlev Line are relevant examples. As per official records, more than 1,00,000 persons attempted to breach the legendary Berlin Wall, 5,000 odd succeeded, and 150 lost their lives in the process. The famed multi-layered Barlev defences across the Suez, linking the Sinai Peninsula, were a hybrid of multiple layers of physical and technical means. Though described as impregnable, the Arabs breached them in the Yom-Kippur War of 1973 using rudimentary and basic techniques. Defensive barriers are increasingly incorporating technical means like surveillance cameras, CCTV, smart fences, and now, surveillance drones, integrated into automated warning and alarm systems. On balance, technology aids but is neither the silver bullet nor panacea for assured impregnability. The bottom line and seminal reality are that no wall or fence can stop a determined attacker, especially when aided by collaborators.

Evolving Trend

While defensive means have evolved, concurrently attackers have kept pace in their tactics, even adopting *fedayeen* tactics. In certain ways, it is a cat-and-mouse game. The very idea of attacking a protected military camp is based on audacity, regardless of near-certain death, but this generates very high visibility. Often it is timed to commemorate certain notable events in Tanzeem's (terrorist group) calendar like the death anniversary of a terrorist, wherein the security personnel are aware of a higher probability of attack, yet the attacker chooses a suicidal approach. Desperation or determination has been evidenced in the Germans storming the Belgian fortress of Eben Emael in 1940 with gliders. Drones currently reflect a nuanced progression in the aerial domain in the current context both for attacks like the Jammu air-base intrusion by mini drones, and for defensive surveillance.

Dynamic Nature of Threats

Starting with the ancient Greek Trojan Horse perfidy in the city of Troy, the threat has now morphed into cyber bugs, also referred to as malware or Trojans. Closer home and in our context, tunnelling is being resorted to by terrorist groups for infiltration, especially in the Jammu-Kathua-Samba Sector. Hence, there is a constant need to analyse the dynamics and evolving trends both in the threat matrix as also in protection measures. Terrorists keep varying their pattern of targeting like heightened attacks in the Jammu-Pathankot belt in 2013–16—three years—Samba (twice), Kathua, Arnia (foiled attempt aimed at Samba), Janglot, Dinanagar, and Pathankot. These have now petered off with the current focus in the last two years (2022–23) in Poonch-Rajouri. It seems like going back to Hill Kaka, Operation Sarp Vinash, and the tumultuous period of 2003. Terrorists also have a choice to shift periodically to attacking convoys and ambush. In this dynamic flux of varying areas of attack and its methodology, security forces tend to slacken down in out-of-focus areas treating them as routine, often violating the basic SOPs, resulting in setbacks like the recent ones in the Poonch-Rajouri sector.

Mapping of Threats in the Indian Context

The information on the number of terrorist attacks was provided in the Lok Sabha by Shripad Naik, the *Rajya Raksha Mantri,* in a written reply in July 2019. It had details of Terrorist Initiated Incidents (TIIs) in the erstwhile state of Jammu and Kashmir and the Northeast. These include all kinds of incidents including attacks on camps as also ambushes and contact incidents. The details tabled in the Parliament are as follows:

Year	J&K	Northeast
2016	9	6
2017	23	10
2018	54	11
2019	13	5

Statistical data is further validated by the tabulated analyses of relevant aspects of incidents from 2013 to 2016 mapping dates, locations and their type, own and terrorist casualties. This tabulation is limited to *fedayeen* on bases and military camps. The information is sourced from the *Policy Brief on Fedayeen Attacks* prepared by Colonel Vivek Chadha from the Institute of Defence Studies in December 2016.

Date	Location	Type of Establishment	Casualties	Terrorist Casualties
Sep 26, 2013	Samba	Cavalry Regiment	1 officer and 2 other ranks, 4 policemen, 2 civilians	3
Jan 2014	Janglot, Kathua	Artillery Regiment HQ	1 soldier	3
Nov 27, 2014	Kathar, Arnia Sector, Jammu	Stopped in vicinity of border	3 other ranks and 4 civilians	3
Dec 5, 2014	Mohra, Uri	Artillery Unit	1 officer, 7 other ranks	6
July 27, 2015	Gurdaspur	Police Station	4 policemen and 3 civilians	3

Jan 2, 2016	Pathankot	Airfield	1 officer, 6 other ranks	4
Sep 11, 2016	Poonch	Brigade HQ	1 policeman	3
Sep 18, 2016	Uri	Brigade HQ	17 other ranks killed	4
Oct 6, 2016	Langate, Kupwara	Battalion HQ, RR	0	3
Nov 29, 2016	Nagrota	Artillery Regiment HQ	2 officers and 5 other ranks killed	3

Major Fidayeen Attacks on Armed Forces Establishments

(Source: Information compiled from open media sources.)

The table analyses *fidayeen* attacks during the last three years including in areas J&K. This is the period when most such attacks have taken place. The relevant details of the period from 2016 onwards are tabulated further.

Time Period and Location	Terrorist Group	Casualties
02–05 January 2016 Pathankot Airbase	JeM 4 attackers – all neutralised.	6 security personnel and 1 civilian, before entry. No damage to critical assets. Details of injured personnel not known.
18 September 2016 Brigade HQ Uri	JeM 4 attackers – neutralised later.	19 soldiers fatal and 50 injured.
27 Apr 2017 Panzgam camp near Chowkibal (Kupwara)	JeM 3 terrorists – neutralised in retaliatory action.	3 including Captain fatal and 7 injured.
10 Feb 2018 Sanjuwan (Jammu) Army Base	JeM 3 attackers – all neutralised. Attack timed with death anniversary of Afzal Guru.	6 soldiers, 1 civilian- fatal, 20 injured. Over 24-hour gun battle.
11 Aug 2022 Dhangri (Rajouri) camp	Lashkar-e-Taiyyaba (LeT) 2 terrorists – neutralised	4 soldiers fatal and 1 injured.

An analysis of the two tables shows that attacks in the Samba-Pathankot belt, which was the main focus in 2013–16, have reduced from 2017 onwards. These attacks don't consider ambushes like Lethpura (Pulwama) on 14 February 2019 on the Central Reserve Police Force (CRPF) convoy, wherein a lone Jaish-e-Mohammad (JeM) suicide bomber caused 40 fatal casualties. More recently, on 21 April 2023, five soldiers were killed and one injured in an ambush on a Rashtriya Rifles vehicle by JeM near Bhimber Gali (Poonch). Another dastardly improvised explosive attack was on the District Reserve Guard, the auxiliary force of Chattisgarh police, by Left Wing Extremists (LWE) leading to the fatalities of 10 jawans and a civilian driver. Fratricide incidents like the recent one in Bhatinda military base on 12 April 2023, leading to four fatalities, are not discussed as they are of different categories, and as these require separate correctives and mitigation measures.

Challenges in Camp Security

Locational Challenges: The British planned the first set of cantonments away from population centres often in climatically-suitable hill stations. Hence, stations like Wellington, Simla, Kasauli, Yol, Panchgani, Mhow, Deolali, etc., came up. Even in cities, cantonment areas were sited at the periphery with a clear demarcation of civilian and military pockets. After independence, the land got allotted, often on political consideration, in places like Bhatinda, Hisar, and Binaguri. The primary threat being conventional wars in the proximity of borders, terrorist threats were not given due importance. Hence, local protection considerations got watered down. This unplanned urbanisation has resulted in the following challenges:

Civilian pockets, encroachments, and residential areas sprout along the periphery of bases.

In some cases, encroachments have taken place in buffer or no construction zones of sensitive installations like ammunition dumps, air bases, and Headquarters (HQs).

Highways and communication arteries have been constructed through military areas, providing easy access and observation.

Dominating high-rise structures have come up in proximity to vital institutions.

Internal Layout of Bases: Most army bases still have only cattle fences and lack perimeter walls provided for airbases and major depots. Uri and Samba camps had only basic cattle fences when they were first attacked in 2016 and 2013 respectively. Post-attacks, some attempts in hardening fences, with Corrugated Galvanised Iron (CGI) sheets and other contraptions have been made. Bases are very green spaces; some are like biodiversity parks. They often have *nallahs*, rivulets, and micro-forests, which are exploited by terrorists to hide, like in the Pathankot and Sanjuwan attacks. Very few bases have continuous and clear perimeter patrolling tracks. Some have overhanging trees providing Tarzan-like entry over the wall or fence, as evidenced in the entry at the Pathankot airbase in 2016.

Satellite and Isolated Pockets: Constraints of land availability have forced the creation of isolated and satellite pockets. As an example, Jammu has as many as eight pockets; each one requires its own security, surveillance and response mechanisms, imposing huge financial costs and human deployment penalties. Three outlying pockets—Sanjuwan, Kaluchak, and Ratnuchak—have borne the brunt of terrorist attacks. Many of these, due to unplanned urban mushrooming, are in stand-alone mode with little mutual support from other pockets. In some cases, highways, further divide these pockets into sectors like Patiala and Bhatinda stations.

Night and Bad Visibility Challenges: Almost all bases and perimeters lack night and low visibility surveillance devices like thermal imaging. Some bases even lack basic flood lighting and even where provided they may be unserviceable as in the case of Pathankot Airbase.

Proximity to Borders: Bases and military posts in the proximity of borders provide terrorists with an opportunity to infiltrate, strike, and ex-filtrate without elaborate logistics support. They also provide opportunities for reconnaissance to detect vulnerabilities.

Criminal Ecosystem in Border Belt: Criminals often find shelter and operate in border areas due to difficult terrain and lax law enforcement system. These areas have shady gangs indulging in human and cattle smuggling, particularly on the Indo-Bangladesh border. Other activities include narco-trafficking, arms smuggling, counterfeit, and illegal mining. An informal media survey in 2016 established that very few all-India cadre officers from the IAS and the IPS are posted in such areas. It will be apt to quote examples of sacked SP Salwinder Singh in Pathankot and Inspector Devinder Singh in the Srinagar Airport in this regard.

Repetitive Routine: Security duties entail long tenures of duty, which are repetitive and mundane causing fatigue.

Coordination: Base security is handled by multiple agencies, which often work in *silos*, creating issues of coordination and accountability.

Lack of Skilling: Troops employed on security-related duties like Defence Security Corps (DSC) and Territorial Army are treated as auxiliary forces, which are sub-optimally equipped. They have human resource-related problems of age profile, lack of initiative, and sub-optimal periodic refresher training. These troops seldom get recognition and lack motivation.

High Cost of Modernisation: Technological surveillance and modernisation of equipment entail very heavy expenditure and dictate prioritisation.

Long Gestation: Construction of perimeter and surveillance systems takes time and entails gestation periods.

Foreign Origin of Equipment: Dependence on foreign-origin equipment, especially Chinese cameras, creates vulnerabilities. There is a need to develop indigenous manufacturing and avoid foreign systems.

Collaborators: It is a considered opinion that most attacks are supported or even vectored by local or in-house collaborators. However, in most cases, these collaborators escape investigation and legal action.

Demographic Pockets: Interested parties have allowed the settlement of vulnerable sections of the population in the proximity of military camps. Rohingya pockets have come up adjoining the Sanjuwan Base and Gujjar settlements in the Samba belt, in close proximity to the installations. These have been utilised by attackers for reconnaissance and logistics, including the staging of their attacks. *Mazars* and such religious shrines have also been misused for access and reconnaissance.

Investigation and Forensic Back-up: It has been seen that investigation is often tardy, slow, and the forensic support inadequate. Evidence, even when available, gets mishandled. For example, the GPS recovered in the Dinanagar attack (on the police post), got mishandled due to tinkering by local *jugaad* (improvisation) type of experts in Mohali.

Symbolic Scapegoating Approach: The investigation loop, after most incidents, fails to fix full accountability, identify, and book collaborators and often lapses into symbolic scapegoating with the fixing of one odd person in the chain, like the base commander and two lower officials after the Pathankot incident. In this incident, no seniors of police and CAPFs, or even collaborators, were identified and held accountable.

Lack of Transparency and Peer Review in Follow-up: Most investigation reports are classified and even non-redacted portions are not put in the open domain. There is total absence of peer review. It is indicative of a fire-brigade response and failure to learn long-term lessons for genuine security audits of bases.

Policy Approaches for Protection

Operational

There could be various macro-operational approaches for the protection of bases and installations, like the following:

Defensive or Reactive Approach: This methodology focuses on boosting protection in terms of walls, fences, surveillance devices, and such defensive measures.

Offensive or Proactive Approach: This format seeks to identify the potential source of the threat and nip it at the origin, ideally, or before it impacts the protected installation. This approach is practised, to a certain extent, by the USA in its Homeland Security of Continental America. It has been used as a justification for the target of terrorist groups like the Talib, Islamic State of Iraq and Syria (ISIS), and Somalian groups. The concept has obvious limitations, both the selection of the target and even its efficacy. The Twin Tower attacks on the World Trade Centre, New York, of 9/11 is a relevant example in this context. After the Uri attack and the Pulwama ambush, surgical raids and the Balakot Surgical Strikes were executed. While they delivered a strong deterrent message and reduced the frequency of attacks, the series of recent incidents in Rajouri, reflect a continued threat and the need for a hybrid or combined approach.

Hybrid or Combination Approach: This is also termed as offensive-defence and is a balanced combination of strong dissuasive protection and an offensive approach articulated in localisation, neutralisation, and targeted punitive response. The Israelis rely on strong, highly automated surveillance and intelligence system backed with assured offensive surgical response.

Physical vs Technical

Another set of policy choices is about the physical hardening *vis-a-vis* reliance on technical aids. It is a decision between a physical wall or a smart fence with electronic surveillance, including CCTV system. Protection, especially surveillance and technical, means entails considerable expenditure, as also considerable gestation. Hence, a due cost-benefit analysis and prioritisation are mandatory due to fiscal constraints. In addition, life cycle maintenance and upgradation are due to obsolescence in technology. In sum, both physical and technical could be utilised to complement each other.

Armed Forces Study and Planned Correctives

Armed Forces Study

After the Pathankot Airbase incident, in 2016, the Government ordered a tri-service study headed by the former VCOAS, Lieutenant General Philip Campose. This panel suggested that perimeter security entails three key ingredients, beginning with quality local intelligence gathering, smart technology for fence management, and ensuring a quick response. The report visualised a sort of buffer or no man's land between the boundary and the inner fence. The idea was that in case there was a breach, the response mechanism should be efficient enough to neutralise the intruders in this buffer strip between the first and second layers of the base perimeter.

Financial Dimension

The study made several highly ambitious recommendations, entailing a huge budgetary expenditure. As per media reports and informed sources, the committee had identified a paucity of funds allocated for base security as one of the main reasons for the Army's inability to secure its camps by installing high-tech surveillance gadgets, including electrified fences, night vision devices, radars and CCTVs for effective access-control, perimeter security-cum-intrusion detection systems and better intelligence response mechanisms. As per reliable estimates, there are more than 600 big and small and isolated camps in Kashmir, and every camp needed at least ₹1–2 crores to upgrade their security to acceptable levels. Media also reported that the Army, Navy, and IAF, in 2017, had sought more than ₹2,000 crores for strengthening perimeter security of their prioritised sensitive bases. There are more than 3,000 such installations, including 600 categorised as sensitive by the three services after the Pathankot Airbase attack in January 2016.

Response Mechanisms

The same study had recommended revamping the designated protection force, DSC with revamped 20,000 strong physically fit soldiers. It also recommended arming them with AK-47s instead of 7.62 mm-SLRs. The equipment upgrade recommended faster vehicles, bulletproof jackets, and night vision devices.

Follow-up and Implementation of the Study

The report didn't receive an expeditious response, and it was only after the attacks on the Uri Brigade in September 2016, Panzgam in April 2017, and more importantly, the Sanjuwan base attack on 10 February 2018, that the Ministry of Defence (MoD) belatedly approved ₹1,487 crores budgetary allocation on the same day, probably forced by the increasing media and social media pressure.

VCOAS-delegated Powers

In July 2017, the Government briefed the media, and also built up a narrative that VCOAS have been delegated with substantial financial powers amounting to ₹40,000 crores. It was claimed in July 2018 that out of these allocations, they were allowed to spend up to ₹800 crores annually towards upgrading the perimeter security of sensitive installations. However, the share allocated towards the up-gradation of security must be balanced with several critical modernisation requirements like armaments, munitions and equipment, already with shortfalls in ten types of armament systems and 45 types of munitions.

Recommended Measures

At the macro level, the policy recommended is a balanced combination of a proactive offensive-defensive approach based on the following:

> Efficient intelligence and surveillance system to predict threats to enable dissuasive measures and gear-up protective barriers.
>
> Defensive measures should be in layers starting with a likely point of infiltration to provide depth and reaction time.
>
> The base should have a well-organised perimeter and an automated protection system manned by requisite well-trained personnel. There should be a perimeter patrolling track acting as a buffer and providing a second layer within the base.
>
> The aim should be to expeditiously detect the intrusion, localise it, and neutralise it by Quick Action Teams (QATs). Ideally, this process should be completed in the buffer zone.
>
> It is recommended that surgical strike or response capabilities should be built up to deliver a punitive message across borders or LOC by nuanced targeting of the source of the attack.

It is necessary that at the base level, the organisation has to be balanced with an optimised and synergistic utilisation of technology and human resources. In a resource crunch reality, at least on an interim basis, hygiene factors and human resources will remain relevant. The following could be considered:

> Have a people-centric approach to make the population in proximate areas partners like the Reliance Mitra program. It will be appropriate to recall the contribution of the carpenter in Arnia in 2015, and residents in Udhampur in 2016, in nabbing terrorists.

Periodic cyber hygiene exercises like Swachh Paridhi should be undertaken to maintain and reinforce the perimeter.

The presence and domination of the perimeter should be boosted by regular training activities like physical training, riding and treks. Western Command had conducted these as Surakshit Paridhi exercises wherein intrusions and response were simulated and tested. Local dogs that have been duly vaccinated can be trained and utilised to boost the alarm system.

Released Agniveers can be inducted into the DSC for a more youthful profile.

In the long term, municipal and civic authorities should play their part by carrying out the demolition of unauthorised structures. They should also create bypasses to reduce civilian traffic and install view cutters, where relocation is not possible. Civil police and intelligence agencies should play a meaningful role in access denial and access control. The Government, on its part, should remain committed to up-gradation and modernisation by making dedicated budgetary allocations.

Conclusion

Protection of bases will remain persistent and a formidable challenge, which will require modernisation and eternal vigilance. A resource-crunch economy and introduction of technological innovations balanced against an obdurate and desperate set of infiltrators; requires a whole-nation approach. The system has to be based on the prioritisation of bases as per sensitivity and a judicious mix of technology and human resources. The bottom line is that base must be prepared and ready to take on any threat.

Lieutenant General K.J. Singh, PVSM, AVSM & Bar, a Cavalry Veteran, is a graduate from the NDC and has commanded an Armoured Division, a Corps in the NE, and the Western Army. He has extensive experience of CI operations in NE, Punjab and J&K, and in perspective planning and capability development at the Army HQ. As the Team Commander of UNPKF in Angola, he was awarded the citation for bravery. He has conceptualised the establishment of think tanks on Strategy in Punjab University and Western Command, laying the foundation for Military Literary Festival in the Tri-city of Chandigarh. A prolific writer and speaker, he has been the CIC, Haryana, and has been involved in other civic body organisations in the tri-city as well. He has several awards to his credit in CI operations and was conferred with Maharaja Ranjit Singh Chair of excellence in PU, Chandigarh.

Endnotes

1. Till 7 July 2019
2. PIB. *Attack on Armed Forces*, Ministry of Defence. 17 July 2019.
3. Katoch, Prakash. "Securing Perimeter of Military Establishments." *Indian Defence Review (IDR), Quarterly Journal, the Brainchild of Former Captain of the Indian Army, Was Launched on January 1, 1986 as a Logical Continuum to Lancer Established in 1979, the First Indian Publishing House Dedicated to Put Forward the Military Experience and Point of View.*, 12 Feb. 2018, http://www.indiandefencereview.com/news/securing-perimeter-of-military-establishments/.
4. Singh, K. J. "Not Just Fences And Walls." *The Indian Express*, 9 Dec. 2016, https://indianexpress.com/article/opinion/columns/terrorist-attack-uri-mumbai-attack-indian-army-pakistan-pathankot-nagrota-4417668/.
5. Singh, K. J. "Of Army Camps, Fortresses, Scapegoats and Accountability." *Times of India*, 21 July 2019, https://timesofindia.indiatimes.com/blogs/generals-jottings/124201/.

6. Samanta, Pranab Dhal. "Lessons from Sunjuwan: Get a Smart, Effective Perimeter Security System at Military Bases." *The Print*, 14 Feb. 2018, https://theprint.in/opinion/state-of-play/lessons-from-sunjuwan-get-a-smart-effective-perimeter-security-system-at-military-bases/35497/.
7. Sen, Sudhi Ranjan. "Pathankot Attack: Commander Faces Show-Cause Notice." *Hindustan Times,* 30 Jan. 2019, https://www.hindustantimes.com/india-news/pathankot-attack-commander-faces-show-cause-notice/story-vmOBCA1QRy3gP44nHEaAoN.html.
8. Staff, Onmanorama. "From Pathankot to Pulwama: Here's a List of the Deadliest Attacks on Indian Military Camps." *Onmanorama*, https://www.onmanorama.com/news/india/2023/04/12/major-military-camp-army-base-attacks-pathankot-pulwama.html. Accessed 11 May 2023.
9. Chadha, Vivek. "Countering Fidayeen Attacks." *Manohar Parrikar Institute for Defence Studies and Analyses,* 15 Dec. 2016, https://www.idsa.in/policybrief/countering-fidayeen-attacks_vchadha_151216.

13

The Andaman and Nicobar Islands: Some Military Strategic Perspectives

Rear Admiral Sudhir Pillai

Only statesmen who can do their political and strategic thinking in terms of a round earth and three-dimensional warfare can save their countries from being outmanoeuvred on distant flanks.

—*Nicholas Spykman*[1]

Geopolitical Contexts

In the 2017 edition of *The Rise and Fall of British Naval Mastery*, the historian Paul Kennedy writes of a rare shift in global power balances being underway: 'Like the one four centuries ago, where power balances tilted from the Mediterranean to the Atlantic, this time, the trend seems to shift towards the east, with Asia rising as the most populous and productive continent, putting it at the centre of the world stage. Countries like India, Indonesia, Korea, and Vietnam have emerged as major economic players. At the same time, China has become the world's second-largest economy and is poised to become the largest in GDP terms.'[2]

In 2008, Holmes and Yoshihara wrote an article in the *US Naval War College Review* which added India as the third side of an emerging strategic naval triangle in the Indian Ocean. They emphasised India's growing dependence on common nautical spaces to protect its trade and external reliance on energy flows.[3] The stability of the Indian Ocean, they argued, will largely depend on how India manages its maritime rise and views its maritime prerogatives, and how the US and China weigh the probabilities of India's nautical success or failure. Their analysis of the Indian Navy included a strategic view from the Indian Maritime Doctrine (2004),[4] which highlighted the importance of the Andaman and Nicobar Islands (ANI) in influencing vital sea lines of communication on the approaches to the Strait of Malacca.[5]

The prospect that India might blockade Malacca against China has attracted significant attention. Chinese analyst, Zhang Ming, described the Islands of the Andaman-Nicobar archipelago as an 'iron chain' that could lock tight the western exit of the Malacca Strait.[6] He reasons, further, that 'once India commands the Indian Ocean, it will not be satisfied with its position and will continuously seek to extend its influence, and its eastward strategy will have a particular impact on China'. Ming said in 2006, 'India is, perhaps, China's most realistic strategic adversary.'[7]

It appears that it is in response to weaknesses exposed during the Taiwan Strait Crisis and fears of being ringed into the first island chain[8] that led the Communist Party of China (CPC) into a major military modernisation and (later) to public statements like the Malacca Dilemma.[9] During Deng Xiaoping's tenure, the Central Military Commission (CMC) was tasked with a military expansion while he publicly advocated for a policy of bide your time and hide your capabilities.[10]

Aim

With the preceding as a background, this article examines specific military strategic and operational considerations to develop policies for the ANI and to fathom deeper military-strategic concepts that policymakers must contend with.

Critically Thinking Strategy

In generic terms, strategy is the art and science of applying all sources of power in peacetime and in war to accomplish strategic objectives. Specifically, a national strategic approach would require the application and coordination of all elements of national power, including military, economic, financial, diplomatic, psychological, technological, and others, to achieve national objectives in peacetime, and to secure these objectives in war.[11]

An ANI strategy requires thinking through various perspectives including its location at substantial distances from the Indian mainland, proximity to important chokepoints and sea lanes, potential for use as a main or an advanced base, ecological considerations, economic potential, etc.

Built to Fight – 21st Century PLA[12]

PLAN is currently the largest in the world, consisting of approximately 340 ships and submarines, including 125 major surface combatants. The CMC has prioritised the growth and modernisation of the PLAN and PLAAF while downsizing and upgrading the PLA. China's domestic aircraft carrier, *Shandong*, was launched in 2017 and commissioned in December 2019, beginning a multi-carrier indigenous programme. The construction of the next generation of aircraft carriers began in 2018. These carriers are expected to have greater endurance and increased striking power. An electromagnetic catapult launch system could enable the launch of both lighter unmanned systems and heavier crewed aircraft. The PLAN has a fleet of logistics replenishment ships to support long-distance, long-duration deployments, and new ships to support aircraft carrier operations. By 2021, the PLAN Marine Corps expanded to six brigades with added aviation and Special Forces. The expanding fleet of large, modern amphibious warships enables a wide range of expeditionary operations. The PLA Rocket Force continues growing its inventory of DF-26 intermediate-range ballistic missiles capable of conventional and nuclear precision strikes against ground and naval targets. Maritime joint operations and integration with the PLA are also an emphasis of modernisation.[13] Based on such assessments, and if one projects into the future, one can portend a PLAN that can match up, if not surpass, the current-day US Navy.

Captain Robert Rubel, USN (Retd), has identified four levels of at-sea aviation capability and categorised the US Navy's and potentially the PLAN's emerging naval air power into an air fleet at a certain level of aggregation. He writes how an air fleet of at least six aircraft carriers operated together in the WWII such that over four hundred aircraft were available.[14]

Could PLAN bring such forces to bear as the Japanese did in WWII? The answer, possibly, lies in the value of ANI as a strategic position.[15] The military importance of a place depends on several factors, including its position, military strength, and resources.

India does not have the luxury to bide its time and hide its capabilities. India needs to increase its efforts and make significant investments in the military maritime space, or it risks playing second fiddle to other powers seeking to dominate in the geopolitical power play. The Andaman and Nicobar Islands could be the Achilles' heel rather than the unsinkable aircraft carrier, as some call it.

History as Prologue

ANI finds mention in the writings of ancient travellers and explorers, such as the Chinese-Buddhist monk I-Ching (7 CE) and Arab travellers. During the post-medieval period, the Islands came under the control of various European powers, including the Danish and British. The British used the Andaman Islands as a penal colony from 1858 (after the First War of Indian Independence) till 1937.

In WWII, the British abandoned the ANI rather than defend them due to the proximity to Japanese-occupied Burma, the vulnerability to Japanese attacks, the excessive resources needed to defend the Islands and the need to prioritise its military efforts in other areas. Japan occupied the ANI during WWII from 1942–45.

The ANI were transferred to independent India in 1947 after Viceroy Lord Mountbatten convinced the British Government not to retain the Islands as a Crown colony. This decision went against the view of the Defence Council in London, which wanted the Islands to maintain air routes to the Far East through Ceylon. The policy papers, since publicly released, don't appear to make any strategic claims for the ANI for imperial purposes in the East.[16]

Suppose one looks deeper into the operational and tactical histories of the mid-twentieth century when naval air power helped achieve objectives in the Pacific against a string of Islands and formidable opposition in maritime scenarios; in that case, one can see with great clarity:

> Why and how could a force, again, seek to occupy the ANI?
>
> What would it take to try and defend the Islands against any efforts to overcome defences and occupy them?
>
> The difficulties in protecting and supporting islands from afar.

If occupied, the campaign plan and force structures needed to retake the Islands.

From Theory to Concepts

India can learn lessons for current contexts through campaign planning, operational defensive and offensive schemes, and force structuring. Traditional concepts of sea and air power would come into play to plan and execute military strategies from near and far shores, and to use forces at sea. These concepts include sea control, sea denial, command of the air, air superiority, and favourable air situation. All of these would be part of the Operational Design.[17] The Army would also bring its concepts for operations from across the shore and into littoral regions. It would require classical joint planning and execution of joint command and control under clearly defined theatre and component commander assignments.

In Operational Concept Development,[18] planners could contend with defining the Bay of Bengal and the Andaman Sea as a primary theatre or theatre of main effort. They could need to factor in the expansive Indian Ocean and other adjoining seas as secondary theatres.

Due to its strategic location at the southern end of the ANI, where sea lanes converge towards the Malacca Straits, the Indian Government has prioritised a project worth ₹72,000 crore ($9 billion) to develop Great Nicobar Island. The project involves the construction of a transhipment port, a dual-use defence-civilian international airport, a power plant, and a township that will be built on over 160 sq km of land over 30 years in line with the national strategic imperatives.

Strategic Analyses

Bay of Bengal

Operating from and defending the island territories such as the ANI, from across the Bay of Bengal, requires considering a range of strategic considerations. Here are a few examples:

Geographical Location: The ANI are far (than near) from the Indian mainland, making them vulnerable to potential threats. This distance means that India must seek to influence its maritime power over a larger area and through intermediate objectives to defend these islands.

Surveillance and Early Warning: Given the Islands' remote location, it is crucial to establish early warning systems and surveillance capabilities to detect potential threats in advance. To improve situational awareness in the Bay of Bengal, the military could undertake various operations, including manned and unmanned scouting, and deploy radar and other sensors to monitor activity.

Response Time: Once a threat is detected, the response time must be fast and effective. Besides forward basing of quick reaction elements, this may involve deploying naval and air assets from afloat and the mainland to intercept incoming threats. The distance between the mainland and the Islands means that response times can be longer than in other scenarios, limiting the options for responding to an attack. Under such scenarios, embarked aviation with real-time presence in the area can be crucial, especially if formidable opposition with large integral air and missile assets brings the battle to the Islands and its Vital Areas (VAs) and Vital Points (VPs).

Logistics and Supply Lines: The Islands' remote location also makes logistics and supply lines a critical consideration. The Indian Navy and Air Force must maintain the infrastructure to sustain island operations, including airfields, ports, and other support facilities.

Intelligence Gathering: India must maintain strong intelligence-gathering capabilities to monitor regional activities and detect potential threats. The military can improve situational awareness in the ANI by deploying increased human intelligence assets and using technological means such as satellite imagery and electronic intercepts.

Coordination with Regional Partners: To effectively manage the security of the Bay of Bengal, coordination with regional partners is essential. This coordination involves sharing intelligence, conducting joint exercises, and coordinating responses to threats with neighbouring countries.

The Bay of Bengal is not a typical narrow sea.[19] It is a large sea covering an area of approximately 2.2 million sq km, surrounded by land on three sides: India to the west, Bangladesh to the north, and Myanmar to the east. Operating naval and air forces in this region can be challenging due to the sea and weather conditions affected by the southwest and northeast monsoons. Additionally, the Islands' narrow north-south orientations and the complex coastal geography of the region can pose weather and navigational challenges. Under the circumstances:

> Defending island territories in the Bay of Bengal requires a comprehensive and integrated approach, accounting for various strategic considerations. The Indian Government and military must be prepared to deploy different assets and capabilities on time to respond effectively to potential threats.
>
> Escorts for logistics streams to the ANI can be critical to ensure the safe and secure transport of supplies and equipment. Naval escorts may need to protect cargo ships from various threats due to the distance from mainland India.
>
> Given the complexities involved, air support may be necessary to ensure safe and expeditious communications and transport of critical supplies.
>
> Using UAVs in fair weather periods and other surveillance technologies can enhance the security of logistics streams and provide early warning of potential threats.
>
> A combination of military assets, technology, and other resources can help support and sustain operations and logistics involving the ANI.

To illustrate the geographical complexity that India must deal with, note that the distance from the east coast of India to approaches to the Andaman Islands (the Northern Group) is around 700 nm (nautical miles), while the approaches to Malacca Strait (south of Great Nicobar Island) is about 900 nm. During the Falklands War, Argentine fighter jets primarily operated from airbases located in Argentina, such as *Rio Gallegos, Rio Grande,* and *Comodoro Rivadavia,* located around 300–500 nm away from the Falkland Islands.

Navies typically seek to develop multiple facilities along their coastlines that serve various operations which may be closer or farther away from potential conflict areas. For operational reasons, bases that serve as primary, secondary, and forward operating bases will all need consideration in the theatre of operations, which is the area of responsibility of the Eastern Naval Command and the Andaman and Nicobar Command.

Additionally, navies and air forces must deploy capabilities to project power beyond their immediate coastal waters by deploying their own or cooperating aircraft carriers, submarines, and other naval assets.

During WWII, the Atlantic Gap was a significant vulnerability for the Allies, as German U-boats could operate freely in the mid-Atlantic, beyond the range of land-based air cover. To close this gap and protect vital convoys of troops, supplies, and equipment, the Allies developed several strategies and technologies as follows:

> Airbases in Newfoundland, Labrador, Greenland, and the Azores, during WWII, helped bridge the Atlantic Gap. The outer radii of aircraft operations to tackle the U-boat threat were about 800 miles.[20]
>
> Additionally, the Allies developed advanced radar and sonar technologies to detect and track U-boats and new weapons such as depth charges and hedgehog anti-submarine mortars to destroy them.
>
> Another critical strategy was convoying, which involved grouping multiple merchant ships and providing them with naval escorts. Such measures made it much more difficult for U-boats to attack individual vessels, as the escorts could use their weapons and sonar to locate and destroy them. Using convoy systems significantly reduced the number of ships lost to U-boat attacks during the war.

Andaman Sea

Located in the northeastern part of the Indian Ocean and to the southeastern end of the Bay of Bengal, the Andaman Sea is a narrow or marginal sea,[21] bound to the east by the ANI, to the north and west by Myanmar and Thailand, and the south by the Malay Peninsula and Sumatra. As a marginal sea:

> The Andaman Sea is connected to the immense Indian Ocean and is subject to oceanic processes such as tides, currents, and weather patterns.

> The Andaman Sea, with strategic chokepoints and potential for territorial disputes, highlights the need for maritime military operations to consider the unique characteristics of this region.

As a case in point, naval and air operations in marginal seas can differ from operations in high open seas in several ways.[22]

> Firstly, marginal seas can have shallower depths and narrower channels, posing navigational challenges to ships and submarines. In addition, these seas can have complex coastlines and numerous islands, which can affect the ability of ships and aircraft to detect and track targets.
>
> Secondly, the oceanographic conditions in marginal seas can differ from those in the open ocean, such as higher water temperatures, different salinity levels, and different current patterns which can affect the performance of ships, submarines, and aircraft as their sensors and weapons systems.
>
> Thirdly, the effects of land-based threats, such as coastal defences and shore-based aircraft, can be more pronounced in marginal seas. To deal with these threats, naval and air forces must adopt different tactics and employ other weapon systems.
>
> Lastly, the political and legal considerations in marginal seas differ from those in the open ocean. Marginal seas are often subject to competing territorial claims and disputes which can affect the ability of naval and air forces to operate freely in these areas. Additionally, the laws and regulations governing maritime activities in marginal seas may differ from those in the open ocean, which can also affect the conduct of naval and air operations.

Operational Level Considerations

Such unique environments could necessitate special force structuring requirements for naval and air forces operating in marginal seas. The following are illustrative:[23]

Naval forces operating in marginal seas often require smaller, more manoeuvrable ships than those in open-ocean operations. These ships are designed to navigate through shallow waters and narrow channels, and can operate close to the shore. They may also need special systems such as mine countermeasures, amphibious assault capabilities, and shallow-draft landing craft. Additionally, specialised units such as riverine forces, trained to operate in the unique environment of rivers, estuaries, and other inland waterways, may be required by naval forces.

Similarly, air forces that operate in marginal seas may require specialised aircraft that can operate in the unique environment of these areas. For example, helicopters may be better suited to conduct search and rescue operations, transport troops and supplies, and conduct anti-submarine warfare. Fixed-wing aircraft may require special configurations to perform surveillance, reconnaissance, aerial refuelling, and air defence from forward bases and advanced landing grounds. Additionally, air forces may need to establish forward operating and maintenance systems for support operations in remote locations. Overall, force structuring for naval and air forces that operate in marginal seas requires careful consideration of the unique characteristics of these areas and the specific mission requirements of the forces involved.

Aligning Strategy with Policy

Policy refers to the collective set of political, diplomatic, financial, social, and military decisions made by a country's political, military, and naval leaders. These decisions impact the country's maritime situation, including the size and composition of its military, the number of personnel and the organisation of its military forces.[24]

In military strategy, one of the primary tasks during peacetime is to build or acquire suitable military bases to enable a country's forces to achieve national and military strategic objectives in wartime. Bases are the primary centres of all military activity in a specific sea area. Fleets and flotillas depend on adequate basing areas to deploy, redeploy, and retreat when necessary. Combat employment is greatly facilitated by having multiple geographically favourable bases that accommodate a significant part of a fleet.[25]

Joint Approaches

While different military services have similarities in how they accomplish strategic or operational goals, they also have significant differences in how they fight. Each service specialises in unique operating environments and employs different tactics, techniques, and procedures to achieve its objectives. Joint approaches are necessary to synergistically address operating and support environments when applying diverse capacities and capabilities.

The selection of Rosyth by the British as the primary naval base in the North Sea, in 1938, is an excellent example of collaborative approaches in maritime theatres. The British Services collaborated, given the strategic significance of the location for Naval, Army, and Air Force operations. In case of war, Rosyth would support land-based operations and protection for the Royal Navy's Home Fleet. The planners intended to support the naval base and Home Fleet with airfields at Turnhouse and Donibristle. Furthermore, Rosyth's location on Scotland's east coast near Edinburgh provided strategic advantages for the RAF. The RAF's Fighter Command viewed Rosyth as a crucial base for defending Scotland, the north of England, and the east coast against enemy attacks, primarily from the German Luftwaffe. The airfields near Rosyth also provided an opportunity to conduct coastal patrols and provide air cover for convoys in the North Sea.[26]

Synergising similar theatre strategies and operational level considerations by the theatre commander, the Commander-in-Chief of the Andaman and Nicobar Command (CINCAN) will serve the deployed, attached, and detached joint forces.

Some Theoretical Concepts

Milan Vego is instructive in putting together relevant naval theoretical perspectives as follows:[27]

> Obtaining permanent and absolute control of seas like the Bay of Bengal, in modern times, can be difficult. In contrast, attaining complete control of the sea surface and to a lesser degree, the subsurface in a typical narrow or marginal sea like the Andaman Sea could be relatively easy.
>
> Control of a narrow sea requires close cooperation among all the services of the country's armed forces, and the control of

the sea is more directly affected by the situation on the land front and in the air.

Control of the sea on the open ocean is obtained primarily by destroying or neutralising a significant part of the enemy's naval forces.

Seizing a stretch of or even the entire length of the enemy coast, along with the military bases, airfields, ports, chokepoints, and vital offshore islands, can also accomplish this objective in a narrow sea.

Naval warfare history reminds us that a balanced military capable of carrying out tasks across the entire spectrum of operational tasks is necessary. For example, suppose a navy cannot build the required force of surface ships, submarines, and craft to operate in open and narrow seas during times of peace. In that case, it must develop and test tactical and operational concepts and train for eventualities with fewer ships in case of a major conflict or general war.

History as Epilogue

Concepts from another day, like Fortress Andaman & Nicobar (FORTAN), are no longer relevant today. Given the unending march of geopolitics, the Andaman and Nicobar Command contours could need revisiting.

Reading about the rise and ruin of the Pacific Island of Rabaul can be very instructive.[28] Military history, far from telling us only about the past, gives us a tool to understand the present and the future. It enables us to appreciate that while human nature changes slowly, if at all, warfare evolves rapidly, and that each generation must acquaint itself with the problems and challenges of war afresh. The study of military history is, therefore, not only the heritage of military professionals but an essential component in the education of informed citizens and more particularly, in the formation of sound public policy.[29]

Conclusion

This article seeks to place specific military-strategic and operational considerations in context to outline the complexity that the ANI present to strategic and defence planners. Often, people approach the debate on the subject from simplistic perspectives. The author has sought to address parts of the puzzle. To thwart every foe, one must examine other considerations that complete the puzzle.

India needs to engage with questions such as:

> What can be the implications for mainland India's follow-on forces and operations in the Indian eastern seaboard if the ANI falls to forces inimical to our interests?
>
> What can be involved in retaking the Islands against medium to significant opposition?

A theory developed ahead of time and sound doctrine is needed rather than improvisation at short notice by when it could be too late.[30]

Are such theories and doctrines daunting? In that case, India must look afresh at the future of the ANI, given its potential as a tourism destination with its pristine beaches and turquoise waters, its rich biodiversity, a unique culture with indigenous tribes, and a mix of Indian and colonial influences, and local cuisine with fresh seafood and unique island flavours!

Rear Admiral Sudhir Pillai, NM, IN (Retd) is a former Flag Officer Naval Aviation, CoS HQ Andaman and Nicobar Command, and Chief Instructor (Navy) DSSC, Wellington.

Endnotes

1. Spykman, Nicholas J. *America's Strategy in World Politics: The United States and the Balance of Power.* Routledge, 2007.
2. Kennedy, Paul. The Rise And Fall of British Naval Mastery. Penguin, 2017.
3. According to the International Energy Agency (IEA), in 2020, India was the world's third-largest consumer of energy after China and the United States and its energy consumption is expected to double by 2040. The country imports about 84 per cent of its oil needs and about 25 per cent of its natural gas requirements. India also imports coal to meet more than half of its domestic coal demand. The dependence on imported energy sources leaves India vulnerable to price volatility, supply disruptions, and geopolitical risks.
4. Government of India. Ministry of Defence (Navy). Indian Maritime Doctrine. Integrated Headquarters, 2004.
5. Holmes, James R. and Yoshihara, Toshi (2008) "China and the United States in the Indian Ocean," *Naval War College Review:* Vol. 61: No. 3, Article 4. Available at: https://digital-commons.usnwc.edu/nwc-review/vol61/iss3/4 p. 47.
6. Angang, Dong. The Indian Navy Energetically Steps toward the High Seas, Modern Ships, no. 267 (July 2006), p. 17. quoted in Holmes and Yoshihara, China and the United States in the Indian Ocean: An Emerging Strategic Triangle? Naval War College Review, Summer 2008.
7. Ming, Zhang. The Malacca Dilemma and the Chinese Navy's Strategic Choices, Modern Ships, no. 274, October 2006, p. 23.
8. The Chinese fears of being ringed into the first island chain were first reported publicly in the early 1990s, specifically during the Taiwan Strait Crisis of 1995-1996. During this crisis, the United States sent two aircraft carrier strike groups to the region, including the USS Nimitz and the USS Independence. This deployment prompted the Chinese leadership to worry about potential encirclement and to begin developing strategies to counteract this perceived threat.
9. Ming, Zhang. The Malacca Dilemma and the Chinese Navy's Strategic Choices, Modern Ships, no 274 October 2006 p. 23.
10. Deng Xiaoping's statement made during a meeting with a group of Japanese businessmen, November 1985, quoted in Ezra F. Vogel, Deng Xiaoping and the Transformation of China (Cambridge, MA: Belknap Press of Harvard University Press, 2011), 370.
11. Vego, Milan N. Naval Strategy and Operations in Narrow Seas. London: Frank Cass, 1999. ISBN 9780714646615. Kindle edition, location 34.
12. The 'built to fight' quote is often attributed to Chinese President Xi Jinping, who used the phrase in a speech during a military parade in 2017.
13. US Department of Defense. (2022). Annual Report to Congress on Military and Security Developments Involving the People's Republic of China, 2022. Retrieved from https://media.defense.gov/2022/Nov/29/2003122279/-1/-1/1/2022-military-and-security-developments-involving-the-peoples-republic-of-china.Pdf

14. Rubel, Robert C. (2014) A Theory of Naval Airpower, Naval War College Review: Vol. 67: No. 3 , Article 6. Available at: https://digital-commons.usnwc.edu/nwc-review/vol67/iss3/6

15. Mahan Hasin *Naval Strategy Compared and Contrasted with the Principles and Practice of Military Operations on Land* postulated that a strategic position is a series of points close to each other that directly impact the outcome of war in a particular theatre. Mahan, Alfred Thayer. Naval Strategy Compared and Contrasted with the Principles and Practice of Military Operations on Land. (Boston: Little, Brown, and Company, 1911), 134.

16. Mansergh, Nicholas. India: The Transfer of Power, 1942-47, Vol. 11. Accessed online at https://archive.org/details/constitutionalre06nich/page/304/mode/2up.

17. Operational Design is a concept in operational art that refers to the deliberate and systematic planning and execution of military operations to achieve strategic objectives.

18. Operational Concept Development is a key step in operational deign that goes towards developing a comprehensive plan that leverages available resources to achieve the desired outcomes.

19. A narrow sea is a type of sea that is defined by its geographic characteristics. It is a relatively small body of water that is surrounded by land on most sides, often with a limited number of access points. These features make it easier to control the sea surface and subsurface compared to larger bodies of water. The Andaman Sea is considered a narrow sea because it is bordered by the Andaman and Nicobar Islands to the east, Myanmar to the north and east, Thailand to the northwest, and the Malay Peninsula to the south. It is connected to the Bay of Bengal and the Indian Ocean. Source: Hall, R. B. Narrow Seas and Great Powers: A Strategic Conception of the Baltic, North, Black and Mediterranean Seas, Journal of Strategic Studies, vol. 23, no. 1, 2000, pp. 140-167.

20. Hampshire, Edward. The Atlantic Gap and the Development of Anti-Submarine Warfare, The Mariner's Mirror (May 2017): 244-259.

21. A marginal sea is a body of water partially enclosed by land and connected to a larger sea or ocean. According to the United Nations Convention on the Law of the Sea, a marginal sea is defined as 'a gulf, sea, or ocean, partly enclosed by land where the width of the sea between the mainland and an adjacent island is not more than twice the breadth of the adjacent channel'. Marginal seas are often shallower than open ocean and can be affected by unique weather patterns and currents. Source: United Nations Division for Ocean Affairs and the Law of the Sea. (n.d.). Marginal Seas. Retrieved from https://www.un.org/Depts/los/LEGISLATIONANDTREATIES/pdffc/marginal_seas.htm

22. Vego, Naval Strategy and Operations in Narrow Waters.

23. Ibid.

24. Ibid., p. 329.

25. Hattendorf, John B. ed., Naval Policy and Strategy in the Mediterranean: Past, Present, and Future, Cass Series—Naval Policy and History 10 (London ; Portland, OR: Frank Cass, 2000).

26. Clarke, David. Rosyth, The Navy, and the Nation: The British Naval Base at Rosyth, 1903-2002. Edinburgh University Press, 2013, p. 108.
27. Vego, Naval Strategy and Operations in Narrow Waters.
28. Samuel Eliot Morison, The Rise and Ruin of Rabaul, Proceedings of the US Naval Institute 77, no. 6 (June 1951): 655-66, https://www.usni.org/magazines/proceedings/1951/june/rise-and-ruin-rabaul.
29. Keegan, John. The Future of Warfare. In The Book of Military Quotations, edited by Peter Tsouras, 239. New York: Zenith Press, 2006.
30. Ibid., location 7676.

14

Theatre Commands: Integrating to Implement National Strategy

Lieutenant General Anil Ahuja

During the Combined Commanders' Conference held recently at Bhopal (30 March–1 April 2023), one of the significant topics discussed was 'Jointness and Theatreisation of the Armed Forces'.[1] This was highly relevant to the overall theme of the conference, which was 'Ready, Resurgent, Relevant (Armed Forces)'.

The PM reportedly advised the senior military commanders, to make sure that joint warfighting concepts are imbibed quickly and implemented expeditiously to be an effective force in the fast-changing global situation. Seemingly, the PM has left it to the military leadership to evolve a roadmap to form joint commands within a reasonable timeframe.[2] This is a welcome development, and a more prudent approach than pushing through a change. Yes, it is a change and not a reform or transformation, since the roadmap has not been crystallised yet, at least not in the public domain! The significance of this measured approach lies in appreciating the challenging security environment, where the country does not have the luxury of getting unbalanced, in the process of transformation.

The Indian Armed Forces have been operating jointly and have acquitted themselves well (the 1971 War, Operation Vijay in Kargil in 1999, and the Maldives, where the generalship has performed outstandingly). The current realities, however, suggest the need to graduate from mere jointness to an advanced level of integration to meet the complex challenges of the current day operational environment, which is spread across multiple domains.

The current organisational structures do not lend themselves to synergised operational planning, coordinated utilisation of resources, and acting jointly to achieve national security objectives. Consequently, each service essentially operates in *silos* defined by its own threat perception and operational doctrine.

The issue, therefore, is not whether the services need to integrate, the answer to which is an unqualified 'Yes'. What needs to be deliberated is how to get such integration right in the Indian context. Another question that merits consideration is, whether this integration needs to be implemented at the national (apex) or theatre level. These considerations will determine the contours of future organisational structures. It would be prudent to pause and tell ourselves that theatreisation is not a *sine qua non* for integration of the Armed Forces. Future wars will be highly specialised in certain fields. A great deal of deliberation will have to be given to the aspect of specialisation and integration. Integration of specialised subjects and forces diffuses their effect. To maximise the effects of the multi-domain war, identifying the areas of integration will be a study on its own.

Integration and Jointness

Though the term 'jointness' and 'integration' are often used interchangeably, there exists a subtle distinction between them. These concepts are not built on a collection of doctrines, platforms, and capabilities, pooled from different services. Instead, they refer to an environment of trust and understanding transcending the core beliefs and assumptions of individual service, resulting in effective integration and employment of different service capabilities and competencies within a unified command structure.

The jointness must be accepted in the minds of military officers since it relies on their mutual understanding. It is more in spirit than in structure, and entails cross-service cooperation in all dimensions – planning, capability development, acquisitions, training, operations, communications, logistics, and more. It entails operating together, seamlessly, while retaining their own organisational, command, and control construct.

Integration, however, entails institutional and organisational amalgamation of relevant constituent elements of all services, to employ their capabilities in concert. It ensures the representation of all services, domain specialists and representatives from relevant military and non-military domains in the organisational construct. This has become necessary because of the change in the scope and the context of wars, entailing high levels of specialisation. The integration enables the harnessing of operational and logistic capability, and integration of sensors, systems, and networks to create a comprehensive cross-domain picture and capability.

Why Do We Need to Integrate?

A perusal of the various pronouncements since 2001 suggests that the focus of defence reforms put into motion belatedly, with the appointment of the CDS in 2020, is on enhancing operational efficiency and optimal utilisation of individual service resources in an integrated manner, eliminating wasteful overlaps. The primacy, however, remains in achieving better operational efficiency.

The problems in the current pattern of single service planning and functioning, which are detrimental to achieving operational efficiency and national security goals, basically arise due to the lack of unity of command at the operational level. The problems that arise from this are:

> The service-specific interpretation of the loosely-defined national security and national defence policy. The Defence Minister's *(Raksha Mantri)* operational directive does not address this issue. This, in turn, results in perception-based and compartmentalised planning.
>
> This is compounded by the absence of political directions from the CCS, leaving each service to interpret its role and asset employment according to its own doctrinal thinking. No doubt there are consultations, but these are driven mainly by individual service perceptions and biases.
>
> Non-existence of a single authority, at the theatre or apex level, to institutionally coordinate inter-service plans, reconciling single service perceptions and expectations, i.e., to make each service speak a language understood by all.
>
> Absence of a common national intelligence picture integrating inputs of all services, and other national agencies like the National Technical Research Organisation (NTRO) or ISRO, etc., that would result in real-time intelligence sharing. This is missing even between the services.

Absence of contingency operational planning based on a visualised escalation ladder, with a distinct possibility of successive rungs of action and response straddling multiple domains, e.g., the action and response may rapidly shift between continental, air, maritime, space, or even strategic domains.

A paucity of overall resources, in particular, air assets, long-range vectors, and force multipliers, and the inability to shake off a sense of ownership to allow resource use by or for the other service(s).

Lack of coordinated, intra and inter-service prioritised capability development and acquisition plans, resulting in sub-optimal utilisation of meagre defence budgets and the inability to develop the desired threat mitigation capabilities. (Despite India being the third largest spender on defence and the largest importer of global arms.)

Non-availability of commanders and staff trained in a joint service environment to function in an integrated manner; the continued inability of the system to impart requisite training, due to lack of institutional capacity and integrated staff appointments.

Inadequate intra and inter-service integration for network-centric warfare.

Recognising the above, there is a definite need for integration of the services to deal with the overall threat envelope by optimising plans and resources. Due consideration needs to be accorded to the core competency, domain specialisation, resources, culture, and ethos of each service, optimised to achieve the defined politico-military objectives.

Cosmetic integration in the form of participation of other service contingents in parades (Army, Navy, and Air Force Day parades), combining service-specific social institutions and facilities, only trivialises this serious exercise, without tangible benefits.

Also, for the many ringside commentators, for whom integration entails reducing 17 single service commands to fewer numbers of integrated commands, it needs to be clearly understood that the reduction of manpower that may accrue by reducing the total number of HQs (although the size of an integrated HQ is likely to be always bigger than single service HQs) is of marginal consequence in comparison to developing integrated operational and capability development plans. Also, at the present juncture, the visualised span of command and control extending across the entire length of the western and northern borders, as well as along the entire coastline and island territories, is too vast to be managed by a single HQ. This attains added significance because:

> Sino-Pakistan collusion will result in the Northern and Western Theatres practically becoming 'one' in threat manifestation; and
>
> The politico-military directives for the nation at war will continue to emanate from Delhi through a real-time interface. Delegation of authority to theatre commanders, in the near future, is likely to remain a *chimaera*.

Towards Integration and Theatreisation

After a long journey towards integration (too well known to be recapitulated), the Government notification for the appointment of the CDS was issued on 24 December 2019.[3] It spelt out the charter, mandate, and functions of the CDS and the newly-created DMA, placed under him.

In over three years, since the appointment of CDS, numerous discussions on theatreisation have been held within and outside the services, though none have been based on any comprehensive approach paper, analysing the need, factors to be considered, challenges, and a timelined road map. The narrative centres around the creation of Northern and Western Theatre Commands on the China and Pakistan fronts respectively; leaving the existing structure of the Army's Northern Command unchanged; and the creation of a Maritime Command. No official communication, however, exists on this. The challenge before the nation and the services is to work out the nuances of implementation, in a reasonable time frame, without creating operational imbalance, and within constraints of affordability.

While many options can exist, one viable option is the simultaneous evolution of jointness and theatre or functional commands, building upon process and resources incrementally, in a phased manner.

The process of implementing this option must commence with the current Service and Command HQs remaining intact, for they have the domain expertise and ownership of single service plans as these exist today. Existing plans, duly optimised, would need to be stitched to formulate mutually reconciled, integrated operational plans.

In the initial phase (Phase 1) of interservice integration, salient steps to be taken are as follows:

> Formulating strategic guidance and promulgating a common military strategy, to achieve collectively-identified national politico-military objectives. This needs to be done even if the National Security Strategy remains a work in progress.
>
> Identifying the character and pattern of future wars in the Indian subcontinent (through scenario-building exercises) factoring in the realities of terrain, disputed borders, emerging technologies, and the evolving capabilities of our neighbours in the continental domain and of regional players in the maritime domain.
>
> Within this construct, each service should evolve detailed plans for the visualised single/two front – multiple domain threat scenarios.
>
> The amalgamation of individual service plans to evolve integrated/lead service response options.
>
> Retain existing Command HQs of all three services, i.e., 17 single-service commands. Within the existing organisational construct, revise the delineation of geographic Areas of Responsibility (AOR) of the Army and Air Force Commands to align their boundaries (e.g., removing anomalies like the Western Air Command [WAC] covering AOR of the Army's Northern, Western, and parts of SW Command). The aim should be that each geographically-aligned theatre (Command) should have an equivalent, three-star, C-in-C level officer from the Army and Air Force (or the Air Force and Navy, where applicable) for the formulation of integrated operational plans for the designated area. In undertaking this exercise, no reallocation or redeployment of assets needs to be carried out.

Extensive wargaming of likely scenarios.

Detailed planning and gaming of the visualised escalation ladder, with responses across domain verticals. An appropriate representation of the Strategic Forces Command (SFC) would be useful, wherever the action or reaction is likely to spill over into the strategic domain.

Based on the integrated operational plans evolved, develop an intra and inter-service prioritised capability development and budget-supported acquisition plan.

An outline plan for the initial deployment or redeployment of limited assets (Air Force, long-range vectors, strategic), and the contingency allotment of these for cross-theatre and strategic tasks.

Overriding emphasis on networking all the services and agencies for seamless communication, and for creating appropriate battlefield management systems.

Evolving a pragmatic joint training doctrine, institutionalising an integrated training curriculum, and the amalgamation of select training establishments.

Detailed consideration of the management of the hinterland, including critical aspects of national mobilisation; assigning responsibilities for rear area security.

Integrating personnel and units of all three services to strengthen the Cyber and Space Agencies, and to commence their upgradation to a tri-service functional command under the Chairman COSC. This would help validate the nuances of exercising operational control at this apex level.

Coordinated, nationwide grid deployment of all Intelligence, Surveillance, Reconnaissance (ISR) assets, with an integrated ISR network linking recipients of all three services.

Merging logistic installations, provost, and medical resources, wherever possible.

Cross attachment and posting of officers and other ranks between the three services, to units and the formation HQs.

This in-house preparatory exercise must be led by the CDS and supported by an operationally-oriented HQ Integrated Defence Staff and the Service Chiefs. The National Security Council Secretariat (NSCS), SFC and the national organisations for cyber and space must also be appropriately incorporated.

Following the above process, at the end of Phase 1, three integrated theatre HQs are recommended to be raised and superimposed over existing command HQs of two or three services. This would entail one theatre Command HQ each, placed over the eastern and central Army-Air Force Commands (Northern Theatre); western, southwestern and southern Army-Air Force Commands (Western Theatre); and one for the Northern Command. These HQs should be staffed by carefully selected officers and headed by a three-star, C-in-C level officer from any of the services, preferably with joint services experience. It would be helpful if these theatre commanders are former C-in-Cs. It would also be appropriate to test bed this concept.

In the subsequent phases, the contours of restructuring and reorganisation can be better evolved after gaining the experience of the Phase 1 transformation. This may entail giving operational responsibility to the CDS or the COSC and restructuring HQ IDS as an overarching Integrated operational HQ (which presently, it is not); placing integrated theatre or functional commands directly under the CDS or HQ IDS; reorganising theatre command and single service command HQs by reducing the number of HQs, and reducing a layer of command; sub-allocation of certain dedicated resources to each theatre and earmarking some superimposed resources for strategic or inter-theatre employment; confining responsibility of the respective service chiefs only to 'raise-train and sustain', and vesting operational responsibilities in theatre commanders and the CDS; raising of the air defence and maritime command. All these should, however, be considered to be tentative as of now. The process of capability development of each service would then have competing stakeholders in the Service Chiefs and Theatre Commanders, and this would require in-depth consideration. This would be a much greater challenge than visualised now, with the heads of arms and services (advisers) concentrated at the apex level.

Conclusion

While inter-service integration and the creation of integrated military commands is a desirable end state, to enhance operational efficiency, the process needs to be progressed diligently. The evolution of the integrated military strategy and doctrine needs to be concurrently developed along with placing the organisational building blocks in place. The existing single service structures have a significant role to play in planning and bringing about integration, and thus, should not be interfered with in a hurry. There also exists merit in first bringing about apex-level integration, before creating theatre commands. Finally, whichever course of action is adopted, it would be prudent to first formulate a policy document and a road map, so that its sanctity persists beyond the personalities at the helm.

Lieutenant General Anil Ahuja, PVSM, UYSM, AVSM, SM, VSM & Bar, commanded a Brigade in CI, a Division, and a Corps facing China, and has been the Deputy Chief of IDS. He has served as the ADG MO, and been Secretary DAC as well as the Co-Chair of India-USA Defence Technology and Trade Initiative. A graduate from NDC and Netherlands Staff College, his forte lies in policy planning, higher defence organisation, theaterisation and perspective planning, and security frameworks. A Fellow of the Delhi Policy Group and Distinguished Fellow VIF, he is a renowned speaker and writer on International Relations, defence acquisition and security organisational policy matters.

Endnotes

1. PIB. *PM Takes Part in Combined Commanders' Conference in Bhopal, Madhya Pradesh*. https://pib.gov.in/PressReleaseIframePage.aspx?PRID=1912929. Accessed 12 May 2023.
2. Gokhale, Nitin A. "Symbolism, Integration & Theatre Commands: Trilateral Approach To Tri-Service Synergy – Strat News Global." *Strategic News Global*, 7 Apr. 2023, https://stratnewsglobal.com/articles/symbolism-integration-theatre-commands-trilateral-approach-to-tri-service-synergy/.
3. Press Information Bureau, Government of India. *Cabinet approves the creation of the post of Chief of Defence Staff in the rank of four-star general.* 24 December 2019. https://pib.gov.in/PressReleseDetail.aspx?PRID=1597425

15

Redesigning Our Counter-insurgency Strategy

Lieutenant General P.S. Mehta

Counter-Insurgency: Any military and political action taken against the activities of guerrillas, revolutionaries, or terrorists and can be considered war by a state against a non-state actor.

Peep into the Past

'The concept of insurgency is restricted to rebellious acts that did not reach the proportions of an organised revolution or armed uprising typically guerrilla in character against the recognised government of a state.'[1] If so, then, the insurgency in J&K fits classically into this definition. The principle of insurgency is that it focuses on the population rather than the enemy forces, because while the enemy is fluid, the population is fixed. This principle was the basis of Pakistan's strategy to foment insurgency in the erstwhile state of J&K. To be successful, both the insurgents and the counter-insurgents need the population to support their operations and acquiesce to their authority. The mind of the population is the battlefield. The insurgents organise a protracted politico-military struggle designed to weaken the control and legitimacy of an established government by occupying power and political authority that controls the population. NATO describes counter-insurgency as a 'comprehensive civilian and military effort made to defeat an insurgency and to address any core grievances'.[2] Insurgency in the erstwhile state of Jammu and Kashmir had reached a level of the fourth generation of warfare, where the distinction between civilians and combatants was blurred, and terrorising became the main weapon to control the population. At a stage, in 1991, the insurgency evolved into irregular forces supported by Pakistan, fighting guerrilla tactics against the Armed Forces of India. In the end, the insurgency can be eradicated by winning over the heart and minds of the population, and generating faith and confidence in the Government. Alternatively, it may be eliminated by waging a coercive battle to intimidate or eliminate a radicalised civilian population suspected of loyalty to the insurgency through controlled violence. The selected strategy must have a fine balance between the two alternatives.

Insurgency in J&K has lingered on for the past 34 years despite fierce actions by the military and constant political dialogue. It becomes important to identify the fault lines that exist in our security system, which has led to the most violent insurgencies in modern history in India. There is no doubt that this insurgency is aided and abetted by the ISI of Pakistan with total military professionalism. To begin with, it was a gross national intelligence failure, wherein thousands of Kashmiri youths crossed over into Pakistan for training and indoctrination from the LoC, undetected by our security forces, which were deployed for preventing such a cross-border movement. No Indian intelligence agency, including the police of the erstwhile state of Jammu and Kashmir, could get a whiff of it; everyone was caught napping. Pakistan's leadership conceptualised this insurgency with exceptional strategic finesse, and this was executed by the ISI with military precision. They sowed the seed of insurrection, which germinated into the idea of *azadi*. The motivation of locals, ex-filtration to Pakistan for radicalisation, indoctrination and weapon training; then the infiltration of these youths to execute massive insurgency operations in J&K was the tool kit of this operation. They were supported by foreign terrorists from Pakistan and Afghanistan to guide and provide leadership. This was the start of the famous Strategy of Thousand Cuts,[3] which has bled India for the past three decades.

Ethnic cleansing and removal of the Kashmiri Pandits from the valley at the start of the insurgency was carried out with skill by a very simple concept of terrorising through fierce aggression, rape and murder, executed with lightning speed and extreme violence, to affect their exodus.[4] The Indian agencies could not handle the exodus of these terrorised Pandits which marked a victory for Pakistan and their agencies. The Sikhs of J&K were lucky to have escaped similar treatment because of the emergence of insurgency in neighbouring Punjab; after Operation Blue Star, Pakistan was under the assumption that the Sikh sentiments were largely anti-India, and they could be exploited as part of their strategy later.

A cursory examination brings out the main strategic reason for the insurgency lasting for the past thirty-four years; that is the lack of political vision and a clear directive to the various security forces deployed in the state. A lack of internal strategic communication between the political leadership and the military led to the Army structuring its own strategy around the policy of an iron fist in a velvet glove.[5] This strategy, surprisingly, was not understood by many military commanders, nor was carried out in totality, which initially led to human rights violations, thus, inviting global attention. This strategic concept could not be converted into operational plans and, therefore, failed to deal with insurgency at the tactical level, which is evident from the fact that force-on-force application continued for nearly 20 years. The one success that can be attributed to this strategy was the eradication of foreign terrorists to a very large extent. The next major reason was the disconnection between operations on the Line of Control and operations in the hinterland. This resulted in uncontrolled cross-border infiltration and ex-filtration despite the installation of modern technological devices and increased patrolling. Pakistan, sensing success, expanded the arc of insurgency to the south of Pir Panjal and into the Jammu Province, not only to execute more cuts, but also to engulf and justify internationally that the so-called Working Boundary[6] is a disputed zone between India and Pakistan.

The failure to eradicate insurgency, and prolonged overt and covert operations, with little accountability, gradually grew as a profitable industry for all agencies operating there. Repeated postings, assured rewards and financial benefits overtook serious operational content. J&K became the so-called promising operational area where even the mediocre climbed the ladder of success[7] The most serious damage this did to the Indian Army was putting the conventional operational requirements in cold storage, and the emergence of an officer clan, who had little exposure or experience in conventional operations for 30 years, but was an expert in policing and fighting lightly armed insurgents. The effect of this was seen as the reduced conventional force ratios between India and Pakistan, which gave great relief to Pakistan in balancing its forces between the Global War on Terror and India's Cold Start Strategy. The initial number of casualties in the Kargil War proves this point, where we confronted the Pakistan Army with counter-insurgency tactics. The raising of Rashtriya Rifles (RR) was yet another toll on the Army by cutting down its own teeth.

The next reason was the failure to identify and predict the phases and stages of counter-insurgency. A strong and consistent strategy would have conceptualised the adaptations in tactics by the phase and stage of the insurgency. Periods of success, wherein militancy was brought down to sub-optimal levels, were not exploited nor taken advantage of by implementing political initiatives by the civil agencies, and exploitation by the security forces. Delhi continued to only carry out crisis management rather than take the Kashmir issue seriously at the strategic level. In the overall assessment, Operation Sadbhavna[8] did not achieve success as expected because it was exploited by the civilians and the locals for personal benefits. It failed to win the hearts and minds of the locals, especially the youth who continued to be radicalised by the Jamiaties and the Hurriyat, besides Pakistan.

Over the last three-plus decades the Awaam, the separatists and the Jamiaties have gained nothing but thousands of Kashmiri Muslims (referred to as martyrs) dead, thousands of families and homes shattered, besides bringing up a generation of psyched youth in an environment of insurgency despite living in a state considered to be heaven on earth. Multiple offers for peace, extensive *sadbhavna* projects, doles of money by Delhi, provision of jobs, employment and repeated elections—Panchayat upwards—were probably seen as a weakness of the Indian Union. People of the valley also overlooked the fact that Pakistan is a weak nation (as proved during the Kargil War), and that it could not do any good for them, but would only foment trouble by propagating the theory of thousand cuts. The Kashmiris also ignored the opportunities offered by the Prime Minister to shun the gun and join the mainstream; possibly they were forced to think that they were close to their ill-conceived azadi. The question arises how did the Kashmiris ignore the massive contingent of security forces present in the Valley and their demonstrated capability to prevent this from happening? How did they fail to understand that the combined strength of all Central Armed Police Forces (CAPF) and the Indian Army together are a formidable force capable of destroying the strategy of Pakistan and its band of terrorists?

The Kargil debacle and the Cold Start strategy evolved by Indian forces in 2004 made it amply clear that Pakistan's forces were no match for India. This aspect was also ignored by the Kashmiri intellectual community. On 5 August 2019, the abrogation of Articles 370 and 35A was declared and the State was reorganised into union territories. This masterstroke from Delhi suddenly brought the realisation that their dream of azadi or a special status would never fructify. The bedrock of azadi that Pakistan was playing upon was removed in one stroke from under their feet.

Pakistan was also stumped, and this created an imbalance within Pakistan, resulting in a serious divide between the Pakistan military and polity. One would like to imagine that had the abrogation and reorganisation of the state been done in, let's say, the year 2000, the insurgency in J&K would have been eradicated for good by 2005, and would have brought Pakistan to a weakened state ten years ago. With ten years of prosperity, imagine the economy of J&K

Redesigning our Counter-insurgency Strategy

Politico-Military Strategy

Taking into consideration our peep into the past 34 years of ongoing insurgency in J&K, our future politico-military strategy has to be given a relook. Some thoughts on redesigning our strategy are given in the succeeding paragraphs.

A pragmatic geopolitical strategy must define the future of PoJK and Gilgit-Baltistan, which historically is part of the state of J&K. The strategy of unification must not create another violent tragedy. The Parliament has already resolved[9] to integrate these territories but the public sentiments, Pakistan's belligerence, and China's influence in the region are major factors in deciding the strategy. One thing is clear—this must be a very long-term strategy and diplomatic actions are the key. On the other hand, this strategy must actively demonstrate a strong political resolve backed by military strength both internationally and in the region. A positive internal opinion must be generated. The resolution of PoJK and Gilgit-Baltistan could be given a timeline, say up to 2030, to suppress Pakistan's agenda. There should be an end to the Kashmir-centric dynastic politics (which is playing to the tune of Pakistan), thus creating a larger canvass of communities that are pro-India to include Mirpur-Bhimber-Rawlakot areas in the Poonch zone.

The security forces must be given a clear central directive, and a mission with converging aims and goals with the politics and governance of the region. The aims and goals must be given a mandate supported with suitable rules of engagement, which pass muster with the law of the land. The Indian Army, RR, and CAPF must be given clear-cut objectives to eradicate insurgency in a phased plan. These objectives should be achieved approximately by the year 2026. The acceptable levels of gradual reduction of insurgency must be analysed within a given timeline, which will then hold the security forces accountable.

The phase of ebbing insurgency in the erstwhile state of Jammu and Kashmir is now discernible. Hence, the security forces must exploit the success. The iron hand must be used against the Over-Ground Workers (OGWs) to eradicate with impunity any form of support to the remaining radicals. The aim should be to isolate these radicals from the population. All forms of indoctrination, especially madrassas, social media, and foreign interference, must be constantly checked. A special task force of experts should be established to monitor indoctrination attempts.

Elections in all five divisions will play an important role to bring peace in J&K, but the date of these elections needs to be carefully arrived at given the state of insurgency, and the political leanings of the old guard of the state. The elections should be delayed so the levels of insurgency and influence in Pakistan are reduced. This could happen somewhere around the year 2030, subject to changes in the environment. Early elections will have their own dangers of a retrograde effect. In the interim, the Union Territories of Jammu and Kashmir should be administered under the provisions of the Governor's rule. Most importantly, we should buy time to bring about the development process to its planned peak, the emergence of representation of all areas into an effective political system. This time must be used to deradicalisation the people and the youth of the Valley. One of the main indicators of harmony will be a situation that permits the return of the Kashmiri Pandits to their homeland. Panchayat and municipal elections may be considered in Jammu where insurgency has subsided as a measure to provide relief to the people of this province, and to meet their demands, aspirations and development of infrastructure, which has been lagging due to Kashmir-centric policies. This should be seen as an incentive by the people of Kashmir division to shun insurgency and militancy, and to join the national mainstream.

Operational Strategy of the Security Forces

The strategy of the iron hand in a velvet glove with a focussed developmental *sadbhavna* can be considered a suitable strategy for the future. The pillars of this strategy should be first, strength and swiftness of military action, secondly, strict adherence to the rule of law, thirdly, respecting human rights, fourthly, isolating the insurgents and, lastly, winning the hearts and minds of the population by genuine empathy. The stated decisive points on both military and civilian lines of operation must be laid down, and the establishment of responsibility and accountability should part of the strategy.

The actions that security forces need to undertake with the full support of the civil administration are:

Effect-based coordinated counter-insurgency operations in coordination with all agencies should be immediately introduced.

Strong coordination should be developed within the Line of Control areas and the hinterland. Night curfew can be resorted to in the border and the Line of Control areas.

Special forces, hit squads, and border action teams are to be positioned all along the critical areas north and south of the Pir Panjal to cover the Line of Control with the capability of strong cross-border operations. The liberty to act and react at the mid-level of operational command, and surgical strikes should be decentralised to local field Commanders.

All intelligence is to be coordinated at one level in each zone with all intelligence agencies establishing their parallel intelligence centres at these zones. Joint interrogation centres should be the responsibility of J&K police.

Ceasefire violations by Pakistan should be responded to with standardised reactions by suitable weapons systems, which could include arty and air force. There should be full freedom of action for local commanders.

IB Sector of J&K from Lakhanpar to Sangam in the Chhamb Sector to be made foolproof for infiltration using electronic devices and suitably supported by explosives. Ditch-cum-bunds in the IB Sector to be part of this denial with forces redeployed from North and South Kashmir, however ensuring no loss of tactical or operational balance. Similarly, the second and third tiers of anti-infiltration grid lines were to be established and occupied by RR troops in the Line of Control Sector.

Deobandi mosques and their maulvis must be monitored for doctrinal propaganda.

Governance and Administrative Actions

The strategy of governance of UTs of Jammu, Kashmir, and Ladakh must be an off-take overall security strategy till full normalcy returns. The basic governance must be based on annual developmental plans, which should be evaluated for success at the end of the year. The selected projects must aim at fulfilling the aspirations of the people of both the UTs. Financial planning, prioritised allocation of work and their PDCs should be targeted and achieved on an annual basis. These must be subjected to technical evaluation and financial audit by nominated teams under the aegis of Central Government specified government officials must be given responsibility and be held accountable at the end of the planning period.

Quotas for all minorities to include educational, employment, food and farming subsidies. It is important to maintain a balance amongst all minorities, and politicians must not be allowed to disturb this balance. Border areas must be developed at superfast speed, and the aim should be to connect all blocks districts by roads, proper electricity and water supply. UTs should not be subjected to power cuts. Money should be allocated to all blocks and essential projects must be achieved on an annual basis. Medical, educational and provision of essential daily required commodities must be ensured by the District Collectors. All pending law cases must be disposed off on a fast-track basis. Encroachments and land grab cases done under the Roshni Act must be taken back or demolished and culprits taken to task legally. Roshni Act must be formally scrapped or discontinued. Deradicalisation drives, especially in the Valley, must be undertaken jointly by the civil administration and the Army. The aim should be to get the youth on the national mainstream as soon as possible.

Electoral Process and Political Representations

J&K was put on the wrong track in 1947 by allowing a single party-political system in the state. The erstwhile Muslim Conference was baptised as the National Conference to drive the state politics and policies on Islamic and Kashmiri agendas. This has been the main cause for the people of the state not meeting their lifestyle and political aspirations. Dynastic politics with Kashmir-centric agendas and policies are the cause of backwardness in all fields in Jammu and Ladakh provinces. Jammu province lost all interest in politics since they were suppressed by Kashmiri leaders. The politics of the state must be run with equitable representation of multiple political parties.There is a definite need to have regional parties with competent and dynamic leaders in all parts of the state who have the confidence of the people. A new allocation of the seats as per the latest delimitation process should be enforced to give the all-region an equitable representation, and to generate competition for the valley-based parties. There is a definite need to groom potential new candidates for the post of chief minister who should hail from different regions and represent all faiths. This will certainly act as the force multiplier as also the most powerful political strategy that will break the back of the retrograde political practices and interference from Pakistan. A good political system and strong governance will also influence and produce that ray of hope for the people of Gilgit-Baltistan provinces that will draw them closer and in favour of India. Toward this, we must ensure to generate processes diplomatically, politically as well as militarily to ensure the resolution of the Gilgit-Baltistan problem.

Return of the Kashmiri Pandits

Fundamental factors of harmony must be established for the return of Kashmiri Pandits to their homeland and reacquiring of their properties must take precedence. The essence of Kashmiriyat must return to the Valley. The Central Government should take on the responsibility of providing relief to this community. A safe environment for their return will depend on the termination of insurgency in the valley. This should be taken up on a defined timeline based on all inputs.

Conclusion

Redesigning our counter-insurgency strategy is the need of the hour, and the bedrock for the final resolution of the Kashmir issue. This must consider the numerous factors described above as they are all interrelated and interdependent upon each other. Success will depend upon a comprehensive approach to be rolled out and followed seriously in a time-bound manner. The dynamics of insurgency being generated by Pakistan and its ISI have to be beaten and squashed by proactive political, diplomatic and military approaches, and stern actions. India must adopt more potent measures to beat Pakistan-generated responses in time and space by undertaking proactive strong operational actions and surgical strikes as and when felt necessary. International pressures should not hinder our plans and effective Indian diplomacy must prevail as prescribed by our stated bilateral policy with Pakistan. The world is seeing changing war dynamics and many past theories and military apprehension have been proven wrong by the Russian invasion of Ukraine. India should not hold back its economic, diplomatic and military strengths and demonstrate that we mean business to retake the areas of PoJK, which are part of J&K, to put an end to the menace of insurgency once and for all.

Lieutenant General P.S. Mehta, AVSM, VSM was commissioned into the Armoured Corps and was a Strike Corps Commander. He has authored various papers on War with Pakistan and capture of areas of PoK, Western Front Strategy cum Operational Plans. He steered a national level seminar on 'Jammu & Kashmir – The Way Ahead'. He has been very closely following the events in J&K for last thirty years and has considerable understanding of socio-political dimensions, intelligence set-up and the psychological impressions of people of Kashmir because of his ancestral roots in the valley.

Endnotes

1. Britannica, the Editors of Encyclopaedia. "Insurgency". *Encyclopaedia Britannica,* 27 Mar. 2023, https://www.britannica.com/topic/insurgency. Accessed 11 April 2023.

2. *U.S. Government Counterinsurgency Guide.* United States Government Interagency Counterinsurgency Initiative Bureau of Political-Military Affairs Printed January 2009. https://2009-2017.state.gov/documents/organization/119629.pdf

3. Gates, Scott, Kaushik Roy (2016), *Unconventional Warfare in South Asia: Shadow Warriors and Counterinsurgency.* Routledge. pp. Chapter 4. ISBN978-1-317-00540-7.

4. Estimated to be 1,90,000 of a total population of 2,00,000. The CIA fact book estimated the number to be 3,00,000.

5. Army chief calls for 'iron fist in a velvet glove' policy in Kashmir, The Indian Express, 11 August 2011

6. From Madhopur to Sangam (approximately 198 km)

7. This can be compared to the problem as given by Richard A. Gabriel and Paul L. Savage in their book *Crisis in Command* which describes the mismanagement in the Army due to prolonged engagement in Vietnam.

8. *Operation Sadbhavana Journals of India,* Manifest Learning Academy 6 February 2023. https://journalsofindia.com/operation-sadbhavana/

9. Pakistan must vacate the areas of the Indian state of Jammu and Kashmir, which they have occupied through aggression; http://www.kashmir-information.com/LegalDocs/ParliamentRes.html

3

The Strategic Neighbourhood

16

India's Military Strategy Against Pakistan: Hits and Misses

Lieutenant General Surinder Singh

Foundations of Military Strategy

Strategy, in simple terms, is a plan of action. The differentiating factor from routine plans being the importance and involvement of the larger project at hand, multitude of variables factors, varied agencies, and the longer-term perspective. Military Strategy is, accordingly, a long-term plan for developing, structuring, training, and employing a military force for achieving the military objectives. It is, thus, the art and science of employing Armed Forces to secure the objectives of National Policy, either by application of force, or just the threat of use of force, to coerce a weaker opponent into accepting favourable terms for peace.

Military Strategy would, thus, emanate from, and would be, a rung in the national strategy to secure national aims. The foundation has to be the national aim, strategy and policy. These would lay down what the nation wishes to achieve over the long term, how it wishes to go about it, and the plan to achieving its aims. While our national aim, derived from the Preamble to our Constitution, would essentially be to provide for its people a sovereign republic which is democratic, socialist and secular, and provides for a society where each citizen can expect justice, liberty, equality, and a fraternity at peace with itself. For these lofty aims to be achieved, the nation must have a strategy, a long-term plan. We have a robust and an inspirational constitution which lays down our national aim and we have cabinet committees on security, political affairs, economic affairs, and other such committees to strategise and guide our national policies, some long term, and cast in the constitutional stone, and others which change with changing geopolitical, socio-political, economical, scientific, and technological realities. Non-alignment, Indus Water Treaty, Land Ceiling Act, reservations for the weaker sections, international and inter-state free trade policies, climate action plan, population control, education and health policies are all examples of national policies.

Unfortunately, there has not been much clarity in the field of national security and defence policy. The erstwhile Defence Policy Group and the subsequent National Security Agency has singularly failed in articulating a National Security Policy and National Security Strategy. The Indian Military Strategy, thus, has no foundations to build upon and is always 'up in the air' swaying with the winds of changing interests of political leadership, and personal experiences and biases of higher military leadership. Whatever consistency that has been there, has been forced by economic factors, bureaucratic inertia, and the large size of the military. With limited defence spending available, no large-scale or revolutionary restructuring or capability enhancement of the military can take place. The bureaucracy's lack of knowledge about military affairs and inability, or unwillingness of political leadership to get intimately involved with military affairs has resulted in painstakingly slow pace of reforms. Even, when all else is working well, the sheer size of the military and its penchant for tradition, results in transformation taking decades to fructify. Such long drawn restructuring is always vulnerable to changes in leadership or environmental factors which could change the course of transformation or halt it altogether. The Indian Military Strategy has, thus, remained an enigma and confusion even to the military officer corps. However, the silver lining is that it has still worked well sometimes, if not always.

1947-48 Indo-Pak War – Shared Spoils

At the cusp of our Independence, the country was grappling with unification of its erstwhile princely states, poverty, hunger, and lack of educated and experienced workforce. The Government's attention was not on defence matters. The military itself was looked at with suspicion by the freedom fighters and politicians for its close association with British military and its ethos. Pakistan's attempt to capture J&K by force in 1947 was the first military challenge for India. The military strategy was simply to secure Srinagar and Leh and secure as much of J&K as possible with whatever was available. The fledgling military, created and trained by the British, rose to the challenge and saved Srinagar, Punch, and Leh, pushing back Pakistani irregulars, and later its army to a line, which exists largely to date. The military strategy and tactics used were primarily the legacy of the British Army. Limited Indian military capability and difficulties of conducting offensive operations in high mountains against a similarly organised, equipped and trained Pakistan Army brought about a stalemate, and a divided Kashmir. This continues, even today, to be a political and military challenge for both countries. The successful military campaign in Srinagar earned for the military the respect of its people and some politicians. The talent and experience in higher ranks was limited, but at the tactical and operational level, the military delivered. Surprisingly, the need for upgrading military capabilities was still not felt. The political goodwill India enjoyed was considered enough to protect us from further threats to our borders.

1962 War – The Himalayan Blunder

The 1962 War with China brought new and insurmountable military challenges. This war brought out the vital necessity of intimate civil-military coordinated decision-making, and the need to have political leadership which understands military capability and conduct of war. It is apparent that there was no defined strategy to defend our northern borders. We even failed to demarcate our national boundary until 1954. The physical infrastructure in Himalayan border regions was insufficient to even support rudimentary defence operations. Military logistic capabilities were rudimentary. Most of the Army remained committed in the West to defend the Line of Control with Pakistan in J&K. Mismatch in political directions and military capability to achieve them, incompetent political and higher military leadership, coupled with political interference in military chain of command led to an unwanted debacle. Indian military strategy of forward deployment was hastily conceived to stop China from occupying Indian territory. The execution of this strategy had inadequate logistic support, delayed deployment, and ill-timed withdrawals. Not employing the Air Force completed the fiasco. The valour and sacrifices displayed by the experienced infantry units was the only silver lining.

Shaken by the loss of geopolitical standing, and finally realising the need to have a minimum deterrent capability, the Government began work on military rejuvenation and strategic deterrence capability. Close civil-military coordination and improved funding led to new units and formations being raised, and weapons being imported. Many logistic establishments, areas, and dumps were set up. The Indo-Tibetan Border Police and the Seema Suraksha Bal were raised for guarding the border, and to relieve Army units. There was positive intent to upgrade military capability, but the progress remained slow due to fund crunch even though defence spending went up from two per cent of GDP in 1960 to four per cent in 1963.

1965 Indo-Pak War – An Honourable Stalemate

Indian military restructuring was underway and many units and formations were still not fully ready when Pakistan, emboldened by India's poor show in the 1962 War with China, and having modernised its forces, felt it had a last chance to capture Kashmir militarily. Taken by surprise, the Indian Forces quickly neutralised the irregular infiltrating forces before Pakistan military joined the conflict. Pakistan's strategy was to limit the conflict to J&K, and capture as much area as possible. Several iconic battles were fought along the Line of Control. Indian success at Hajipir Pass in the Uri sector, and the Pakistani attacks to capture Chhamb, were noteworthy. Operations being restricted to J&K were unfavourable to India, and the Western Army Commander, Lieutenant General Harbaksh Singh, decided to take the battle to the Pakistani heartland of Punjab. This strategy of counter offensive forced the enemy to redeploy its forces and the offensive in Kashmir lost steam. Several battles in the counter offensive were fought, notably, in Burki, Dograi, Khemkaran, and Asal Uttar in the plains of Punjab, and the forces eventually reached a stalemate with Pakistan having failed in its military aim of capturing Kashmir, having suffered huge losses of manpower, its modern tanks, and aircraft. The credit for a successful military strategy should largely go to Prime Minister Lal Bahadur Shastri, who gave the military a free hand, and to Lieutenant General Harbaksh Singh, who managed his resources in a large operational theatre from Ladakh to Rajasthan admirably. He adopted the strategy of indirect approach. When faced with reverses in Chhamb, he opened the Punjab front, and pushed his formations hard in the face of superior enemy forces. Starting with the clarity of strategic vision shown by Lieutenant General Harbaksh in the 1965 War, the next three decades were probably the best years for the military. The negative and defensive mindset that had become a part of the Indian Army after 1962 was once and for all removed, and a new conceptual idea of an offence defence was slowly set into motion.

1971 Indo-Pak War – Exemplary Strategy

Faced with a deluge of refugees from Bangladesh in 1971 caused by Pakistani clampdown and genocide, all organs of the state worked in synchronisation. A well-thought national and military strategy was formulated. The Government went on a worldwide outreach to sensitise governments to the atrocities committed by Pakistan Army, the plight of refugees, and the social and economic costs being suffered by India. Signing a peace and friendship treaty with Soviet Union gave India a safety backstop in its intent to liberate Bangladesh. The intelligence agencies coordinated well with the Army to successfully create the Mukti Bahini, a Bangladeshi volunteer force, which provided invaluable intelligence and logistic support. There was close coordination, and full faith between the Prime Minister and the Army Chief, which helped overcome political and bureaucratic hindrances. Adequate time was given for preparing the military for war, funding was made available, shortages were made up, troops and formations trained well, intelligence field work done meticulously. Since the political aim was to create a homeland for Bengali refugees in Bangladesh, Eastern Theatre was declared the main theatre of operations, and strike formations from the Western Theatre were shifted to the Eastern Theatre. The strategy was to hold the Western front with a minimum defensive force while concentrating offensive capabilities in the East. Once the military rolled into Bangladesh, the three services displayed a very high standard of inter-services cooperation and coordination. Finally, the strategy of bypassing hardened defences in the border region and heading for depth areas proved to be successful in quickly crossing formidable rivers and isolating enemy formations. Employing vertical envelopment by helicopters to close in on with Dhaka were some masterstrokes of Indian strategy that left the enemy confounded. While the higher military leadership displayed great operational art, the intermediate formations and units displayed initiative, adaptability, and courage of the highest order to bring about a spectacular victory. There are no other examples of an Army routing the adversary, taking nearly 1,00,000 prisoners of war, and liberating a country the size of Bangladesh in two weeks. This was probably the finest hour for India, its military, and the way the entire national security apparatus worked seamlessly in unison.

Transformative Years – From Defensive to Offensive

Reduced to its western half, Pakistan remained a security concern. Indian military strategy continued to be defensive in nature against this security concern. Fixed line defences based on ditch-cum-bunds and canals were developed. The offensive capability remained stagnant till much later. In 1975, India conducted an underground nuclear explosion signalling its capability and intent to develop a nuclear deterrence. Pakistan, now fearful of its territorial sovereignty, supported by its western allies, continued to modernise its military arsenal, and began a surreptitious program to develop nuclear weapons. Pakistan could not stomach the loss of half of its territory in 1971, and the humiliation of defeat and surrender. An entire generation of embittered Pakistani Army officers swore revenge and it embarked upon a policy of death by a thousand cuts. The militancy in Punjab in early '80s gave Pakistan a tool to destabilise India. The consequent involvement of the Army in internal security and border sealing spread it thin, and reduced its offensive options. The military strategy *vis-a-vis* Pakistan remained defensive deterrence.

The later half of the '80s brought about the most significant and far-reaching changes in Indian military restructuring, modernisation, and a doctrinal shift from defensive to offensive operations. General K. Sunderji, the Army Chief from 1986 to 1989, pushed mechanisation and modernisation of the armoured fleet. The T-72 tanks from Russia were now being inducted in larger numbers and the Mechanised Infantry, equipped with the BMP Infantry Combat Vehicle, expanded significantly. Indian Artillery was getting equipped with 155 mm Bofors Guns. The Army Aviation Corps and Special Forces were made operational. Mirage aircraft were inducted and were a counter to Pakistani F-16 aircraft. For the first time, the military had the resources to adopt an Offensive Defence Strategy against Pakistan, based on manoeuvre warfare, involving large mechanised formations capable of traversing large distances over under-developed terrain. The concept of employment of Armoured and Mechanised Divisions along with specially formed Infantry Divisions with integral armoured brigades as Combat Commands, groups, and teams brought about the most significant restructuring and doctrinal shift. Operation Meghdoot had successfully wrested and secured the Siachen Glacier; the Sumdrong Chu incident, and the follow up Exercise Chequer Board, displayed a new found confidence. The military began to talk about fighting a 'Two-Front' war with both Pakistan and China, even if it was premature.

IPKF – Failure of National Security Architecture

Things began to unravel with the ill-conceived India-Sri Lanka Peace Accord of 1987 and the subsequent involvement of over 80,000 Indian troops in Sri Lanka under Operation Pawan. The political aims were not clearly thought, and the Army, pushed into the conflict zone in a hurry, were unprepared. The IPKF was soon fighting the Liberation Tigers of Tamil Elam, an organisation created, and continued to be armed and supported, by Indian intelligence agencies. Three years later, after suffering 1,200 soldiers killed and over 3,000 injured, the IPKF returned unceremoniously with none of the military or political objectives achieved. The immense valour, bravery, and sacrifice displayed by the units went in vain due to a dysfunctional National Security Structure. There was no detailed war gaming, nor extensive thought given to political or military objectives to be achieved, and it can be said that there was no strategy or doctrine in place. The military was neither consulted nor given time to prepare for the operation. Within two decades, all the lessons learnt from the Bangladesh War seemed to have been forgotten.

Kashmir – The Low Intensity Trap

Even as the military was recovering from the IPKF fiasco and Punjab militancy had ebbed, political mishandling in Kashmir provided Pakistan another opportunity to destabilise Kashmir, a vital defence region bordering both Pakistan and China. For the next three decades, J&K has totally occupied the Army's mind space. The military strategy effectively comes down to managing the internal security situation in J&K, often at the cost of conventional capacity building. Strengthening the multi-tiered anti-infiltration grid, raising of the tailor-made Rashtriya Rifles battalions, and controlling headquarters, to fight the militants or terrorists in the hinterland, and the creation of a border fence along the entire Line of Control are some of major policy actions which have successfully managed violent incidents and restored the writ of the state. The strategy of conducting military operations with a human face, 'Iron Fist in a Velvet Glove', winning hearts and minds of the civilian population through civic action projects, and maintaining zero tolerance to human rights violations, has been the long-standing military strategy in internal security operations. The strategy has stood the test of time and helped manage a conflict to a stalemate. In absence of any significant political steps to resolve the conflict, stalemate in J&K continues. Recent political moves to bring the state under direct central rule have not affected the military situation in J&K, which remains in a state of NWNP.

Kargil War: Nuclear Deterrence and Space for Conventional Operations

The year 1998 saw nuclear deterrence being firmly established in India-Pakistan military balance. Indian nuclear weapons tests, followed immediately by Pakistani nuclear weapons tests, established both countries as nuclear weapon states. While Pakistan seeks to use nuclear deterrence as a shield against superior Indian conventional forces, India insists there is adequate space for conventional operations below the nuclear threshold. These hypotheses have been tested during the Kargil conflict, and the more recent air duel between the two Air Forces. In Kargil, Pakistan mistakenly believed that India will be constrained by its nuclear deterrence to launch conventional attacks to recapture areas occupied by it. India correctly assessed that attacks to recapture own areas will not invite nuclear response. India employed several battalions of infantry, hundreds of artillery guns, rockets, and air power to throw out the Pakistan Army. In the end, an alarmed United States of America intervened to bring the conflict to a quick closure. The Kargil War set new benchmarks of bravery and valour of Indian soldiers, and the effectiveness of artillery support. Inter-service synergy, however, left much to be desired. Lack of adequate ammunition stocks was exposed, leading to hurried imports. In 1999, after a devastating suicide attack killing 40 Indian paramilitary soldiers, the Indian Air Force launched attacks across the Line of Control into a Pakistan border village housing terror training camps. Pakistan Air Force responded by an attack into the Indian side. However, both sides were careful not to escalate any further. It is, therefore, clear that the space for minor 'Tit for Tat' ground, air, or naval operations may exist between the two adversaries, but it is very small, and escalation control will be a priority at the level of top leadership. The Military Strategy will have to revert to deterrence, defensive or offensive.

China – The Main Threat and a Two Front Scenario

Emergence of China as a global economic, technological, and military power, willing to use military muscle to achieve its political objectives, is already posing significant threat along the contested and un-demarcated Himalayan Frontier. China has reorganised its military into Integrated Theatres Commands, and equipped them well. Substantial military infrastructure, airfields, highways, railways, logistic bases, and military habitat have been constructed which has greatly enhanced its capacity to station and employ large formations all along the borders. Its incursions into Eastern Ladakh in 2020, increasing belligerence, and willingness to use force to alter the status quo have created a significant military challenge for India. While India matched deployments, and is in the process of building military infrastructure to deter further incursions, it's going to be a long haul. Indian military had to divert resources from the western front to increase its capacities along the Northern borders, further restricting military options against Pakistan.

With China-Pakistan friendship, the 'Two-Front' scenario is a real possibility. China Pakistan Economic Corridor running through Pakistan occupied Kashmir and presence of PLA personnel in Gilgit region does not augur well. In a limited India-Pakistan conflict, China may not directly get involved, but will likely provide weapons, ammunition, intelligence, and financial support. In the event of an India-China conflict, Pakistan is sure to meddle directly or indirectly with irregulars. A two-front war will be unfavourable to India. The overall strategy will have to be based on creating a strong deterrence or a strong diplomacy to avoid a collusive war against Pakistan and China. In case of a failure of such a strategy, Indian military must have the strength to hold one front while solving the other. Military Diplomacy will play an important role in such a strategy.

Capacity Building and National Security

Defence Budget: The defence spending is an important indicator of government priority to defence, and has a direct bearing on military capacity, capability, and the robustness of military strategy. From 1960 to 1990, the defence spending remained around three per cent of GDP, spiking to four per cent after 1971 War and 1989 Kargil conflict. Thereafter, it has remained below 2.5 per cent of GDP, and is now almost at two per cent of GDP. Increase in overall GDP of the country in recent years meant that even as the defence budget has remained below 2.5 per cent, in real terms, there has an increase, and this is cited often. However, six to seven per cent increase in defence budget every year is offset by inflation, increase in pays and pensions, and the phenomenal increase in the cost of high-tech weapon systems. The capital acquisitions and military modernisation has, therefore, suffered over the years. Without resources, the military strategy will remain hamstrung. A minimum of three per cent of GDP is required to modernise the military, and build up the requisite military capacity to counter threats along both Western and Northern Borders. Indigenising defence production will be a force multiplier.

Inter Services Synergy: Besides compromising operational effectiveness, lack of integrated functioning consumes more resources. The appointment of Chief of Integrated Defence Staff, and bringing an act in Parliament for the creation of Integrated Theatre Commands has signalled the Government intend. Greater synergy among the three services builds the capacity to fight integrated and prolonged wars in the new multi-domain battle space, and is a positive step in cost effectiveness.

Whole of Government Effort: There has been substantial improvement in bringing about synergy and coordination among various agencies to overcome security challenges. National Investigating Agency has done a commendable job in controlling terror funding and over-ground supporters of militancy in Kashmir. The Paramilitary forces have stepped up to take over low threat sectors, and political and administrative measures are trying to reduce disaffection among population. It's time to bring to battle the non-military resources to change the narrative in fighting a war, and fighting insurgency and proxy war in Kashmir. Political, diplomatic, economic, technological, and cultural power of a rising India can, eventually, achieve the political aim of coercing a weakening Pakistan to shun violence and hatred. A peaceful South Asia region will spur our economic growth, and development will come faster than as imagined today.

Lieutenant General Surinder Singh, PVSM, AVSM & Bar, VSM retired as the GOC-in-C of the Western Command. He has been a patron of Gyan Chakra. He is an alumnus of the Staff College, Camberley (England), and is a former Chairman of the Punjab Public Service Commission.

17

Pakistan: Treading a Difficult Journey

R.K. Kaushik, IAS

Pakistan is in full precariousness. The political and economic situation has become more important than the military in Pakistan. The extremely weak but establishment's protégé Government is moving towards its closure on 17 August 2023. After the dissolved assemblies of Punjab and KP (Khyber Pakhtoonkhwa), even the caretaker governments have crossed their 90 days limit. There is a visible unrest, frustration, depression, and turmoil in the state of Pakistan.

Pakistan was born out of the two-nation theory propagated by the Muslim League and its leader Mohammad Ali Jinnah. The two-nation concept was opposed by the Congress, but was discreetly encouraged, nay, abetted by the British. The demarcation of boundaries and the communal acrimony resulted in an unprecedented violence in which about a million people died a violent death, and 14 million others crossed borders. As a result of this theory, the newborn Pakistan had two wings—East Pakistan, made up of East Bengal, and West Pakistan, made up of districts of West Punjab, Sindh, North West Frontier Province, Baluchistan, and 10 Princely States—mostly areas with conspicuous presence of Muslims. The violence and migration were of such magnitude that this tragic episode can be regarded as the first example of ethnic cleansing in history. In fact, it was a surgery without anesthesia. During the first six months, the Central Government of Pakistan relied on the assets and the liabilities of the 1947-48 all-India budget, and on the whole, was insufficiently solvent.

The budgetary deficit during the period from August 1947 to March 1948 reached INR 234 million. In all this, the provincial and princely states' governments accounted for a significant part of the public expenses.

In early 1948, the Nizam of Hyderabad extended a loan of INR 200 million to Pakistan. This, to a large extent, enabled the Central Government to finalise its first annual budget, whose defence component accounted for 70 per cent, while the comparative figure in India's first budget was almost 40 per cent.

The founding father, Quaid-i-Azam, Jinnah was very perspicacious when he addressed 60 members of the constituent assembly on 11 August 1947 at Karachi. He said, 'You are free, you are free to go to your temples, you are free to go to your mosques, or to any other places of worship in this state of Pakistan. You may belong to any religion or caste or creed—that has nothing to do with the business of the state.' But communal tensions-leading to riots were uncontrollable. Jinnah died on 11 September 1948 in Karachi. After nine years of efforts, Pakistan succeeded in framing a constitution which became effective on 23 March 1956 proclaiming Pakistan an Islamic Republic.

Khwaja Nazimuddin and Ghulam Mohammad were poor replacements of Jinnah. Whereas Mohammad Ali Bogra, Hussain Shaheed Suhrawardy, I.I. Chundrigar, and Feroz Khan Noon were no match for the first Prime Minister Liaquat Ali Khan who was in power till October 1951.

It is said that 'No constitution can bc absolutcly safc from a rcvolution or from a *coup d'etat*'. General (Later Field Marshal) Ayub knew fully well that the constitution contained no provision for its own abrogation, and that it contained no provision for declarations of Martial Law and appointment of a Chief Martial Law Administrator. That's why, he called his military takeover on 8 October 1958—a revolution. Field Marshal Ayub Khan became President of the Islamic Republic of Pakistan the very same day.

Ayub introduced a range of reforms in the hope that the benefits flowing from these reforms would reach the people, and they would come to recognise the merits of his system of government. Some of the reforms never got off the ground, others like the land reforms, lost their purpose in the course of implementation. Still, the introduction of the reforms created an atmosphere of rethinking, which constituted a challenge to vested interests.

Ayub would also be remembered for the development of the Atomic Energy Programme in Pakistan which received a shot in the arm when he converted the Pakistan Atomic Energy Commission from a semi-government body into a statutory body in 1965.

Ayub Khan fought a fiercely contested election with Fatima Jinnah (Mohammed Ali Jinnah's sister) as opponent. He defeated her and got elected as the President in 1964. Thereafter, in August-September 1965, Operation Gibraltar failed, and the 1965 War started. The Tashkant Agreement, in January 1966, lead to the resignation of Zulfiqar Ali Bhutto as the Foreign Minister, and the foundation of the PPP in September 1968. The political dexterity of Bhutto lead to massive mobilisation of students, labour, employees, and people in general.

Field Marshal Ayub Khan resigned on 25 March 1969, and handed over powers to General Yahya Khan. The 1970 elections lead to the majority going to Awami League of Sheikh Mujhhur Rehman. Yahya Khan refused to hand over the Government to him. The December 1971 War with India ended with the fall of Dhaka, and the surrender of a Pakistani Army of 93,000 troops, paramilitary forces, and civilians. Zulfiquar Ali Bhutto took over as Chief Martial Law Administrator on 20 December 1971, and like Churchill, on the eve of acquiring power in the state, Bhutto felt as if he, too, was walking with destiny, and that all his life had been but a preparation for that hour and the task that lay ahead. On 2 January 1972, he nationalised 10 basic industries. On 11 March 1972, he introduced land reforms in which a person could own 150 acres of irrigated and 300 acres of un-irrigated land. On 1 April 1972, he took over the management of most of the private colleges and schools in Pakistan. On 10 March 1972, he dismissed more than 1,700 civil servants for being inefficient and corrupt. He took decisions with alacrity, and was a leader in a hurry. He signed the Shimla Agreement with India on 2 July 1972.

In June 1972, he helped in organising a discreet visit by Dr Henry Kissinger to China to meet Mao Tse Tung and Chou En Lai. Bhutto received credit, appreciation, and gratitude from the Chinese Communist Party.

The 1973 constitution, which had the approval and support of all political parties in the country, was undoubtedly one of Bhutto's greatest achievements. Bhutto violated its sanctity by a series of unilateral amendments in the teeth of opposition from his political opponents. In June 1974, Bhutto called all prominent scientists of Pakistan at Multan, and directed them to start the process of building of a nuclear device. He gave them *carte blanche* regarding budget and all sorts of help. Immediately thereafter, Bhutto himself visited China and decided to consolidate relations with the communist neighbour. In March 1976, General Tikka Khan, the Army Chief retired, Bhutto, in his imperiousness, ignored the first seven generals, and chose General Zia-Ul-Haq, who was number eight in the seniority. All seven generals resigned. His conduct of the 1977 elections was controversial and filled with rigging allegations. On 5 July 1977, General Zia-Ul-Haq conducted his army coup and took over the power in the country. The operation of taking over the country by the Armed Forces was code named as Operation Fair Play. He registered a murder case against Bhutto, and executed him on 4 April 1979. He declared that Pakistan could not survive without Islam, and that the sole justification, the *raison d'être* for the establishment of Pakistan was the introduction of the Islamic system. There had been military coups before, but now for the first time, a deeply religious person was the head of state, the head of the Government, and the Army Chief—a frightening combination, and he seemed determined to recreate the Islamic legal and social order which had originated in Tribal Arabia more than a thousand years earlier.

General Zia established a federal Shariat Court with powers to declare invalid any law or provision of a law as repugnant to the injunctions of Islam as laid down in the Holy Quran and the Sunna of the Holy Prophet (PBUH). Zia held party-less elections in May 1985 in which Mohammad Khan Junejo became the Prime Minister. Zia subsequently dissolved the National Assembly on 29 May 1988, and dismissed Junejo's Government. General Zia died in plane crash on 17 August 1988. It is pertinent to mention that he dexterously handled the situation created for Pakistan by the Soviet intervention in Afghanistan, which had taken him and everybody else completely by surprise. Everyone had proceeded on the assumptions that the Soviets would never cross the Oxus and enter Afghanistan. Zia refused to accept that *fait accompli.* He sponsored Mujahideen groups to fight the Soviet Union and fought an eight years long war as an American proxy. Also, he got benefits in the form of political, international, economic, and defence support.

The National Assembly elections were held in November 1988. PPP emerged as the largest party, and Benazir Bhutto became the Prime Minister. The Bhutto Government lasted till 6 August 1990, and was dismissed by the President Ghulam Ishaq Khan under Article 58(2)(b). In general elections held in October 1990, Mohammad Nawaz Sharif became the Prime Minister. His government was dismissed on 17 April 1993 by Ishaq Khan. On 19 October 1993, Benazir Bhutto started her second term as the Prime Minister. Her government was dismissed on 5 November 1996 by President Farooq Leghari. When Benazir came into power for the second time, it was hoped that she had learnt her lessons. But the performance of the Government was, once again, very disappointing.

In the general elections held on 3 February 1997, Mohammed Nawaz Sharif became the Prime Minister for the second time. On 28 May 1998, Pakistan carried out five nuclear tests. In September 1998, Nawaz Sharif met Atal Bihari Vajpayee in the UN. Vajpayee visited Lahore in February 1999. However, the Bonhomie was short lived as Pakistan Army created the Kargil crisis.

After India's victory in Kargil, Nawaz Sharif had to cut a sorry figure. On 12 October 1999, General Pravez Musharraf arrested Nawaz Sharif and his party leaders, and took as over as the Chief Martial Law Administrator. He also made efforts to normalise relations with India, and visited Agra in August 2001. The general elections were held in Pakistan. The overall voter turnout was 40.69 per cent, and Zafrullaha Khan Jamali became the Prime Minister followed by Shaukat Aziz. On 27 December 2007, Benazir Bhutto was murdered, and the elections for Pakistan Assembly were held on 18 December 2008. Musharraf resigned on 16 August 2006 as President, and Asif Ali Zardari took over as the President.

Meanwhile, there were massive terrorist acts in Pakistan leading to more than 304 incidents of terrorist violence in a span of six years (2008 to 2013). The Pakistan Army conducted operations against some militant groups in FATA and North Waziristan called Zarb-E-Azb.

Nawaz came back to power on 5 June 2013 in his third term. He was initially soft on India, and wanted close interactions and relations, without caring for hiccups in his endeavour to mend fences, but needless to say, the GHQ was not pleased by his forays in friendship with India.

After General Ashfaq Parvez Kayani retired on 29 November 2013, he chose General Raheel Sharif as COAS when Nawaz was attending Prime Minister Modi's oath taking ceremony in May 2014. General Raheel Sharif had ordered a crackdown on Karachi, Hyderabad, and Sindh. The Ranger's were deployed, and they killed 85 MQM fighters and arrested more than 900 of them. Thereafter, there were reports of some surreptitious meetings between GHQ and Imran Khan leading to a *dharna* in Islamabad from 14 August 2014 till December 2014 when Tehrik-e-Taliban Pakistan killed about 175 school children in an Army school in Peshawar. The year 2015 was full of bitterness between the establishment and Nawaz, who was trying to create his own space in the polity of Pakistan. The love-hate relationship had its own highs and lows between Nawaz and the Generals. Western observers had observed that Nawaz wanted a soft line on Afghanistan and India, which was pertinaciously opposed by the GHQ.

Nawaz faced problems in his cabinet and party because the powerful Interior Minister Chaudhary Nisar Ali Khan was not on speaking terms with the Defence Minister Khwaja Asif and Petroleum Minister Shahid Khaqan Abbasi leading to difficulties in governing. The animosity could not be mellowed down. It was in these precarious circumstances with terrorists hitting at will that the relationship started inching towards the worst, and Nawaz started realising that the heat was being put upon his government in the form of agitations, *dharnas,* and serious charges of corruption, especially in the purchase of power plants. There were the *Dawn Leaks* allegations that Nawaz had spoken against the Pakistan Army in his interview with journalist Cyril Almeida of *The Dawn* newspaper and in a way supported the Indian narrative that Pakistan regularly sent terrorists in India to kill Indians and create terror, and conducted the 26/11 attacks in November 2008. It was a vaulting embarrassment to Pakistan's establishment.

It was on 4 April 2016 that the Panama papers showed the involvement of Sharif's family in offshore companies. Soon, thereafter, Sharif asked the Supreme Court to form a commission to investigate the Panama leaks after staggering pressure from the opposition. Cricketer-turned-politician Imran Khan demanded an independent probe. It was on 2 November 2015 that the Supreme Court agreed to set up a Judicial Commission to probe corruption allegation against Sharif and his family. The Commission, consisting of three Judges of the Supreme Court (Justice Ejaz Afzal Khan, Justice Gulzar Ahmed, and Justice Ejaz Afzal Khan), further forwarded it to the Joint Investigation Team (JIT) to investigate the charges of corruption, and gave its report to the three-judge bench on 11 July 2017 indicting Sharif and his family. The Supreme Court found him guilty of violation of People Representation Act 1976 of Pakistan that punishes the non-disclosure of assets, and does not allow a Prime Minister to hold an office of profit while he is the head of the Government. In Nawaz Sharif's case, he had a work permit of a company registered in the UAE. The Supreme Court also ordered the National Accountability Bureau (NAB) to conduct investigations against Sharif and his family within six months, and in case found guilty under Articles 62 and 63 of the Constitution of Pakistan, it would be proven that he was neither *sadiq* (truthful) nor *ameen* (honest).

Sharif launched a number of development projects, including the multi-billion CPEC. Another major achievement was the launch of military operation Zarb-e-Azb in 2014 to ameliorate the militants from North and South Waziristan—a hub of terrorism.

Shahid Khaqan Abbasi took over as the Prime Minister of Pakistan on 1 August 2017. It is worth mentioning that the Kashmir Policy, India

Policy, Nuclear Policy, China Policy, US Policy, Afghanistan Policy, and Defense Policy are very brashly controlled, and dictated by the Army and the ISI. Now, even social media, press and TV channels have joined this list.

The establishment, under General Kayani and the ISI Chief, Lieutenant General Ahmed Shuja Pasha, had decided to support Imran Khan from the 2011 onwards. Massive support was given to Imran and his PTI on 20 October 2011 when the public meeting organised by him in Lahore, had a crowd of about 2,00,000 attending and animatedly cheering him. The indication was noted by the various political parties, their leaders and workers.

The membership of PTI started increasing in districts, tehsils, and villages. Financial support from businessmen started flowing. In the 2013 elections, Imran had won 35 seats in National Assembly (total seats 342), and had a vote share of 16.92 per cent.

In the next general elections in July 2018, Imran won 149 seats for his party, and formed the Government with the support of smaller parties.

Initially, the hybrid experiment was seemingly successful, and it was exuberantly said that the Imran Government and the powerful establishment lead by General Qamar Javed Bajwa were on same page. However, slowly the differences started. The misunderstandings multiplied. General Bajwa's powerful father-in-law, Major General (Retd) Ijaz Amjad, started hobnobbing with Shahbaz Sharif and Pakistan Muslim League (Nawaz). Thereafter, General Bajwa ensured the release of Nawaz Sharif from jail, who then travelled to London on 18 November 2019 and is still there.

After Imran gave a three-year extension to General Bajwa till 29 November 2022, General Bajwa started active interference in the Government. He ensured that all serious corruption cases against Sharif family and his ministers got delayed.

He also wanted a change in the Chief Ministership of Punjab Province where a lame-duck, Usman Buzdar, Imran's choice, ruled. However, Imran refused, and General Bajwa felt humiliated as he had promised Aleem Khan—a real estate tycoon—about the post. Then Covid-19 hit the world in March 2020, and Pakistan's fragile economy faced serious problems. The growth went negative. The foreign exchange reserves dwindled, and unemployment increased. General Bajwa was also not happy with Imran's closeness with Lieutenant General Faiz Hameed, the ISI Chief, who was Bajwa's junior colleague from the 16th Baloch Regiment.

General Bajwa shifted Faiz to head 11 Corps in Peshawar, and brought Lieutenant General Nadeem Anjum, who was GOC 5 Corps in Karachi, as the ISI Chief in October 2021. Imran resisted this move. The differences with General Bajwa further deteriorated. However, the powerful establishment had its way.

In March 2022, the PDM led by Muslim League (Nawaz) brought a no-confidence motion in the National Assembly. This PDM by opposition parties was formed on 20 September 2020. At present, it has 13 political parties. The major success of PDM came after reportedly 20-plus members of Pakistan Tehreek-e-Insaf surfaced in Sindh house on 17 March 2022. Pakistan Tehreek-e-Insaf claimed that these MNAs were bribed and had violated the law. However, PDM refuted these claims, and termed the decision of dissent members as their own choice. Nevertheless, dissent of members allowed PDM to negotiate with government-allied parties —Muttahida Qaumi Movement and Pakistan and Balochistan Awami Party, proving to them that the government had gone weak and PDM already had a reasonable number to win the no-confidence motion. Ahead of the vote on the motion, Balochistan Awami Party and Muttahida Qaumi Movement-Pakistan joined the opposition alliance on 29 and 30 March 2022 respectively. As a result, opposition alliance won the vote of no confidence with 174 votes without using dissenting members, and saving the use of Article 63(A) against them. The tenure of Imran Khan as Prime Minister ended on 9 April 2022, while Shehbaz Sharif was elected as Prime Minister of Pakistan by the National Assembly of Pakistan.

In recent years, Pakistan's reliance on the West has been replaced by dependence on their close strategic allies—China, Saudi Arabia, and the Gulf states, who have provided financial help to bail out the country from economic and liquidity crises. Rollover of debt and deposits in the Central Bank to shore up reserves has been among the ways this has been achieved. Recent announcements from the UAE and Saudi Arabia stand as examples.

It, again, underlines the intersection of foreign alignments and financial help to overcome economic crisis. It also demonstrates how governments continue to look outside to rescue the country's economy when it teeters on the brink of insolvency. That Pakistan is now in its 23rd IMF programme is another testimony of this.

The habit of depending on others has become so deeply entrenched in the country's political culture that there is little, if any, questioning of this among those in power, or for that matter, in the establishment, whose leaders join in and often spearhead the effort to seek 'lifeline' funds from friendly countries. This reflects the failure of economic governance, as it involves lurching from one crisis to another with no ability to avert the next one, and with outsiders seen as stopgap answers to the cash-strapped country's perennial economic problems. Above all, this approach reduces the country to the unfortunate status of a supplicant whose economic survival depends not on itself but on others.

Pakistani leaders do not realise that living off other people's money is hardly a national achievement.

Imran Khan faced a murderous attack in November 2022, which he escaped, but still received bullet injuries. The November attack on Khan's life only intensified the burning sense of injustice in members of PTI, who have since clashed with police in escalating street battles involving slingshots and tear gas. Although, an avowed religious fanatic was arrested for the shooting, Khan continues to accuse an assortment of rival politicians of pulling the strings: incumbent Prime Minister Shehbaz Sharif, the brother of Khan's longtime opponent, former Prime Minister Nawaz Sharif, as well as Interior Minister Rana Sanaullah, and Major General Faisal Naseer. All of them have denied the accusation.

In addition to bullets, Khan has also been hit by charges—143 over the past 11 months by his count, including corruption, sedition, blasphemy, and terrorism—which he claims have been concocted in an attempt to disqualify him from politics. After Sharif's Cabinet declared on 20 March that the PTI was 'a gang of militants' whose 'enmity against the state' could not be tolerated, the police arrested hundreds of Khan's supporters in raids. 'Either Imran Khan exists or we do,' Interior Minister Sanaullah said on 26 March.

That Pakistan is moving away from the US, and closer to Russia and China is a moot point; the bigger question is who actually wins from embracing Pakistan. The $65 billion China-Pakistan Economic Corridor was supposed to be the crown jewel in President Xi Jinping's signature Belt and Road Initiative, linking China via roads, rail, and pipeline to the Arabian Sea. But Gwadar Port is rusting, and suicide bombers are taking aim at buses filled with Chinese workers. Loans are more regularly defaulted than paid.

Pakistan faces an uncertain future with TTP (Tehreek-e-Taliban Pakistan) starting its terrorist activities since January 2023 and Foreign Exchange Reserves at $4.6 billion. GDP growth is at minus 5 per cent (in negative). External debt stands at $141 billion and internal debt at Rupees (Pakistani) 63 trillion. The caretaker governments in Punjab and Khyber Pakhtunkhwa have crossed their 90-day limit but are still continuing. The term of National Assembly is ending on 17 August 2023.

The establishment lead by General Asim Munir is supporting the Shahbaz Government, and delaying the election to Punjab and KP. The orders of Pakistan Supreme Court are being flouted with impunity.

Jinnah's dream called Pakistan has surely gone sour, and traversed a difficult journey in last 76 years.

Ravinder Kumar Kaushik, IAS completed his MPhil on Pakistan from Punjab University. He joined the Civil Services in 1987 in the Punjab Cadre. Kaushik has written more than 100 articles on Pakistan in various newspapers. He also visited Pakistan multiple times for further research and study. He has been regularly addressing seminars on Pakistan in Lal Bahadur Shastri National Academy of Administration, Mussoorie, Indian Business School, Mohali, Western Command, Chandigarh, and Punjab University. He is also a fellow of the South Korean Development Institute, Seoul.

18

Comprehensive Strategy for the Northern Borders

Lieutenant General Pradeep Bali

India has an inimical neighbourhood both in the west and the north. While the western adversary has been a constant irritant, it does not pose a major threat by itself. The main issue of concern is, and will remain, China, with whom the unsettled land borders stretch across the Himalayas. China has always been difficult to comprehend by external observers, and under the rule of the CCP, it has acquired a mystique which shrouds its intent. Added to this is a complex play of words in stating policy and diplomacy, with its political trajectory firmly in the control of the communist regime.

The 20th National Congress of the CCP in October 2022 saw not only the emergence and endorsement of the paramount leader, but also was a clear pointer of how China would conduct its business on the global stage. Xi Jinping's strident stance at the G-20 summit in Indonesia, and his visit to Moscow earlier this year, in 2023, was not only a reflection of his perceived dominance as a powerful leader, but also how China now views the world. In March this year, in 2023, China's rubber-stamp parliament, the NPC, voted unanimously for Xi Jinping to be President of the country. Since he is also the Chairman of the CMC, Xi continues as the triple-hatted helmsman of communist China, at least for the foreseeable future. At the CCP Congress, the official line was very clear about the approach to local (neighbourhood) conflicts and how China intends to deal with them. These are mainly regarding Taiwan, disputes in the South China Sea (SCS), island territories with Japan, and the Trans-Himalayan conflict on the LAC with India.

While Taiwan and other maritime disputes can well be managed by a combination of deft brinkmanship, coercion, and economic influences, a major concern for China will remain the plethora of issues with India. India's ongoing security problems with China are land-centric. The unsettled land border stretching for 3,488 km along the LAC has well-identified disputed and sensitive areas. This border, which is contested all along due to the ambitiously manufactured Chinese claim lines, has become alive, or rather lively, due to their testing the waters in Eastern Ladakh with indifferent results. This uneasy state is likely to continue with new pinpricks emerging by the day. A case in point is the recent statements by the Bhutanese Government, which provide legitimacy to China, to get fully involved in settling boundary lines at the sensitive Doklam plateau, bordering Eastern Sikkim. The presence of the Dalai Lama and the Central Tibetan Administration-in-exile on Indian soil has always been a sore point in bilateral relations. Added to all this, China sees India as the sole challenger to its regional domination in Asia, which it aspires to as a prelude to global superpower status. Resolving these irritants with India on its terms would therefore gain priority for the CCP leadership in the days ahead.

As an emerging superpower, which seeks parity with the USA on the global stage, China needs to have Armed Forces with matching capabilities. Whether it can meet the self-imposed deadline of a fully modernised PLA by 2027 or not, the world is likely to witness an increasingly assertive China, which will tend to seek and take on a more influential role far beyond its shores, and this will need the backing of military muscle. A clear pointer is the timeline of the PLA Navy for acquiring a sizeable number of aircraft carriers, which would be a prerequisite for expeditionary forces.

A superpower that dominates the world through its influence and impact on geopolitics and strategic issues should have a safe and secure homeland, well insulated from any threat or disputes, at least on its immediate borders. The US is the prime example of this, as fortress America has never experienced any direct dangers except the terror attack of 9/11. In this vein, China would want to ensure its dominance in the region with no nettlesome issues affecting its own borders.

To safeguard our national interests, and to deter China from inimical actions, whether military or non-military in their scope, India needs to adopt a comprehensive strategy, some of which is already falling in place but at a slow and limited pace. The military dimension of such a strategy can only be a sub-set of the whole, which must necessarily include diplomatic and economic strategies, as well as a technological underpinning, which is apace with the latest developments in that field. A comprehensive approach, and not a strait-jacketed military formulation of strategy, is what is required.

First and foremost, India must be proactive in dealing with the Northern adversary. Militarily, we have always been reactive, whether it was the debacle of 1962, or even when the PLA got a bloody nose in 1967 at Nathu La and Cho La in Eastern Sikkim. At Sumdrong Chu in Arunachal in 1986, Doklam in 2017, and presently in Eastern Ladakh, the responses were a consequence of aggressive actions by the PLA. China, apart from maintaining a belligerent military posture, would amply harness media and psychological propaganda to look for every opportunity to keep India in a reactive mode while dragging on with any dispute resolution mechanisms.

For India, being pro-active does not necessarily imply being aggressive, but rather being pre-emptive in our planning and actions, to counter any perfidy by outguessing the adversary. It also means having credible deterrence capabilities, which, in fact, is the desired state against China. Here, it is essential to understand some ground realities relevant to our national security, and the geo-political situation as it exists. To be a great power, India needs a large and modern navy with a trans-oceanic reach, adequately equipped with surface, sub-surface, and aerial platforms for varying roles. While the Navy is a potent player in furthering diplomatic reach, it also needs to be counted while tabulating force parities and deterrence capabilities, especially against our northern adversary. The maritime role is not a standalone exercise, and acquisitions like aircraft carriers should amply complement the efforts of the land forces deployed along the Himalayas. In the same vein, the Air Force must possess the capability not only to guard our vast air space but also to provide operational reach and effective air support to the field army, thereby enhancing its deterrent value.

Further, credible deterrence should not be viewed in quantifying military capabilities alone. Military preparedness must be in concert with diplomatic efforts of the same, if not greater, intensity, if they have to be meaningful and credible. A proactive thought process, which is in sync with the efforts of our Armed Forces on the borders, should be the defining character of our diplomacy. The other organs of the state should be similarly aligned whether in harnessing technology for defence needs, development of infrastructure, or generation of material resources. This whole-nation approach is a must when dealing with a country like China.

India's three-pronged approach to resolving the stalemate in Eastern Ladakh—disengagement, de-escalation, and de-induction of troops—does not seem to be gaining any traction with the Chinese political and military leadership. The billeting capacity for PLA units in this high-altitude sector of Southern Xinjiang has increased exponentially for well over 1,00,000 soldiers. There have been some major military and infrastructure improvements by the PLA in the last three years since the stand-off began, which include commissioning long-range artillery and rocket systems, upgrading air defence systems, expanding runways, and hardening blast pens to house fighter aircraft in the area. While a military conflict, even a limited one, seems unlikely, the Chinese army is in no hurry to de-induct from the contact points along the LAC.

China is also planning to build another highway through Aksai Chin, running opposite the Indian border, and connecting Xinjiang with Tibet, expected to be completed by 2035. The G-695 national expressway will be the second highway through the disputed Aksai Chin region, where China controls 38,000 sq km of land claimed by India, since the controversial construction of the G-219 highway in the 1950s.

While the Chinese forces may have been deterred from any misadventure across the LAC, having seen the reactions of the Indian army, both at Doklam in 2017 and now in East Ladakh, they will continue to jockey for a position of strength. The most glaring example is the way they have circumvented any blockade by the Indian Army at Doklam. Having made rapid progress with their road construction along the Amo Chu on the eastern flank of Chumbi Valley, the PLA has reached the southern tip of this valley, outflanking Doklam from the east and are now poised close to the Jampheri Ridge from where the strategic Siliguri corridor, connecting India to its northeast, is just around 40 km. The construction and inhabitation of three Chinese border villages, well inside Bhutanese territory in the Amo Chu river valley, which is very close to the Doklam border conflict point, is now virtually complete. The economic and cartographic clout that China is attempting to wield over Bhutan was apparent in the ambivalent statements emerging from the 'Hermit Kingdom' with the tacit acceptance of involving China in resolving the tri-junction with India at the Doklam plateau.

For ensuring an effective deterrence strategy against China, we have to look both within and outside. There should be no shying away from highlighting our own capabilities and vast experience in high-altitude warfare. Along the 3,488 km India-China LAC, there are areas where the terrain and deployment are quite favourable for us. There is a definite need to be more assertive in such dominating locations, and give clear signalling of intent when required, by stressing *quid pro quo* options. Infrastructure development and induction of equipment need not only to be prioritised, but also publicised, to ensure a more balanced narrative than what it is now. While a game of brinkmanship is fraught with dangers, the Army must resolutely continue facing up to the PLA. The Indian Army of 2023 is not what it was in 1962, and is quite capable of staring down 'the dragon', with an unblinking stance. This struggle will be ours alone as other nations will have little interest in calling out Chinese intransigence along the LAC. Therefore, we cannot be just reactive. We must clearly visualise our capabilities and demonstrate a readiness to use these.

There is no gainsaying that the Chinese military focuses on regions away from our borders would be in our interest. All policymakers must meet competing demands over limited resources, including long-term investments in future capabilities, and short-term spending on readiness. The PLA's modernisation goals appear affordable, at least over the next decade, and it can maintain, expand, and improve its regional defence forces. However, to match its self-image as a great power, China is investing in building a range of power projection platforms for global operations, including aircraft carriers, cruisers, destroyers, blue water logistics vessels, submarines, and long-range aircraft. The PLA, particularly the Navy, will face increasing strain from operations and maintenance costs over the next decade due to its rapid procurement of large surface combatants. The sequencing of China's force structure investments indicates the prioritisation of its strategic objectives. This indicates that Taiwan and the SCS continue to have precedence over China's wider global ambitions. Its threatening language and actions, in trying to dissuade any contact between Taiwan and US political leaders, further highlights its edginess on such matters. To pay for investments in its priority categories, China may go for reduction and cuts in the ground forces of the PLA. Despite large reductions of PLA Army personnel and units over the last several decades, further downsizing may be needed to free up funds sufficient to realise China's strategic goals in the maritime direction. This is where the Quadrilateral Security Dialogue (QUAD) strategic grouping of India, the United States, Australia, and Japan can play a key role by being militarily more visible in the SCS, to which China would always be hypersensitive. It would well serve Indian interests to support and encourage quadrilateral naval exercises in the region. The increasing presence of QUAD navies in the SCS would impact Chinese planners in recalibrating defence spending more towards the PLA Navy with a relative reduction for the ground forces.

India also needs to hedge its bets by not only remaining militarily prepared against China, but also looking for meaningful strategic partnerships. While it makes sense to be in concert with dominant and leading world powers on strategic issues that are aligned with our national interests, what would be of great significance is to invest in a wholesome manner in deepening our relations and partnerships with countries in Asia with whom we can have a convergence of views vis-à-vis China. Vietnam, a very proud country that has a history of getting the better of France, the USA and China, should be top of the list. The other big player of significance in Asia is Indonesia. Its size, strategic location, and history of being colonised make Indonesia a country capable of standing up to the crude bullying that China has made its weapon of choice to realise its maritime claims. The relationship with this country, in the context of China, needs a major overhaul, and should be the focus of our foreign policy. Singapore, though not a nation which is likely to get militarily embroiled in any conflict, has key advantages in aligning with India. With the present political leadership in Bangladesh, bilateral relations have remained on an upward trajectory. The positives of this relationship need to translate into permanency, which goes beyond changes in political leadership. Relationships with countries mentioned are national assets that we can build on as a counter to China.

China, under the Communist rule, has built up a large technological base for military use, and claims niche capabilities next only to the USA. Its economic linkages with most European nations have also seen the flow of technology into China. It has taken very rapid strides in the fields of robotics, quantum computing and communications, artificial intelligence, energy capture and storage, smart sensors, and biomaterials. All these would be the primary drivers in any multi-domain non-contact warfare against an adversary.

How does the Indian Military match up? Budgetary constraints and labyrinthine processes have undoubtedly been a dampener in the acquisition of military weapons and equipment. However, this is not something which cannot be corrected. What is relevant here is a look at our capacities and capabilities in the technological fields related to contact, and more importantly, non-contact warfare. Indian scientists have made remarkable progress in the fields of space research and missile technology. Similar momentum is required in other dimensions of non-contact conflict. The leading technical education institutions of India are populated by faculty and students who can provide top-rate technical solutions to the plethora of technological problems and requirements for developing equipment related to different domains of warfare. As this gains momentum, systems will have to be put in place for the transfer of technology, from prototype to assembly line products.

The border stand-off in Eastern Ladakh with the PLA, which began in mid-2020, has entered a stalemate phase, with the latest round of talks achieving little progress, and the Indian Army formations committed to the bleak and hostile terrain for the long haul. The only time these talks were followed up in right earnest was when Indian troops occupied the important features on the Kailash range, south of Pangong Tso, which effectively dominated forward posts of the PLA. The Chinese were quick to concede on a *quid pro quo* basis, and even dismantled habitat and other structures while pulling back along the north bank of Pangong Tso. This was a clear indicator that China respects and listens when spoken to from a position of strength. The rapid PLA withdrawal after the brawl at Yangtse in the Tawang sector appeared to be in the same vein.

The fact of the matter is this unease will continue along the LAC and we have to live with it as the PLA will endeavour for a more aggressive approach in gaining positions of advantage anywhere along our northern borders. At the same time, China will continue to stress de-linking border scuffles from overall bilateral relations, while India will emphasise on a holistic approach with peace on the borders as a pre-requisite. The meeting between the Defence Ministers of India and China, as a precursor to the Shanghai Cooperation Organisation dialogue at New Delhi in April 2023, was on much the same lines. The Minister for External Affairs has adequately highlighted in various forums the current abnormality of India-China relations due to the disturbed situation on the borders. The on-ground implication is for the Indian Army with increased year-round deployment in hostile terrain and weather.

India is neither expansionist nor covets foreign territory or aspires to act as a global security provider on its own. The primary role of our Armed Forces is to deter war against the country and prosecute operations to safeguard our territorial integrity in case deterrence fails. Given the adversarial relationships with our northern neighbour, it is imperative to maintain and equip the three services with state-of-the-art weapons, technology and platform-centric systems, so that desired deterrence levels are maintained. With this in place, if the disputes along the LAC are managed with resolve and sagacity, actual occurrence of a large dimension conventional conflict may well be deterred. At worst, face-offs and intrusions could lead to local clashes, which would lie in the domain of the army with support from the air force. It is within these parameters that the creation of theatre commands must come about, achieving greater synergy and optimisation of the national assets and capabilities.

The only panacea against this threat to national security is being prepared on all counts, be it militarily or diplomatically, including pre-emption when required. We need a pro-active mindset to deter China, as the Chinese Communists are firmly committed to maximising their power in the world, and we happen to be their neighbours, with a turbulent relationship between us.

Lieutenant General Pradeep Bali, AVSM, VSM commanded the Army Corps in Sikkim during the Doklam crisis with the PLA, and oversaw its aftermath. He also served as a Military Diplomat in Japan and South Korea. He writes extensively on strategic and military issues for newspapers and defence publications.

4

The Strategic World

19

Russia-Ukraine War: Military Strategy and Operational Art

Lieutenant General Jasbir Lidder

The art of war is of vital importance to the state. It is a matter of life and death, a road either to safety or to ruin. Hence it is a subject of inquiry which can no account be neglected.

—*Sun Tzu, The Art of War*

Russia's territorial aggression, referred to as a 'special military operation' by President Putin more than a year ago, has made the world insecure and unstable, something not been witnessed since WWII. Efforts to stop the war have not succeeded. Though the conflict has been restricted to Europe, the unintended and undesirable consequences have impacted the entire world.

The Russia-Ukraine war has given traction to deglobalisation and hardened the 'Western' versus 'Russian' geopolitical narratives. Security and economic priorities have relegated to other conflict landscapes and exacerbated humanitarian impact, particularly in food and energy. Before the war commenced in 2022, the estimated global economic growth was five per cent, which now stands at just 3.1 per cent, and is expected to be 2.2 per cent in 2023. The war has had the greatest shock effect on Europe's economy, where growth in 2023 is projected to be just 0.3 per cent.[1] The reconstruction cost would be between $350–500 billion.

The war has transformed Europe from an economic cooperative continent to a Euro-Atlantic strategic construct. Russia has survived the war despite diplomatic isolation and economic sanctions. Russia's GDP contracted by 2.1 per cent in 2022, much less than the predicted five to six per cent – the gap having got cushioned by the subsidised oil and gas sales and revenues from hydrocarbon production and exports.[2]

Wars are the best teacher of war. The Russia-Ukraine war has thrown up stunningly unexpected results, carrying important strategic and operational lessons for both policymakers and warfighters. The analysis is based on assessed operational effectiveness following a top-down approach. There are three caveats: Firstly, since the war is ongoing, the operational status and deductions are subject to review. Secondly, with the lack of clarity from the Russian side, many accounts are based on available data. Thirdly, the main effort is to deliberate on matters military, which in no way undermines other instruments of war.

The Conduct of War

> *Tactics teaches the use of armed forces in the engagement; strategy the use of engagements for the object of the war.*
>
> —*Carl von Clausewitz, On War*

Force Structures

Russia vastly outnumbers Ukraine's military in the defence budget, active military personnel on duty, fleet size, and other military hardware. Russia has more than 9,00,000 active military personnel on duty compared to Ukraine's 3,61,000. Russia's military spending in 2020 was $61.7 billion, ten times more than that of Ukraine's $5.9 billion, as per Stockholm International Peace Research Institute.[3]

Russia deployed roughly 1,42,000 troops on land for the attack. They comprised 110 Battalion Tactical Groups (BTGs), each structured on one tank company of 10 tanks (mix of T-72, T-80 and a few T-90) and three infantry companies of 30 armoured personnel carriers (20 tracked and 10 wheeled)[4]—the majority of the equipment being twentieth-century vintage. The troops comprised the regular army, irregular forces, and militias from Donetsk and Luhansk. The ground forces were augmented by air, naval, and cyber support.[5]

Ukraine had 10 brigades covering the entire line of contact, with limited reserves for counterattack and ammunition. The Ukraine Armed

Forces (UAF) fielded about 30 tank battalions at the start of the conflict numbering 900 tanks, comprising T-64 and up-gunned T-72. Ukraine fielded the largest artillery force in Europe after Russia, comprising 152 mm guns, howitzers, and Multiple Launch Rocket Systems (MRLS). The difference in numbers between Russian and Ukrainian artillery was not so significant at the beginning of the conflict—2,433 barrel artillery systems against 1,176, and 3,547 MLRS against 1,680.[6]

The Campaign

Russia's strategic objective was to capture Ukraine through a swift offensive, estimated to last a few days. The military build-up commenced in March 2021, to muscle-flex annexation on the lines of Crimea – 2014. The 'special military operation' looks conceived around a few key assumptions—firstly, speed being critical to success to render the response of the international community irrelevant; secondly, to defeat an inferior Ukrainian military using multiple advances, causing attrition, and generating surrenders; thirdly, having captured Kiev and major towns, remove Ukraine's governance and mobilise pro-Russian Ukrainians to support the occupation; lastly, coerce the non-supportive population into submission by denying basic civic amenities.[7]

The Russian ground forces invaded Ukraine on 24 February 2022, activating four main fronts (see map) – Northern (pushed toward Kyiv from Belarus, employing three combined armies), Northeastern (moving west toward Kiev from Russian territory by two combined armies), Eastern (towards Kharkiv and out of Donbas by a tank army and two combined armies), and Southern (from Crimea West towards Odesa, north towards Zaporizhzhia and east towards Mariupol by air assault division, air assault brigade, and three combined armies).[8]

The secrecy attained through the political posturing of 'no attack' appears to have achieved strategic deception, with the Russian military making swift gains. However, Kyiv could not be captured—the major contributor towards the stout defence of the capital being the Irpin River, a water obstacle exploited militarily against invaders for centuries.[9] The tactical deadlock led to a strategic crisis.

Under operational outstretch, Russia began to withdraw forces from Kyiv around April 2022, and concentrated its efforts on eastern and southern Ukraine. Thereafter, the 'West' became Ukraine's strategic depth and the UAF seized the initiative, recapturing Kherson and Kharkov. Concurrently, Russian logistics started to come under long-range bombardment.[10]

Original Russian Axes of Advance

The Ukraine theatre stands deadlocked in a war of attrition, akin to the trench warfare of WWI. The strategic stalemate is corroborated in the recent American war leaks, which predict a higher level of mutual attrition, with neither side capable of mustering superior military capability to gain any decisive advantage.[11]

The battle line frontage is roughly 600 miles that extends just west of Kherson along the Black Sea, and moves east through Melitopol, Mariupol, and other southern cities. It then cuts northeast through the Donbas in eastern Ukraine, including the cities of Luhansk and Donetsk, continues northwest near Izyum, and then intersects the Russian border north of Kharkiv.[12] Bakhmut grapples in a prestigious confrontation where months of vigorous fighting left thousands dead.

In attrition warfare, a successful side is one that can replace its soldiers and equipment more readily. As the war prolongs, the Russians hope their industrial depth and larger manpower mobilisation will provide long-term strategic advantage. Meanwhile, Ukraine fights for its existential survival, with its resolute population as the force multiplier, supported by a sustained flow of modern war inventory. The long-term dilemma on both sides is to fund the stagnating conflict or improve their economies.[13]

Doctrine and Military Strategy

> *Battle then is the means of the operation. Tactics are the material of operational art. The operation is the means of strategy, and operational art is the material of strategy.*
>
> *—N.E. Varfolomeev, Russian Strategist, 1933*

Geostrategic Context: NATO has come out strongly to support Ukraine and is treading the right line in providing the weapons they need, while avoiding too high a risk of escalation with Russia.[14] For the sagging American arms industry, the war is a boon, with sales of over $46 billion. The latest deliveries include M1 Abrams tanks, infantry combat vehicles, Patriot and S-300 missiles, and various forms of artillery.[15]

NATO stands expanded and strengthened, with Finland as the newest member, and Sweden awaiting entry. Brussels has also intensified engagement efforts in the Western Balkans. However, differences exist in the EU on the level of involvement in the war, which may get recalculated with domestic politics. There are also differing perceptions on Europe's 'strategic autonomy' while emerging as the 'third power', in particular, on balancing relations between America and China.

The war has shifted European thinking about Russia as an enduring military threat, leading to increased defence spending and the decoupling of the economy. The blowing up of 1224 Nord Stream pipelines under the Baltic Sea has severed Euro-Russian energy relations, as Europe looks for alternative supply chains.[16] Europe's eastern flank countries are rearming on a major scale. Poland and the Baltic states have been at the forefront in resisting Russia, while Hungary and Belarus have maintained a pro-Russian stance.

Russia's defence collaboration and economic relationships, in particular with China, India, and South Africa, have helped to garner support. China's lead in sponsoring a ceasefire through a 12-point peace plan has received limited endorsement.[17] Notwithstanding, the 'strategic friendship' with Russia (driven by common US rivalry) is being demonstrated through diplomatic and economic assistance.

Beijing's reach may, nevertheless, remain short of lethal military transfers requested by the Russians, as President Xi walks the tightrope on China's geoeconomic impact. Closer home, Belarus is proving Russia's most willing partner, offering bases, including for nuclear weapons.[18]

Russia's inability to achieve a swift and decisive victory, with pronounced battle reverses and equipment failures, has bruised its military professionalism and modernisation reforms. The reputational damage carries significant strategic implications, and can impact future defence engagements and arms transfers, as partnering countries search for alternative alliances or technologies.

Strategic Culture

Russia issued its updated version of the National Security Strategy (NSS 2021) two years ago, based on which its military doctrine is developed. Military action forms an integral part of political objectives.[19] Russian operations have historically developed in the conventional military spectrum for territorial conquest. The 'deep battle' doctrine is based on the concentration of mass, mobility, and firepower with operational manoeuvre on the 'extended battlefield'. The doctrine conceptualises *Operativnoe Iskusstvo* (operational art) for depth in space and time, *Maskirovka* (surprise, security, and deception), and operational shock.[20]

Unconventional operations are critical to Russia's successive theories of victory, even as its conventional forces fail to achieve their objectives on the battlefield.[21] Russian military campaigns from 2008–2022 have, thus, been marked by swift employment of heavy conventional force, comprising highly survivable tank forces.[22] There was clearly a desire to achieve both military and political objectives in Ukraine within a short time frame using asymmetric advantage.

Nuclear deterrence is an important constituent of Russia's doctrine. Hence, the periodic threats of tactical nukes for brinkmanship. The suspension of participation in the New START demonstrates Moscow's leverage in dismantling all treaties and formats for dialogue.[23] If ever President Putin decides to cross the nuclear threshold, it may get justified as a 'weapon of last resort' against the existential threats to Russia.[24]

The military strategies of Russia and Ukraine have been divergent. Russia initially engaged in some fast-moving manoeuvres to attain rapid and decisive victory, but over time changed its strategy to mass strike weapons with extended ranges. UAF has been comparatively adaptive to the changing warfare, and exploited precision-guided weaponry.

Ukraine has also been fighting on its own territory, and limited itself to targeting Russia's military, while the Russians have been targeting Ukraine as a whole. These contrasting approaches—the 'classic warfare' pursued by Ukraine, and the 'total warfare' adopted by Russia—have deep roots in the wars of the twentieth century.[25]

Legitimacy and Ethics

The Russian aggression violates the UN Charter, notwithstanding any historical or ideological rationality. While the Security Council remained inactively polarised, the General Assembly was vocal in passing resolutions on March 2022 and February 2023, calling for an end to the war, and demanding Russia's immediate withdrawal from the country. Notably, there were absentees messaging non-consensual ambivalence.

Moscow has been accused of breaching International Humanitarian Law (IHL) in its pursuit of military objectives, going beyond 'military necessity' in the use of force. While the primary fire delivery has been on the Ukraine military, the breadth of Russian strikes has led to heavy civilian casualties and targeted damage to economic infrastructure. President Putin has since been indicted by the International Criminal Court (ICC) for war crimes with warrants issued for arrest.[26] As the war subsides, military excesses warrant scrutiny across the board, cutting across geography and nationality.

Cognitive and moral dimensions are fundamental to military effectiveness and fighting power. A factor differentiating professional armies from mobs is battlefield discipline, enforced through principled training and ethical accountability. The use of private military and security companies (PMSC), like the Prigozhin-led Wagner Group, comprising mercenaries and non-national volunteers, raises the worrying issue of battle commercialisation and criminalisation.[27]

Operational Art

Strategy without tactics is the slow road to victory but tactics without strategy is just noise before defeat.

—Sun Tzu[28]

The Prussian general and military theorist, Carl von Clausewitz, wrote that war is filled with unpredictability and that 'in war more than anywhere else in the world things happen differently to what we had expected'.[29] The political objective of overthrowing the Kiev government appears to have triggered the 'special military operation', aimed at blitzkrieg seizure of the capital. Though swift advance gave Russians a 12:1 force ratio advantage north of Kyiv, the offensive could not result in operational success.

Complex wars demand a comprehensive assessment of the national perspective. This process should help conceptualise an integrative military strategy, translating war objectives into operational plans. Russian plans for the war appear to have been drawn by a group of selected officials close to President Putin.

Whether the invasion was strategically converged by the Russian General Staff for protracted long-drawn campaigning, or war-gamed for non-sequential scenarios with attacking troops. remains ambiguous. The gaps in the planning and initial execution are now becoming difficult to fix.

Having stalled in the initial forays, the Russian higher leadership made a faint effort to challenge the battle evidence and revise the operational course. This could be due to diminished capability, excessive conventional warfare confidence, or overdependence on the unconventional tools of covert operations which form an integral part of campaigning.[30] With operational reversals, top commanders have been frequently changed. General Valery Gerasimov is in command, having taken over a few months back from Sergey Surovikin, who, too, had been appointed for the job a few months before.

Within the strategic culture of centralised command and control, and sequential application of force, Russian BTGs found it difficult to obtain operational agility for seizing and holding territory. The Russian ground units are now being reorganised into smaller assault detachments with increased infantry content for enhanced survivability. Ironically, most attacking troops in the initial phase were mobilised, briefed, and equipped for collective training, therefore, not mentally conditioned for combat.[31]

The UAF has acquitted itself reasonably well against a force with a significant advantage in material resources and battle experience, motivated by a spirit of survival nationalism and adaptation to Multi-Domain Operations (MDO).[32] Ukraine's convergence of new capabilities in command and control, pervasive surveillance, and mass precision fires may prove to be the game-changer in this war.[33]

Events in Ukraine indicate that a planned swift-and-decisive war may prolong, testing strategic patience and human perseverance. Both sides appear to have reached the 'culminating point' (described as a *Kulminationspunkt* by Clausewitz in his book *On War*), as neither side can muster resources to maintain their operation (an assessment endorsed in the US war leaks too).[34]

The war is redefining urban warfare, with major cities of Mariupol, Sievierodonetsk, Lysychanskand, and Bekhmut being designated as strategic and operational objectives. Extended sieges with high-intensity warfare have inflicted major damage to Ukraine's life and property. Amongst this, the Ukrainian citizenry has risen to fight a 'whole-of-societal war', with women playing a variety of crucial roles in the resistance, including participation in combat.[35]

The captured enclaves are difficult to hold against a hostile population, and with prolonged stand-offs, these could turn into hubs of guerrilla-based urban insurgency. The success in urban warfare is not through methodical clearing, but by combined-arms manoeuvre, integrating fire, armour, infantry and engineers, and by finding, fixing, and destroying hidden or embedded enemy with innovative tactics.[36]

Manoeuvre and Firepower

The 'return of the tank' has evoked mixed attention. The Russian fleet of 2,800 (mix of T-72, T-80 with few T-90) with superior protection and sensors has a distinct advantage over the updated Ukrainian fleet in short-term engagements. Yet, the Russians lost tanks in hundreds. The armour met success in open terrain and where the defences were thin but got bogged down in areas offering restricted mobility, becoming targets to precision anti-tank weapons. Within the land forces, the battle results have reignited the debate between a tank being pushed into obsolescence or remaining a protected lethal offensive weapon system for mobile warfare.[37]

The unexpectedly large tank losses are being attributed to three factors—lack of warning and preparation, conceptual weakness in the employment of BTGs with inadequate infantry and logistics follow-ups, and vulnerability to long-range drones and anti-tank weapons. While US-supplied top-attack Javelin missiles and UK's NLAW took the publicity, Carl Gustav recoilless rifles and Rocket-propelled Grenades (RPGs) remained effective.[38]

With sizeable losses of modern fleet, including the most advanced T-90, the Russians are increasingly equipping their newly-mobilised battalions with obsolete T-62 and T-80B.[39] So, while Russians may still have enough machines to fight, they are likely to face technological asymmetry against the new Ukrainian fleet of M1 Abrams (USA), Leopard 2 (Germany), Challenger 2 (UK) and T-72 M1 (Poland). As and when these heavy tanks get properly integrated into other additions of infantry fighting vehicles, air defence systems, and longer-range artillery, options for a counter-offensive by Ukraine exist.[40]

With airpower absent, artillery (Stalin's 'the god of war') has taken centre stage.[41] The Russian doctrine advocates the use of massed guns to weaken and demoralise the enemy before sending in large numbers of infantry to seize territory. Artillery duels comprising precision-ammunition cannons and long-range precision high mobility artillery rocket systems (HIMARS) are being witnessed extensively in cities, infrastructure, and depth areas, with heavy to very heavy ammunition expenditure.

The future of artillery lies in high rates of fire, cross-country mobility, reduced or simplified maintenance, and long tube life.[42] Artillery's employment beyond a stage needs recalibration as the defender discovers measures to protect, and the resupply of precision-ammunition stocks becomes logistically strenuous. To win battles, physical captures by infantry-armour-engineer task forces remain an operational necessity.

Maritime and Air

The war is seeing expeditionary maritime and air assets become vulnerable to the electromagnetic spectrum and long-range precision-guided weaponry, leaving land forces to fight battles with their integral firepower. This has generated comments on strategic beliefs in such costly defence investments.[43]

The conflict theatre has been largely absent of airpower, the Russians having failed to achieve air superiority. The Russian Aerospace Forces (VKS) conducted extensive fixed-wing strike operations during the initial stages, where Ukrainian ground-based air defence (GBAD) got suppressed.[44] The attempt to establish an airbridge by capturing the Antonov airport, through a special operation (reminiscent of Arnhem 1944, a bridge too far), failed.[45] VKS, thereafter, lost its ability to operate in the battlefield space, except at very low altitudes—contested by Ukrainian surface-to-air missile (SAM) systems.

Russia's big fleet of aircraft looks inadequately maintained, and faces outstretched logistical support in fuel and spare parts. In the absence of air superiority, ground-based missiles and drones are getting recognised as key instruments of air power.[46] Russia's strategic attacks have, accordingly, shifted to cruise and ballistic missile barrages, but on a much more limited scale. These could not inflict the required decisive damage during the first seven months. However, in the latter part of 2022, there appears to be a more focused bombardment of the Ukrainian electricity grid and other larger targets.

The Russian Black Sea Fleet had the ability to operate in close proximity to Ukrainian shores. However, the successful attack on the fleet's flagship, *Moskva*, with UAF's indigenous Neptune anti-ship cruise missiles, and the subsequent Russian defeat at Snake Island, reduced the naval threats.[47] The Black Sea grain initiative of July 2022 is allowing Russia and Ukraine to export essential humanitarian food through a safe shipping channel. Russia can, however, shift its military focus to a naval blockade if ground operations continue to face failures.

Strategic Communications

The ambitious plan to invade the largest country in Europe must have been based on years of intelligence gathering and military planning; yet, it looks that Russian military planners either overestimated their ability to achieve strategic objectives, or underestimated the level of Ukrainian resistance that they would encounter.[48] Astonishingly, the Russians embarked on a major war using cell phones and old-fashioned radios, which were successfully intercepted by the UAF, resulting in targeted fatalities, with overreliance on technology becoming a single point of failure.

The UAF have, by and large, maintained an edge in both strategic and operational intelligence, the inputs being provided by a vast variety of AI tools, commercial satellites or drones, NATO inputs, and open-source extraction. The cellphone-based Delta system provides the UAF with an understanding of the battle space in real-time, by integrating intelligence, and command and control functions.[49]

The multi-domain spectrum of space, cyber, and electromagnetic (EW) is underutilised and unintegrated.[50] Russian forces failed to conduct effective EW during the war's opening phase, their unencrypted communications providing a wealth of intelligence to Ukraine. The UAF learnt to manage its cyber defence as the war progressed, actively supported by NATO cyber security systems, commercialised sources (Starlink satellite terminals), and a volunteer Ukraine vigilante cyber-army.[51]

Information is the dominant instrument of war, with credible narratives influencing impressions and opinions in cyberspace. Ukraine gained an 'information advantage' by projecting itself as a war victim, done by proactive messaging through commercial media. Social media is flooded with stories, live images, and videos communicated by influencers and soldiers directly from the battlefront.[52] Contrarily, Russia's narrative or counter-narratives are on restricted platforms, and carry credibility risk due to authoritative control of information flow.

Operational Logistics

Logistics win wars – perhaps the greatest lesson of 2022. The developments in Ukraine are an example that if a nation has to go to war, it must align its operational plans with necessary resources in logistics and sustainment. Wars demand large stockpiles and significant slack capacity. There is no sanctuary, and with extended reach, the enemy can strike throughout the operational depth. Ukraine successfully evaded Russia's initial wave of strikes by dispersing its aircraft, critical arsenal, ammunition stocks, command and control headquarters, and maintenance areas.

The Russian military is facing logistics challenges. Its vintage rail-and-road-based support system has proved unsuitable for high-attrition expeditionary operations. The supply lines have not supported deep thrusts, and without access to rail transport, and with roads clogged with destroyed vehicles, forward troops have run out of fuel, munitions, and spare parts.[53]

Further, plans to wage war along the entire Ukrainian border not only exacerbated the aforementioned logistical problems, but hindered the objective of concentrating capabilities and achieving overwhelming mass and firepower in given sectors. Russia's ability to regenerate residual combat power and produce critical war equipment by revitalising its long-term economic growth to pre-war levels is essential.[54]

An important part of Kyiv's battlefield performance is informal security assistance, coming in a wide range of non-lethal equipment from non-state channels. Since no formal procedures are involved, the deliveries are timely. Such provisioning of logistical support for warfighting could classically be termed within irregular warfare.[55]

Leadership – The Final Frontier

> *In its ultimate relationship to the human understanding, the central idea or doctrine is nothing else than common sense – that is action adapted to circumstance.*
>
> —*JFC Fuller, 1926*

War is the art and science of strategy influencing politics, the military, and the economy. Yet, inherently, it remains a people-centric activity, requiring leaders who handle complex human behaviour. In blurred conflicts, victory may not necessarily be objective, but based and projected on population's emotions and perceptions of political leaders. But for the military, the results are objective and transparent – success or failure. President Putin's war objectives have been driven by his political ambition, and have undergone multiple changes—occupation of Kyiv, military victory in Donbas, energy shortfall, and presently to exhaust Ukraine as a state. The narrative of 'victory' is being adapted to influence the host and Russian sympathetic populations.[56] For Volodymyr Zelenskyy, the war is being fought on his own territory, and being directed empathetically on the spirit of nationhood survival—a classic case of 'leading with a cool head and a warm heart'.[57]

There is a need to draw the right lessons from historical experience. The Russian army is inclined to template WWII prescriptions, hesitating to restructure and re-strategise. Unfortunately, many in the senior military leadership got killed by battle casualness—cellphone tracking, partisans, and informants.[58] The Russian Army is in the process of recruiting fresh manpower through 'partial military conscription', which carries huge responsibility for turning the tide.

The battles are won by junior leaders. Ukraine's investment in developing an empowered non-commissioned officer corps is proving to be the edge. The UAF has transformed over the years with socio-economic contracts, and built a command climate that encourages operational innovation and specialised skills demanded by modern conflicts.

At the end of the day, rivets and steel are not as important as flesh and bone on the battlefield.[59] Militaries require competent and morally upright commanders who understand the character of contemporary wars and 'romanticise' warfare for victory.

Lieutenant General Jasbir Lidder, UYSM, AVSM, a Grenadiers 1971 war veteran, commanded a brigade on the LoC and a counter-insurgency force in Kashmir. He has been UN Force Commander and Deputy Special Representative of the Secretary General (Political) in Sudan. An expert in conflict management and peacekeeping, he is sought as a speaker, mentor, and author in UN institutions and international think tanks.

Endnotes

1. Rand, *Consequences of War in Ukraine: The Economic Fallout,* Brain Michael Jenkins, 7 March 2023
2. Aljazeera, *Russia After a Year of Sanctions*, Sergey Aleksashenko, 28 February 2023
3. GlobalData.com, *Russia and Ukraine Military Comparison;* https://www.globaldata.com/data-insights/macroeconomic/russia-and-ukraine-military-comparison-overview/
4. Forbes, *How Many tanks Does Russia Have in Ukraine and How Many has it Lost so far?* David Hambling, 15 March 2022
5. Centre for Strategic and International Studies (CSIS), *Russia's Ill-fated Invasion of Ukraine: Lessons in Modern Warfare,* Seth G. Jones, 1 June 2022
6. RUSI, *Preliminary Lessons in Conventional Warfighting from Russia's Invasion of Ukraine,* Mykhaylo Zabrodskyi, Jack Watling, Oleksandr V. Danylyuk and Nick Reynolds, 20 November 2023
7. Ibid
8. Centre for Strategic and International Studies (CSIS), *Russia's Ill-fated Invasion of Ukraine: Lessons in Modern Warfare,* Seth G. Jones, 1 June 2022
9. The Guardian, *Ukraine's 'Hero River' helped Save Kyiv; But What Now for its Newly Restored Wetlands?* Vincent Mundy, 11 May 2022
10. Centre for Strategic and International Studies (CSIS), *Russia's Ill-fated Invasion of Ukraine: Lessons in Modern Warfare,* Seth G. Jones, 1 June 2022
11. ACNA, *Commentary: Pentagon Leaks Paint Gloomy Picture of Long Ukraine War that Can't be Won, but Must not be Lost,* Stefan Wolff, 15 April 2023
12. Ibid
13. Wall Street Journal, *Putin Wouldn't Win a War of Attrition in Ukraine,* Douglas London, 24 March 2023
14. Crisis Group, *Global Politics in the Shadow of Ukraine,* Comfort Ero, 22 March 2023
15. BBC News, *Ukraine Weapons: What Tanks and Other Equipment are the World Giving?* David Brown, Jake Horton and Tural Ahmedzade, 22 February 2023
16. War on the Rocks, *Permanent Rupture: the European-Russian Energy Relationship has Ended with Nord Stream,* Emily Holland, 3 October 2022
17. Firstpost, *Ukraine's Volodymyr Zelensky to meet Xi Jinping after China Proposes Peace Plan: What is Beijing's 12-point Proposal,* explainers, 27 February 2023
18. Reuters, *Belarus Says it Will Host Russia Nuclear Weapons to counter NATO,* Andrew Osborn, 28 March 2023
19. NATO Defense College, *Russia's Updated National Security Strategy,* Julian Cooper, 19 July 2021
20. Strategic and Combat Studies Institute, *The Occasional Number 30: The Development of Soviet Military Doctrine,* John Erickson, September 1997
21. RUSI, *Preliminary Lessons in Conventional Warfighting from Russia's Invasion of Ukraine,* Mykhaylo Zabrodskyi, Jack Watling, Oleksandr V. Danylyuk, and Nick

Reynolds, 20 November 2023
22. NATO Defense College, NDC policy brief No 12, June 2022
23. Chatham House, *Nuclear Stability for all put at Risk by Putin's Speech, Patricia Lewis, Marion Messmer,* Julia Cournoyer and Emma Saunders, 22 February 2023
24. BBC News, *Ukraine War: Russian Air Strikes Cut Power at Zaporizhzhia Nuclear Plant,* 9 March 2023
25. CCLP Week 4, *The War in Ukraine, Debating Point 2: The Changing Nature of Warfare,* Lawrence Freedman February 2023
26. International Criminal Court, *Situation in Ukraine: ICC Judges Issue Warrants Against Vladimir Putin and Maria Alekseyevna Lvova-Belova,* press release 17 March 2023
27. Euronews, *What is the Wagnergroup and Who is Behind the Kremlin's Shadow Army?* Marta Rodriguez Martinez, 31 March 2023
28. Study.com, *The Art of War by Sun Tzu; summary, analysis and quotes*
29. Clausewitz.com, *On War,* the Clausewitz homepage
30. RUSI, *Preliminary Lessons in Conventional Warfighting from Russia's Invasion of Ukraine,* Mykhaylo Zabrodskyi, Jack Watling, Oleksandr V. Danylyuk, and Nick Reynolds, 20 November 2023
31. Business Insider, *Russian soldiers drafted to Ukraine were told they wouldn't have to actually fight anyone, report says. Many were swiftly killed,* Alia Shoaib, 18 December 2022
32. Modern War Institute, *Who 'Does' MDO? What Multi-dimensional Operations will Mean for - and require of - the Army's Tactical Units,* Rebecca Segal, 10 March 2023
33. Atlantic Council, *Game Changers: Implications of the Russo-Ukraine War for the Future of Ground Warfare,* Thomas X. Hammes, 3 April 2023
34. Russia Matters, *Has Russia Reached its Culminating Point in Ukraine?* Simon Saradzhyan, 20 July 2022
35. Reader's Digest, *Women of Ukraine Fight Back: How They are Revolutionising the Role of Women in War,* Elizabeth Yuko, 13 March 2023
36. Modern War Institute, *Twelve Months of War in Ukraine Have Revealed Four Fundamental Lessons on Urban Warfare,* John Spencer and Liam Collins, 23February 2023
37. War on Rocks, *The Tank is Obsolete and Other Observations About the Future of Combat,* Rob Lee, 6 September 2023
38. Atlantic Council, *Game Changers: Implications of the Russo-Ukraine War for the Future of Ground Warfare,* Thomas X. Hammes, 3 April 2023
39. Insider, *Russia Says its T-90 is One of the Best Tanks in the World but it is Having Trouble in Ukraine,* Wesley Culp, 12 August 2022
40. RUSI, *The Ukrainian Offensive Must Come in Stages*, Jack Watling, 2 September 2022
41. New Atlas, *Invasion of Ukraine Shows Artillery Still Rules the Battlefield,* David Szondy, 20 November 2022
42. Atlantic Council, *Game Changers: Implications of the Russo-Ukraine War for the*

Future of Ground Warfare, Thomas X. Hammes, 3 April 2023
43. RealClear Defense, *Lessons from Ukraine Many Don't want to Hear,* Matthew Van Wagenen and Arnel P. David, 11 March 2023
44. RUSI, *The Russian Air War and Ukrainian Requirements of Air Defense,* Justin Bronk, Nick Reynolds, and Jack Watling, 7 November 2022
45. Modern War Institute, *An Airfield Too Far: Failures at Market Garden and Antonov Airfield,* Jeremy Kofsky, 5 May 2022
46. Atlantic Council, *Game Changers: Implications of the Russo-Ukraine War for the Future of Ground Warfare,* Thomas X. Hammes, 3 April 2023
47. The EuroAsian, *Russian Navy Crippled in Ukraine War; Top US Military Official Sas Kyiv Effectively Used Weapons 'We Provided Them',* Tanmay Kadam, 1 March 2023
48. BRASIDAS Group, *Failures in Intelligence: Russia's Invasion of Ukraine,* 8 April 2022
49. Mezha, T*he Unique Situational Awareness System Delta was presented at the Annual* NATO Event, Oleg Danylov, 28 October 2022
50. Centre for Strategic and International Studies (CSIS), *Russia's Ill-fated Invasion of Ukraine: Lessons in Modern Warfare,* Seth G. Jones, 1 June 2022
51. DW, *Inside Ukraine's Cyber Guerilla Army,* Janosch Delcker, 24 March 2023
52. War on Rocks, *The Ukrainian Army is Leveraging Online Influencers. Can the US Military?,* Todd C Helmus, 1 March 2023
53. RAND, *Will Logistics be Russia's Undoing in Ukraine?* Bradley Martin, 10 February 2023
54. Wall Street Journal, *Russia's Economy is Starting to Come Undone,* Georgi Kantchev and Evan Gershkovich, 28 March 2023
55. War on Rocks, *More than a Hobby: Informal Security Assistance to Ukraine,* Jahara Matisek, William Reno, and Sam Rosenberg, 17 April 2023
56. Modern War Institute, *What is Russia's Theory of Victory of War in Ukraine?* Marnix Provost, 31 March 2023
57. Current Psychology (2022), *Leading with a Cool Head and Warm Heart; Trait-based Leadership,* Anna Maria Daderman, Petri Juhani Kajonius, Angela Hallberg, Sandra Skog, Ake Hellstorm, 2 November 2022
58. The New Voice of Ukraine, *Russia Already Lost over 20 Generals in War against Ukraine Believes Japanese Intelligence,* 9 February 2023
59. US Department of Defense, *NCOs Key to Ukrainian Military Success against Russia,* Jim Garamone, 28 February 2023

20

India's Strategy in the United Nations

Ambassador Asoke Mukerji

India's membership of the UN, as an original founder-member, is primarily due to its major military contribution to the Allied victory in WWII, in which 2.5 million volunteer Indian soldiers participated in campaigns across Europe, Asia, and Africa. India's diplomacy at the UN has been directed to make the organisation reflect and respond to India's priorities for peace, security, and development, anchored in the UN Charter. During the past seven and a half decades of India's diplomatic engagement in the UN, the effort to make the UN universal in its relevance has thrown up major challenges that affect India and the wider membership of the UN. As the UN nears its eightieth anniversary in 2025, India has adopted the strategy of reformed multilateralism to respond to the traditional and new challenges confronting India and the UN.

The UN Charter

The Preamble of the UN Charter highlights the three pillars supporting the multilateral structure of global governance.[1] The political pillar provides the commitment of UN member-states 'to save succeeding generations from the scourge of war', and is anchored in the UNSC. The economic pillar gives focus to the principle of international cooperation to 'promote social progress and better standards of life in larger freedom,' and is anchored in the United Nations Economic and Social Council

(ECOSOC). The human rights pillar reaffirms 'faith in fundamental human rights, in the dignity and worth of the human person, in the equal rights of men and women and of nations large and small', and has been anchored in the United Nations General Assembly (UNGA) and its Geneva-based Human Rights Council (HRC). The obligations of the UN Charter on its member-states emphasise the human-centric character of multilateralism and stress the equitable application of the core principle of international cooperation.[2]

Decision-making in the United Nations

India has consistently supported the provisions of Article 18 of the UN Charter on how the UNGA takes decisions. This process is democratic and transparent, with each member-state of the UN having one vote. In case it is necessary to decide on an issue on which there is no consensus, the Charter provides for a decision by majority vote among UNGA member-states, with 'important questions' requiring a majority of two-thirds (which translates today into 129 votes in favour in a 193-member UNGA).

The first challenge to India's expectation of the UN as an equitable organisation arose while the UN Charter was being negotiated, and has not been resolved till today. This is the derogation from the democratic principle of decision-making by the UNSC. While the UNGA's decisions are recommendatory, the decisions of the UNSC under Article 25 of the UN Charter are mandatory for compliance by UN member-states.

The current text of the Charter allowing the five self-selected Permanent Members (P5)[3] of the proposed UNSC to take decisions based on their veto power was objected to by several delegations, including India and Australia, during the San Francisco Conference in 1945. The P5 had made their support for the UN Charter conditional on it, including their secretly agreed understanding giving each one of them the veto. This became Article 27.3 of the UN Charter.

The text of the veto provision, requiring each P5 member to cast a concurring vote on UNSC decisions, had been proposed by the United States before the San Francisco Conference during a meeting between the United States, the United Kingdom, and the Soviet Union at the Crimean resort of Yalta in February 1945.[4] This privilege was extended to their principal wartime allies, France and the Republic of China. Primarily due to the urgent need for a framework of international cooperation between the P5 in the UNSC to maintain international peace and security, India and other dissenting delegations agreed to accept the P5's text on the veto on the understanding that the provisions of the UN Charter would be reviewed ten years after the Charter came into effect, i.e., in 1955. This compromise agreement was set down in Article 109 of the UN Charter.[5]

At the first session of the UN General Assembly, on 18 January 1946, India had recorded this linkage explicitly. It said that it looked 'willingly to the great powers to discharge their responsibilities, not to exercise their rights; let us hope that during the next ten years, on the one hand, our apprehensions and fears we may not have, will not be realised either, so that, at the end of the ten years when we reexamine the Charter, there will be unanimity again, and that this United Nations Charter will not require all the safeguards which big nations sometimes claim and small nations so unwillingly give'.[6]

To date, the promised review of the Charter's provisions, under Article 109, has not taken place. Instead, the UNSC has been increasingly gridlocked while taking decisions by the use of the veto by its P5 members, a practice that began in 1946 itself with the onset of the Cold War[7] The veto has been used 293 times by the P5 members between 1946 and 2020.[8] The Soviet Union cast the veto 120 times, the bulk of these used to block applications by states to join the UN during the 1940s and 1950s; the majority of the 82 vetoes cast by the United States have been used to protect the interests of Israel since 1970; the United Kingdom has used its veto 29 times, France 16 times and China 13 times, including a veto against Bangladesh's application for membership of the UN cast on 25 August 1972. The adverse impact of the vetoes has been inevitably felt most by developing country members of the UNGA.[9]

Amending the United Nations Charter in 1963

When the promised review of the UN Charter provisions did not take place by 1955, India endorsed the strategy of tabling a UNGA resolution to expand the membership of the UNSC by amending the provisions of the UN Charter. This strategy was considered a major challenge, since the inbuilt double veto in the UN Charter, under Article 108, requires any UNGA resolution to amend the Charter to be also unanimously ratified by all the P5 countries.

In December 1960, developing countries, including India, achieved a major breakthrough in democratising the UNGA, when the UNGA unanimously adopted its historic Decolonisation Resolution to fast-track the entry of former colonial countries into the UN.[10] This opened the door to a surge of new member-states of the UNGA, almost all of them developing countries.

In December 1963, this new ground reality in the UNGA enabled the tabling and adoption of a composite resolution by a recorded two-thirds majority vote to amend the UN Charter. This resolution amended the provisions of Articles 23 and 27 of the UN Charter to increase the number of elected non-permanent seats in the UNSC from six to ten. There were 97 votes in favour, including the Republic of China and Taiwan—11 against, including France and the Soviet Union, and four abstentions including the United Kingdom and the United States. The same resolution also amended the provisions of Article 61 of the UN Charter to increase the number of elected seats in the ECOSOC from 18 to 27. This received 96 votes in favour, 11 opposed, including France and the Soviet Union, and there were five abstentions including the Republic of China and Taiwan, the United Kingdom, and the United States.[11] Contrary to the expectation of the use of their double veto contained in Article 108, all the P5 countries, including those which had opposed or abstained from the resolution, ratified this UNGA decision. The amended provisions of the UN Charter came into effect in 1965.[12]

Integrating Developing Country Perspectives into the Charter

When the UN Charter was negotiated and signed, India was among the minuscule number of member states that could be considered a developing country. India's vision of its expectation as a member of the UN was articulated forcefully in the UNGA on 19 September 1947, soon after India attained independence from British colonial rule. In a far-sighted statement, India said that 'the great powers, instead of coming closer together, are drifting farther apart. There is tension, suspense and anxiety, and an uneasy awareness that things are perhaps moving towards some new and annihilating disaster for mankind...'. Rejecting attempts to make India part of the ideological confrontation of the Cold War, India said that 'ideology is less important than practice. We cannot eat an ideology; we cannot brandish an ideology and feel that we are clothed and housed. Food, clothing, shelter, education, medical services – these are the things we need'.[13]

This perspective required a major reorientation of the existing mindset in the UN, which was dominated by its West European member-states. After the UNGA adopted its resolution in 1963, amending the UN Charter to expand the ECOSOC and give greater representation to developing countries, India took the lead in calling for a platform within the UNGA to network and negotiate the priorities of developing countries. The consolidation of developing country coordination in the UNGA resulted in June 1964 in the formation of the Group of 77 (G-77), and the adoption of the Group's Charter of Algiers aimed at creating a new international economic order at its ministerial meeting in Algiers in 1967. India was elected the first Chair of the G-77 in 1970. The group currently has 134 developing country members in the 193-member UNGA.[14]

The strategy of India as a G-77 member has fundamentally changed the ground-level dynamic of the UN, with issues of sustainable development that encompass all major aspects of human activity becoming the UN's core agenda. Between 1964 and 2015, India's most significant success, as one of the leaders of the G-77, has undoubtedly been the unanimous adoption of Agenda 2030 on Sustainable Development by the UNGA.[15]

The world leaders meeting in New York to adopt Agenda 2030, with its 17 Sustainable Development Goals (SDGs), clearly pointed to the interlinkage between sustainable development and the need for peace and security. The Preamble of Agenda 2030 states: 'There can be no peace without sustainable development and no sustainable development without peace'. Recognising the significance of the interlinkage between sustainable development and peace for developing countries, SDG 16.8 specifically committed UN member-states to broaden and strengthen the participation of developing countries in the institutions of global governance.

Peace, Security, and Development

The interlinkages between peace, security, and development dominated the sixtieth anniversary summit of the UN held in New York in September 2005. The summit mandated early reforms of the UNSC 'to make it more broadly representative, efficient, and transparent and thus, to further enhance its effectiveness and the legitimacy and implementation of its decisions'.[16] However, this mandate had failed to be implemented through Inter-Governmental Negotiations (IGN) launched in the UNGA in 2008, primarily due to stiff resistance of the P5 led by China.[17] China's open support of a small group of UN member-states in the UNGA, known popularly as the Coffee Club or Uniting for Consensus Group, resulted in their insistence on broadest consensus on UNSC reforms. This stand ignored the precedent set by the UNGA vote in 1963 with a two-thirds majority to amend the UN Charter and reform the UNSC.

The deadlock on negotiating UNSC reforms through the UNGA has proved to be a major obstacle to the national efforts of developing countries to implement Agenda 2030. For India, this casts a shadow on its ambitious effort to transform India into one of the major powers of the twenty-first century. Today, over 50 conflicts in Asia, Africa, and Latin America fester on the agenda of the UNSC primarily due to P5 polarisation. This has impacted adversely on the attempts by the UN to resolve these crises through diplomacy and mediation (as in Libya, Syria, Yemen, Palestine, Afghanistan, and Myanmar), or the deployment of Peacekeeping Operations (PKOs).

The four largest PKOs deployed by the UNSC today are in Africa. Over 70,000 UN troops (out of a total of 96,000 UN troops on the ground), mainly from developing countries, have been deployed in MONUSCO[18] (Democratic Republic of Congo), UNMISS[19] (South Sudan), MINUSMA[20] (Mali), and MINUSCA[21] (Central African Republic). These PKOs annually cost the UN member-states US$ 4.68 billion out of a UN PKO annual budget of about US$ 6 billion. Despite this, the UNSC has been unable to broker a sustainable political settlement to these conflicts.[22]

The absence of any permanent member from Africa and Latin America in the UNSC has been a major factor in overcoming the veto of the P5 on decisions taken by the UNSC. As the single largest troop contributor to the UN PKOs since 1948,[23] India has consistently called for reforms in the UNSC's decision-making process to overcome this failure, including on the key issue of how troops contributed by India and other troop-contributing countries are deployed on the ground by the UNSC under Article 44 of the UN Charter.

The Strategic Implications of an Ineffective United Nations Security Council

Three ongoing crises illustrate the strategic ineffectiveness of the UNSC.

The Covid-19 Pandemic: The Covid-19 pandemic, identified in January 2020 by the WHO, a UN specialised agency, was not addressed as a priority by the UNSC, which failed to adopt a unanimous political resolution until 1 July 2020.[24] This contrasted sharply with the UNSC's immediate unanimous response to earlier pandemics, such as the HIV-AIDS crisis of 2000.[25] The lack of political leadership by the UNSC has imperilled the lives and livelihoods of millions of people. The World Bank estimated that the Covid-19 pandemic had pushed 150 million additional people into poverty, mainly in developing countries, by the end of 2021.[26] The decision of the United States to formally withdraw from the WHO in July 2020 effectively sent a signal for the revival of entrenched protectionist sentiments in several Western UN member-states, revolving around their profits from the intellectual property right patent protection of anti-Covid vaccines. India and South Africa were compelled to lead efforts in the WTO, and not the UN, to focus on the need to respond to the urgent demands of developing countries through a vaccine waiver initiative.[27]

Afghanistan: The abrupt and chaotic withdrawal, in August 2021, of the United States and its NATO allies deployed in Afghanistan under UNSC resolutions removed, overnight, the peace and security framework of UNSC-overseen peace-building in this vulnerable developing country since 2001, including the effective use of over $3 billion in development assistance provided by India to Afghanistan. The abdication by the UNSC of its responsibility to uphold the unanimously adopted UNSC resolution 2513 of 10 March 2020 committing to an 'inclusive, negotiated political settlement'[28] has resulted in the massive violation of the fundamental human rights to education and employment of over 20 million Afghan women (half the country's population) by the Taliban regime in Kabul.

Ukraine: The failure of the UNSC to prevent the outbreak of an armed conflict between Russia and Ukraine, on 24 February 2022, despite the clear and unanimous commitment of UNSC Resolution 2202 adopted on 17 February 2015, is yet to be called out by the UNGA. UNSC Resolution 2202 specifically upheld the sovereignty, independence, and territorial integrity of Ukraine, and endorsed the political settlement of the conflict in the framework of the Minsk Agreements, including a political devolution of power to eastern Ukraine.[29] According to the UN, the conflict in Ukraine has already led to the flow of about nine million Ukrainian refugees out of Ukraine's 43 million population, including 2.8 million Ukrainian refugees fleeing to Russia.[30] A UN HRC resolution sponsored by the 120-member Non-aligned Movement on the negative impact of unilateral sanctions on developing countries was adopted on 3 April 2023 by a huge majority of 33 votes in favour, with 13 opposed (all of which were NATO-aligned countries) in the 47-member HRC.[31] The resolution condemned 'the continued unilateral application and enforcement by certain powers of such measures as tools of pressure, including political and economic pressure, against any country, particularly against least developed and developing countries, to prevent these countries from exercising their right to decide, of their own free will, their own political, economic and social systems'.

United Nations Security Council and NATO

Both the Afghanistan and Ukraine conflicts also brought into focus the calibration by the three permanent members of the UNSC belonging to NATO (France, the United Kingdom, and the United States) of replacing the UNSC's functions with that of NATO on selected issues of peace and security on the UNSC's agenda. Addressing a public press conference in Washington, DC on 22 December 2022, US Secretary of State, Anthony Blinken, acknowledged such a NATO approach when he said, 'When it comes to Russia's war against Ukraine, if we were still in Afghanistan, it would have, I think, made much more complicated the support that we've been able to give and that others have been able to give Ukraine to resist and push back against the Russian aggression'.[32]

In April 2023, a US White House briefing paper on the US (and NATO) withdrawal from Afghanistan stated, 'On the global stage, America is leading. We have rallied our allies and partners to support Ukraine and hold Russia accountable for its aggression—and to rise to compete with China. It is hard to imagine the United States would have been able to lead the response to these challenges as successfully—especially in the resource-intensive way that it has—if US forces remained in Afghanistan today.'[33] This is an ironical comment on the existing UN Charter provisions mandating the UNSC with the primary responsibility of maintaining international peace and security and a harbinger of the weaponisation of the UN Charter provisions by NATO.

Reformed Multilateralism

Having just completed its eighth innings as an elected non-permanent member of the UNSC and experienced the way the veto privilege of the P5 consistently overrides any UNSC decision not in their interests, India's strategy is to forge common ground with other developing countries on the need to reform not only the UNSC as mandated by world leaders in September 2005 but also the entire multilateral system. This holistic approach underlies Prime Minister Narendra Modi's statements calling for 'reformed multilateralism' during the seventy-fifth anniversary of the UN.

In his three major addresses to the UN on its seventy-fifth anniversary in 2020, Prime Minister Narendra Modi placed the implementation of Agenda 2030 at the heart of the call for 'reformed multilateralism', saying, 'We cannot fight today's challenges with outdated structures. Without comprehensive reforms, the UN faces a crisis of confidence. In today's interconnected world, we need a reformed multilateralism—that reflects today's realities, gives voice to all stakeholders, addresses contemporary challenges and focuses on human welfare.'

On 12–13 January 2023, India hosted a virtual Voice of the Global South for Human-centric Development Summit to formulate a plan of action in the UN from a developing country's perspective. A measure of the importance of India's initiative can be gauged from the fact that 125 countries responded to this initiative, including 47 from Africa, 31 from Asia, 29 from Latin America and the Caribbean, 11 from Oceania, and seven from Europe. Participating countries were linked by common concerns regarding issues of sustainable development of priority to them on which existing multilateral institutions have failed to provide significant outcomes for human-centric development.[34]

India's strategy would be for the outcomes of the New Delhi Voice of the Global South Summit to be integrated into the preparations for the UN's Summit of the Future, planned to be held in New York in September 2024.[35] The objective would be for the UN's Summit of the Future to convene a General Conference of the UN, as provided for in Article 109 of the UN Charter. Such a General Conference, held in 2025, when the organisation marks its eightieth anniversary, would become a San Francisco 2.0[36] moment, enabling India and developing countries to implement the objectives of 'reformed multilateralism' by reviewing and updating the provisions of the UN Charter.[37]

Ambassador Asoke K. Mukerji, IFS, has been India's Permanent Representative to the UN, High Commissioner to UK, Ambassador to Kazakhstan, Deputy Mission Chief to Russia and CG of India-Dubai. He has extensive experience of Central Asia and WTO's working, handling India's trade relations, and founding political and economic relations with newly independent Central Asian Republics in the 1990s. Also having worked in Washington DC, Belgrade and Soviet Russia, he is a highly regarded writer in Indian and foreign journals on trade policy matters. As Special Secretary MEA, he has intensive experience in dealing with strategic and security matters in India's extended neighbourhood, as well as on issues of Cyber Development and Human Rights. He is a distinguished fellow with VIF, and a well-known speaker at various think tank fora.

Endnotes

1. United Nations Charter, Preamble. https://www.un.org/en/about-us/un-charter
2. United Nations General Assembly Resolution 2625 dated 24 October 1970. https://treaties.un.org/doc/source/docs/A_RES_2625-Eng.pdf
3. The P5 specified in Article 23 of the Charter are the Republic of China, France, the United Kingdom, the Union of Soviet Socialist Republics, and the United States of America. On 25 October 1971, the UNGA adopted a voted (and not unanimous) resolution to give the seat of the Republic of China to the communist People's Republic of China. In 1992, both the UNSC and the UNGA agreed unanimously to the Russian Federation continuing with the membership of the USSR in the UNSC and UNGA.
4. U.S. Department of State, Office of the Historian, The Yalta Conference, 1945. https://history.state.gov/milestones/1937-1945/yalta-conf
5. Note 1. Article 109.
6. *Permanent Mission of India to the UN*, New York. Statement by Mr Ramaswamy Mudaliar, 18 January 1946. https://pminewyork.gov.in/pdf/uploadpdf/80686lms1.pdf

7. The National WWII Museum, New Orleans. *Winston Churchill's Iron Curtain Speech*–5 March 1946. https://www.nationalww2museum.org/war/articles/winston-churchills-iron-curtain-speech-march-5-1946#:~:text=Then%2C%20on%20March%205%2C%201946,for%20the%20next%2050%20years.
8. United Nations, Dag Hammarskjold Library, Security Council Veto List. https://research.un.org/en/docs/sc/quick/veto
9. Security Council Report, The Veto, 16 December 2020. https://www.securitycouncilreport.org/un-security-council-working-methods/the-veto.php
10. United Nations, *The United Nations and Decolonization.* https://www.un.org/dppa/decolonization/en/about
11. United Nations General Assembly Resolution A/1991/XVIII/A&B dated 17 December 1963. Available in Handbook on Security Council Reform, Permanent Mission of St Vincent and The Grenadines, New York, 2018. Pages 33-34. https://pminewyork.gov.in/pdf/menu/pdf/L69InteractiveHandBook_11feb.pdf
12. The most likely reasons for the P5 to agree on ratifying the 1963 UNGA resolution are the strategic interest of both the blocs in the Cold War to influence the new additional elected members to align with them in UN decision-making, using their bilateral political and economic levers of power.
13. Permanent Mission of India to the UN, New York. Statement by Mrs Vijayalakshmi Pandit in the UNGA on 19 September 1947. https://pminewyork.gov.in/pdf/uploadpdf/64080lms2.pdf
14. G-77. About the Group of 77. https://www.g77.org/doc/#:~:text=The%20Group%20of%2077%20is,all%20major%20international%20economic%20issues
15. United Nations, *Transforming our world: the 2030 Agenda for Sustainable Development.* https://sdgs.un.org/2030agenda
16. United Nations, UNGA Resolution A/RES/60/1 (paragraph 153), 16 September 2005. https://www.un.org/en/development/desa/population/migration/generalassembly/docs/globalcompact/A_RES_60_1.pdf
17. Permanent Mission of China to the United Nations, Statement by Ambassador Liu Jieyi, 7 November 2016. http://un.china-mission.gov.cn/eng/chinaandun/zzhgg/201703/t20170321_8412088.htm
18. MONUSCO, is an acronym based on its French name Mission de l'Organisation des Nations Unies pour la stabilisation en République démocratique du Congo.
19. UNIMISS stands for United Nations Mission in South Sudan
20. MINUSMA stands for United Nations Multidimensional Integrated Stabilisation Mission in Mali
21. MINUSCA stands for United Nations Multidimensional Integrated Stabilisation Mission in the Central African Republic
22. United Nations Peacekeeping, 2022. https://peacekeeping.un.org/
23. According to the Ministry of Defence, India has so far contributed over 2,64,000 troops to 51 of the 71 UN PKOs so far. Indianarmy.nic.in
24. United Nations Security Council Resolution 2532 dated 1 July 2020. https://

documents-dds-ny.un.org/doc/UNDOC/LTD/N20/169/84/PDF/N2016984.pdf?OpenElement
25. The UN Security Council's Response to Covid 19 by Jeremy Farrall, Australian National University, 28 May 2020. https://law.anu.edu.au/research/essay/covid-19-and-international-law/un-security-council%E2%80%99s-response-covid-19
26. The World Bank, Covid-19 to Add as Many as 150 Million Extreme Poor by 2021, 7 October 2020. https://www.worldbank.org/en/news/press-release/2020/10/07/covid-19-to-add-as-many-as-150-million-extreme-poor-by-2021
27. *WTO TRIPs Waiver and Covid-19 Vaccine Equity,* Rajeesh Kumar, 12 July 2021. MP-IDSA. https://www.idsa.in/issuebrief/wto-trips-waiver-covid-vaccine-rkumar-120721
28. United Nations Security Council resolution 2513 dated 10 March 2020. https://documents-dds-ny.un.org/doc/UNDOC/PRO/N20/063/35/PDF/N2006335.pdf?OpenElement
29. United Nations Security Council resolution 2202 dated 17 February 2015. https://documents-dds-ny.un.org/doc/UNDOC/GEN/N15/043/71/PDF/N1504371.pdf?OpenElement
30. UN High Commissioner for Refugees, Ukraine Refugee Situation, 11 April 2023. https://data.unhcr.org/en/situations/ukraine
31. UN General Assembly, Human Rights Council Resolution A/HRC/RES/52/13 dated 3 April 2023. https://www.ohchr.org/en/hr-bodies/hrc/regular-sessions/session52/res-dec-stat
32. U.S. Department of State, Secretary Anthony J. Blinken at a Press Availability, 22 December 2022. https://www.state.gov/secretary-antony-j-blinken-at-a-press-availability-27/
33. United States, The White House, *U.S. Withdrawal from Afghanistan,* page 11. https://www.whitehouse.gov/wp-content/uploads/2023/04/US-Withdrawal-from-Afghanistan.pdf
34. Government of India, Prime Minister's Office, *PM's closing remarks at the inaugural Leaders' Session of Voice of Global South Summit 2023*, 12 January 2023. https://www.pmindia.gov.in/en/news_updates/pms-closing-remarks-at-the-inaugural-leaders-session-of-voice-of-global-south-summit-2023/
35. United Nations, *The Summit of the Future in 2024.* https://www.un.org/en/common-agenda/summit-of-the-future#:~:text=Having%20welcomed%20the%20submission%20of,will%20take%20place%20this%20year.
36. Such a General Conference would resemble the San Francisco Conference of 1945, but bring developing country issues into the overall review of the UN Charter by applying the UNGA's rules of procedure including on taking decisions.
37. *Advancing Reformed Multilateralism in a Changing World* by Asoke Kumar Mukerji, Indian Council of World Affairs, 2021. https://icwa.in/pdfs/AdvancingReform.pdf

21

Military Diplomacy: A Powerful Force Multiplier for Statecraft

Lieutenant General Kamal Davar

Diplomacy and defence are not substitutes for one another, either alone would fail.[1]

–John F. Kennedy

India, according to many strategic analysts, both at home and abroad, since its Independence in 1947, has not accorded adequate priority to one of the most powerful tools which can contribute to enhancing its national strategic interests, namely, Military Diplomacy. Traditionally, as a nation with a firm belief in peaceful coexistence, Military Diplomacy has not been an overly popular term in the nuance and lexicon of Indian statecraft. However, all powerful nations do fully appreciate the time-honoured dictum that no country can achieve its foreign policy goals and security interests in today's highly stressed strategic environment if it disregards the effective employment of its military instrument.

A nation's capability to counter the myriad challenges to its economic well-being and security interests rests primarily on the strength and sustainability of the constituents of its Comprehensive National Power (CNP)—both military and non-military. Deft diplomacy is a vital ingredient, which also enhances a nation's CNP. Thus, it merits a holistic institutionalised appraisal in the nation to gauge whether a rising power like India has a well-conceived policy and suitable structures to make use of Military Diplomacy as a vital instrument to further the nation's strategic interests.

Definition of Military Diplomacy

Since time immemorial, nations have employed their militaries to achieve national objectives using kinetic means. On the other hand, diplomacy is just the opposite. Normally, diplomacy is a peaceful engagement and an effort to establish cordial relations between states. If diplomacy or Military Diplomacy fails, the resultant action may involve the use of force. While there is no universally accepted definition of this form of statecraft, Military or Defence Diplomacy (the terms Military and Defence are interchangeable) connotes the peaceful, non-kinetic employment of military capabilities and military resources in the pursuit of national foreign policy objectives. Noted strategic analyst, Anton Du Plessis, goes on to give a broader definition of Military Diplomacy as 'the use of Armed Forces in operations other than war, building on their trained expertise and discipline to achieve national and foreign objectives abroad'.[2] It is also pertinent to point out that powerful nations do demonstrate their military capabilities by a threat of force, a form of coercive diplomacy popularly captioned 'gunboat diplomacy,' a term that has been talked about since the eighteenth and nineteenth centuries. However, Military Diplomacy enhances foreign policy and defence cooperation amongst nations and is primarily an extension of a nation's soft power. It must not be confused with military interventions like India's actions in the Maldives (Operation Cactus) or the dispatch of IPKF to Sri Lanka.

Military Diplomacy encompasses high-level ministerial and military commanders meetings, transfer, or sale of military equipment and platforms, including joint production ventures, goodwill visits, training, both at military institutions and in the field, operational cum logistical exercises, regional defence forums (like Shangri La and Raisina Dialogues, ASEAN Security Forum, etc.), confidence building measures, humanitarian assistance during natural disasters, cooperation in combating sea piracy, the establishment of air and sea traffic control, communication facilities, construction of specialised infrastructure like ports, airfields, bridges, exchange of specialist military personnel, participation in each other's military parades, fleet reviews or air shows, and the like. Cooperation in the emerging realms of warfare, including in the fields of cyber, hi-tech, artificial intelligence, space etc., will also get enhanced with proactive Military Diplomacy endeavours.

The exchange and positioning of military attachés of the three services in each other's diplomatic missions have been, for years, an important ingredient of global Military Diplomacy. In today's terror-afflicted world, the exchange of timely terrorist-related intelligence will also fall under the purview of Military Diplomacy.

Military Diplomacy – Objectives

Military or Defence Diplomacy is undertaken to achieve overall national security as well as our foreign policy objectives. Overall, the Military Diplomacy environment has certainly improved in India but in the recent past, some observations by well-informed media and authors were not complimentary with regards to India's forays in Military Diplomacy. The London-published *The Economist,* in its March 2013 issue, under the article *Can India Become a Great Power?* had succinctly observed that the 'Indian Armed Forces have grown exponentially since Independence, but no civilian leader has the faintest idea how to use India's growing military clout!' Dr Marc Faber, the well-known author of the bestseller, *Gloom, Boom and Doom*, had also opined that 'India continues to be ambivalent about power and it has failed to develop a strategic agenda commensurate with its growing economic and military capabilities. Throughout history, India has failed to master the creation, deployment, and uses of its military instruments in support of its national objectives'. Thus, the goals of Indian Military Diplomacy need to be adequately tailored to further national objectives in today's highly complex regional and global security challenges. Over the past couple of decades, India certainly has improved in its Military Diplomacy postures.

On the face of it, the term 'Military Diplomacy' appears to be an oxymoron, for diplomacy and the military rightly belongs to different realms. Nonetheless, it must be clearly understood by all stakeholders that Military Diplomacy does not replace the nation's foreign or security policies but supplements them for greater dividends for the nation. It works towards confidence-building and the development of closer ties between nations and conflict prevention is one of its primary objectives. Secondly, it aims at substantial accretions in the knowledge and progress of the latest techniques and technologies in weapons, equipment, and domain awareness in emerging concepts of warfare. Thirdly, training, both theoretical and in the field, with joint exercises is a significant feature of this form of diplomacy. All these goals contribute to a nation establishing and increasing its sphere of influence both bilaterally and even multilaterally.

Cooperation in non-traditional security areas like disaster management, anti-piracy threats, meeting pandemic threats, or assistance in mass evacuations of own and other people from foreign countries in emergencies are also part of defence diplomacy. A major spin-off of this form of defence cooperation is that, in emergencies, including while engaging in UN or other internationally constituted operations, participating nations work towards understanding each others' tactics and strategies, equipment, logistics, and SOPs, thus, attaining the important advantage of interoperability.

It needs no emphasis to state that the success of Defence Diplomacy in a nation will solely depend on the political, security, and strategic dialogues to be in sync and complement each other.

It will be pertinent to note that both the US and China are notable examples in the utilisation of their militaries for the execution of their respective foreign policy initiatives. The US has pacts, alliances, and military partnerships with many nations while the Chinese Military Diplomacy has been developing close security ties with its client states. Its over-ambitious BRI is a classic example of China's grandiose thrust in its Military Diplomacy.

Evolution of India's Military Diplomacy

Immediately after independence in 1947, India was confronted with the realities of the Cold War and the continuous jostling for global dominance between the two superpowers, namely, the USA and the USSR. However, for sound geopolitical reasons then, India's first Prime Minister, Jawaharlal Nehru, was a staunch votary of non-alignment, and all of India's foreign policies were centred on chartering a path independent and virtually equidistant of the two competing power blocs. Consequently, India's defence cooperation and Military Diplomacy too remained 'isolationist' in its orientation, and military linkages with other nations were frowned upon by India's new rulers. The exception to this rule was, however, mercifully, India's willing participation in UN peacekeeping endeavours. In addition, during Nehru's prime ministership, India chaired the UN Neutral Nations Repatriation Commission in 1953, and sent a small contingent and field ambulance to Korea. Moreover, during the 1950s, India did engage in Military Diplomacy with Nepal and Bhutan but any noteworthy military initiatives with other nations, apart from visits of Service Chiefs and attendance at some military institutions, hardly materialised.

Former Army Chief, General V.P. Malik, in his seminal book, *India's Military Conflicts and Diplomacy*, has commented that 'India started poorly in making use of Military Diplomacy as a national security and foreign policy tool'.[3] He opines that among the many reasons for this malaise, 'the foremost being a steep erosion of every aspect of India's military capabilities; civil-military relations, military capabilities, leadership and morale'.[4] General Malik further lamented that 'Nehruvian India was distrustful of the Armed Forces and kept them out of the Ministry of Defence and important decision making...South Block ensured that policymaking was crafted by bureaucrats and strategy by diplomats. Both lacked military expertise or perspective'.

As is well-known, Nehru's pacifist orientation was craftily manipulated by his bureaucracy and, thus, the Indian Armed Forces were kept out of the decision-making loop even on matters of national security – an anomaly for which the nation had to pay heavily in later years. However, after the end of the Cold War, in the 1990s, and commencing the early part of this century and till date, India's Defence Diplomacy has undergone a major transformation both in its span and scale in keeping with emerging foreign policy challenges.

Before fast-forwarding to the current years, it will be worthwhile mentioning that meagre efforts at fostering Military Diplomacy have existed since the early 1950s. Since 1950, India's prestigious Defence Services Staff College (DSSC), Wellington (Tamil Nadu), has hosted officer students from the three services of friendly foreign nations. Beginning with officers from the UK, the USA, Australia, Canada and Burma, officers from non-aligned and newly-independent nations such as Sri Lanka, Malaysia, Nigeria, Kenya, Egypt, Indonesia, Ethiopia, Bhutan, Bangladesh, and Ghana, among others, sent their student officers for this renowned military course each year. A fair number of these officers who attended the course reached the top positions in their service hierarchies in their respective nations. Others from the DSSC and India's National Defence College (NDC) have risen to be heads of state of their nations. Dealing with such heads of state is much easier, and the probability of success in mutual ventures is accordingly much higher.

Notwithstanding the bureaucracy and inadequate emphasis on the benefits of Military Diplomacy, India, for decades, has been one of the largest contributors of troops on various UN peacekeeping missions around the world, and its record in this form of Military Diplomacy has been second to none. It is also worth mentioning here that the Indian Armed Forces also enjoy a sterling professional reputation among other

Armed Forces in the world. Thus, India has been requested many times by friendly foreign nations to send military training teams. Some of these nations where Indian military training teams have been sent are Nepal, Bhutan, Iraq (where I, too, served for two years), Botswana, Angola, and Malaysia, among some other nations.

Current Status: Military Diplomacy

Overall, India's Defence Diplomacy has undergone a gradual, yet qualitative change, especially after the early 1990s. Currently, 73 nations from across the globe have their military representation with a total of 120 officers from the three services stationed in New Delhi. On the other hand, India has a total of 71 military officers as defence, military, air, and naval attacheés posted to 44 nations with an increase in the near future planned as regards their numbers and the nations to be represented in.

India's diplomatic relations and military cooperation with the world's sole superpower, the US, have been steadily improving over the last three decades or so. The formulation of the Kickleighter proposals[5] in 1991–1992 gave a fillip to expanded cooperation among the armed forces of the two democracies after decades of being indifferent to each other. This protocol enabled the first ever military-to-military India and US paratroopers exercise in February 1992. This was followed by exercises by the navies of the two nations dubbed Malabar I, II, and III, which have now become a regular biennial feature. The last 10 years, in particular, have seen an unprecedented strengthening of the US-India Defence relationship. In June 2005, India and the US signed a new framework for expanding their defence relationship for the next ten years. This agreement was further extended for another 10 years in 2015. India is today the US military's biggest training partner, with the US conducting the maximum number of military exercises with India than with any other nation. In addition, the US has now become the third-largest supplier of arms and equipment to India. Gradually, irksome differences between the two nations, like the transfer of technology, export to India of dual-use technology, and India signing some strict protocols regarding employment of weapons provided by the US, or inspections, etc., are being smoothened out. In the last few years, India has acquired several systems, including the LPD (Landing Platform Dock) ship *Trenton*, modern transport aircraft like the C-130 (Hercules) and C-17, Chinook and Apache helicopters, AWACS, latest drones, P-8 maritime surveillance aircraft, etc. India is currently also exploring the latest fifth-generation fighter aircraft that the US is offering for making up for India's depleting air power.

The signing of the India-US Nuclear Accord between President George Bush and then Indian PM, Dr Manmohan Singh, in 2009, took India-US ties to a new level. India-US defence ties are on the upswing and were given a comprehensive thrust by Indian PM Narendra Modi with former US President Donald Trump and current US President Joe Biden. Both the Indian Navy and the Indian Air Force are now regularly participating in US-conducted exercises like the Rim of the Pacific multilateral and Red Flag exercises respectively. The much-heralded US-India Defence Technology and Partnership Agreement will take defence ties between the two nations to another level of defence engagement. The signing of the Logistics Agreement between the two nations enables them to utilise each others' bases and logistics. Indeed, a radical departure from the past relationship!

Over the last few years, in particular, the US has also been trying to push India to assume a much larger collaborative role in the Indian Ocean with Japan and Australia having an eye on Chinese expansionist inclinations in the South China Sea and the East China Sea. Thus, in the immediate future, the militarisation of the QSD is well on the cards with these four nations joining hands together to keep China's unbridled ambitions in the Indo-Pacific at bay.

China's naked aggression in India's Eastern Ladakh sector, since April 2020, has brought India and the US further together, with the latter supporting India's stand, and criticising China openly for its expansionist tendencies. India hopes that US President Joe Biden will continue to re-energise the US no-nonsense stance as regards China. Meanwhile, the US and India must step up their cooperation as regards combating China's unleashed global pandemic, COVID-19, and its newer variants. In addition, both nations must impress upon the world to ostracise China for its devious role in bringing misery to the world owing to China's likely foray into biological warfare or experimentation with various types of viruses in their Wuhan-based laboratories.

With Russia, defence relations have been a critically significant pillar of our long-standing strategic partnership. The MoD opines that 'the two countries have a robust, multi-tiered institutionalised mechanism for regular interactions for deepening longstanding defence cooperation'. The India-Russia Governmental Commission on Technical Cooperation needs to be given further impetus by both nations. High-level visits to discuss various issues between the two nations especially regarding weapons, equipment, ammunition, and efforts to manufacture Russian equipment in India, like the Kamov 226T helicopter, have been going on intensively. It is important to mention here that with the deepening of defence relationships of India with Israel and the US, defence cooperation with Russia may take a hit in the years ahead as India diversifies its sources of importing equipment, including for its Make in India programmes. We will have to diplomatically ensure that Russia maintains its historical fraternal ties with India—not an easy call by any standards—with it being cash-strapped and having large-scale defence cooperation ties with China! High-level military-to-military consultations, including upgrading our Military Diplomacy efforts with our long-standing defence partners, are also the need of the hour.

It merits mention here that the Indian Navy has been at the forefront of lending a military dimension to India's Look East policy that was unveiled a couple of decades back. The policy, renamed Act East by the present NDA dispensation, has directed the Indian Navy to vigorously reach out to the Indian Ocean littoral nations. 1995 onwards, our Navy had been conducting multi-national cooperation exercises, code named Milan, reaching nations in the Bay of Bengal. The International Fleet Review conducted in February 2016 by the Indian Navy at Vishakhapatnam, attended by 99 warships from 50 nations, was a spectacular display of India's Military Diplomacy at work. In addition, the Indian Navy also conducts the Malabar exercises regularly with the navies of the US, Australia, and Japan to give a fillip to the Quad formation and send out a strong message to China. Former Indian Naval Chief Admiral, Arun Prakash, has expressed that 'an important component of India's evolving naval diplomacy has been the creation of a strong maritime domain awareness capability.'[6] Indian Armed Forces, the MoD, and the MEA should take a leaf out of the Indian Navy's 2007 Maritime Strategy, which had clearly declared that 'the main business of major navies in the twenty-first century is to use warships to support foreign policy'.[7] Many nations in the region do recall, with gratitude, the Indian Navy's humanitarian assistance and disaster management endeavours over the last few decades. We need to further develop such capabilities to come to the help of many such smaller nations in the Indo-Pacific region.

As regards its neighbours, India has cordial military relations with all except, of course, Pakistan with whom not much should be expected in the foreseeable future. Despite countless efforts by India to normalise relations with Pakistan, the latter continues to zealously follow an anti-

India agenda in all its strategic and security formulations. Accordingly, India must further step-up Military Diplomacy with its other neighbours far more vigorously than hitherto fore. China, as part of its grand design, in collusion with its protégé, Pakistan, will do, whatever it can, to dampen India's efforts at establishing healthy relations with its neighbours.

Recommendations and Conclusion

India today stands at a defining moment in its inevitable rise as an important global player. India's rise is concomitant with the well-conceived and determined steps the national government takes to attain that goal. As stated earlier, the nation, thus, will have to energise all the constituents which contribute to the enhancement of India's Comprehensive National Power. Military strength and Military Diplomacy are both vital and irreplaceable components, which will go to enhance the nation's ascent in the comity of nations. Admiral Arun Prakash, however, has pithily expressed that 'unfortunately, neither India's political establishment nor its bureaucracy—defence and diplomatic—fully support the concept of the military entering the domain of diplomacy'.[8] It is a well-known fact that some Indian diplomats do not subscribe to the Armed Forces playing a greater role in projecting Indian interests abroad. Regrettably, they fail to understand that Military Diplomacy is just a part of the overall national diplomacy endeavours, and will, thus, conform to the strategic mosaic of India's foreign interests.

Foremost, the Government must give adequate impetus to national strategy and national security issues with the defence services in loop. It will be in the larger interest of the nation if, in the formulation of national strategy, the requisite synergy between the MEA, MoD, and the Armed Forces is achieved. The energetic pursuit of Military Diplomacy and defence cooperation with nations of interest to India will thence be a natural corollary. Secondly, India must step up its Military Diplomacy and defence cooperation in a substantial manner with its neighbours like Bangladesh, Afghanistan, Sri Lanka, Iran, Bhutan, and, importantly, Nepal, with whom our relations do fluctuate from time to time. As maritime Asia assumes increasingly larger strategic significance in the years ahead, Indian Military Diplomacy will have to touch the shores of East Asia and better naval cooperation achieved with nations like Japan, South Korea, the Philippines, and importantly, Vietnam. Our military representation, currently restricted to just 44 nations, must be substantially increased and span continents like South America along with nations along the Indian Ocean and Africa.

Importantly, our structures and the Governmental or Services HQ set-ups to conduct Military Diplomacy are not at all adequately geared for the pursuit of Military Diplomacy. With the establishment of the appointment of the Chief of Defence Staff in the last two years, it will be appropriate to accord to the Defence Intelligence Agency (DIA) under him with the responsibility of conducting Defence Diplomacy in all its manifestations. On behalf of the MoD and the three services, the DIA can foster Military Diplomacy in concert with the MEA and any other ministries involved. A much larger number of military officers must be seconded to the MEA to give a fillip to our Military Diplomacy efforts worldwide. Officers, from the MEA, too, must be posted to the Integrated Defence Staff in adequate numbers.

The Government of India may wish to note that in today's world, there exist a large number of nations being ruled by military or quasi-military governments, and a large number of heads of state have a military background. It will be in the nation's interests to send some suitable retired senior officers from the three services as high commissioners or ambassadors to such countries, for e.g., sending a suitable retired senior officer from an Indian Gurkha Regiment to Nepal as our envoy will pay handsome dividends to the nation. Lieutenant General S.K. Sinha, many years back, had made a very successful Ambassador to Nepal.

As India strives for its deserving seat on the global high table, the South Block has to undergo a radical mind change and integrate Military Diplomacy as an inescapable constituent of its global diplomacy. As most nations look up to India for increasing security assistance to it, India will have to speedily establish integrated institutions, and expertise within to comprehensively reach out to the growing demands and aspirations of friendly foreign nations including augmenting defence cooperation with India. We must not punch below our weight but reach out to smaller nations in more ways than one. Military Diplomacy remains, for India, a viable instrument whose potential for national strategic endeavours remains grossly untapped and, thus, this anomaly needs to be speedily rectified in the larger interests of the nation. Leveraging Military Diplomacy must be accorded its due importance for the attainment of the nation's foreign policy and security objectives.

Lieutenant General (Dr) Kamal Davar, AVSM, a Cavalry Veteran, battle wounded in the 1965 war, has been the first DIA Chief and Deputy Chief of the IDS. His experience includes War College, IMT Iraq, and the command of a Division in Ladakh, and a Corps in Punjab. A highly reputed writer and speaker on security, terrorism and intelligence issues, he is the Convener of Strategic Studies think tank in Kasauli, and a member of HLMG, monitoring Israeli operations in Gaza and West Bank. He is also engaged with Track II dialogue with Pakistan, and is the president of the Delhi Forum for Strategic Studies.

Endnotes

1. Kennedy, John F. Address at Washington University's 100 years anniversary 16 November 1961.
2. Plessis, Anton Du, *Defence Diplomacy: Conceptual and Practical Dimensions with Specific Reference to South Africa*, Strategic Review for Southern Africa, November 2008,
3. Malik, General V.P. *India's Military Conflicts and Diplomacy.* Harper Collins, 2013
4. Ibid.
5. Sood, Rakesh. *The India-US defence partnership is deepening,* Observer Research Foundation, Commentaries, 30 October 2020
6. Admiral Arun Prakash in the Jerusalem Strategic Tribune—March 2023
7. Ibid.
8. Admiral Arun Prakash in the Jerusalem Strategic Tribune–March 2023

22

India's Strategy in the Emerging Geopolitical World Order

Major General Pushpendra Singh

Emerging Geopolitical Landscape

Power-Shift

As China became the world's factory and leader in many emerging, cutting-edge technologies, it experienced four decades of spectacular economic growth. In 2022, China's GDP reached 71 per cent of US GDP.[1] Peoples' Republic of China (PRC) leveraged this remarkable growth to pose a direct challenge to US supremacy through its BRI global infrastructure projects, and international organisations in over 150 countries. It also embarked on the largest ship-building exercise the world has ever seen to emerge as the world's largest Navy by 2021.These initiatives have instigated an epic power-shift from the West to the East which has been accelerated by the Russia-Ukraine conflict.

Iran, CAR, and De-dollarisation

Three months after Biden took office as POTUS in Jan 2021, China finalised a 25-year Comprehensive Strategic Partnership with Iran, which, in violation of the Iranian Nuclear Deal, had been isolated by US sanctions. In sharp contrast to India's abject know-towing to Trump by stopping oil imports from Iran, the Sino-Iranian Partnership included supply of Iranian oil at concessional rates (in Chinese Petroyuan) in return for $400 bn worth of Chinese investments to upgrade Iranian manufacturing and infrastructure among others. A month later, in April 2021, Biden made his first visit as POTUS to the UK and EU, which the *Washington Post* described as an American bid to support UK, EU and NATO, to confront the 'harmful activities of Russia and China'. Soon, Russia and China responded by renewing their July 2001 strategic friendship and cooperation treaty for another 20 years. Next, in January 2022, Xi Jinping hosted the five Central Asian Republic (CAR) leaders where he announced a trade target of $70 billion worth (mostly in RMB). Thus, China has lynch-pinned the Eurasian landmass as an Anti-West Bloc (US, UK, EU and Japan) solidly under Chinese influence.

Sanctions on Russia and Belarus

In February 2022, after Ukraine ignored the Minsk-II Agreement by again seeking inclusion into NATO, Russia launched its Special Military Operation to 'de-militarise and de-Nazify Ukraine.' This aggravated the friction between the West and the Eurasian Bloc. The West responded by imposing punishing economic sanctions on Russia and Belarus. The sanctions froze $640 billion of Russian reserves, and banned Russia from the SWIFT international payment system. However, unexpectedly, this gave added impetus to de-dollarisation. China is spearheading efforts to promote the Yuan as the new global currency by exploiting Petroyuan. India too is seeking to internationalise INR for bilateral trade.[2] On 1 March 2023, China and Belarus concluded an 'all-weather, strategic cooperation'. Thus, China now has a trade and economic 'bridgehead' into NE Europe through the China-developed Great Stone China-Belarus Industrial Park near Minsk.

Islamic Rapprochement

On 14 March 2023, Xi Jinping was re-elected President of PRC and Chairman of the powerful CMC for a third time. Thus empowered, Xi lost no time in pursuit of expanding the Chinese hold over the Eurasian Bloc by getting the leaders of Sunni and Shia Islam—Saudi Arabia and Iran—to normalise diplomatic relations. UAE too followed suit with Iran. Hence, Turkey was spurred to mend its fences with Saudi Arabia as well as Egypt. Thus, the stage is now set for peace with Syria and a possible end to the civil war in Yemen. Hence, the Eurasian Bloc's influence has now expanded to include the Middle East as well, while US Influence stands correspondingly diminished. Saudi Arabia and UAE have commenced oil or LNG trade with China in Petroyuan, thus giving another fillip to de-dollarisation—a major blow to USA. With peace in sight, the stage is also set for Chinese 'help' in reconstruction of war-ravaged nations.

Xi in Moscow

Xi followed this up by his three-day visit to Moscow, on 20 March 2023, to stand by his beleaguered 'dear friend' Putin. The subsequent statement supported Russia's position in toto by calling on all sides to respect the legitimate security concerns of all countries, prevent bloc confrontation, and avoid fanning the flames (of the conflict). 'Responsible dialogue' was advocated as the best way for appropriate solutions. This statement indirectly implicated the West's pernicious role in instigating the war.

Great Change

While leaving Moscow, Xi reportedly remarked to Putin, 'We're on the cusp of change that hasn't happened in a hundred years and we are driving this change together.'[3] This clearly indicates that PRC views the Ukraine conflict as a war between the West and the Eurasian powers.

Europe

Therefore, many analysts concluded that the statement would preclude a Chinese role in mediating peace. But surprisingly, Zelensky invited Xi Jinping to visit Ukraine (29 March 2023). Meanwhile, leading European economies are facing severe economic repercussions from sanctions on Russia. Some of these countries are reconsidering their position *vis-a-vis* the US in the Ukraine conflict. On 6th April 2023, French President Macron visited Beijing along with the European Commission (EC) President. They urged Xi to 'reason with Putin' to end the war, while EC President, Ursula Gertrud von der Leyen 'welcomed Xi's openness to talk with Zelensky'.

Germany

Germany, too, is facing severe economic headwinds, and consequent public anxiety from its Russian sanctions. It is, therefore, seeking to boost partnerships in order to give it greater economic leeway. Accordingly, German Chancellor Scholz visited India on 25 Feb 2023 accompanied by a large business delegation. His talks with the PM focussed on expanding cooperation in the areas of trade, defence, clean energy, climate change and new technologies. Hence, Indo-German economic and security partnership holds great promise, not only in boosting our economies through increased Indo-European trade, but also in strengthening security in the Indo-Pacific.

Chinese Aggression

South and East China Seas

Chinese aggression against the littoral and island nations in the South and East China Seas has had the following reactions:

QUAD: The four democracies (India, Japan, US and Australia) came together to oppose Chinese violation of the International Law of the Sea. They formed the QUAD with a focus on enforcing a 'Free and Open Indo-Pacific.' However, both Russia and China are wary of the QUAD – the so-called Asian NATO. Consequently, India being sensitive to Russia's concerns, as also to avoid provoking China, had so far fought shy of joining a militarised QUAD, preferring alignments over alliances.

AUKUS: The Anglophone countries—Australia, UK, US—perceived that they needed to counter Beijing's use of its military power to achieve its ends more effectively. They formed a trilateral military alliance with a focus on 'Free and Independent Indo-Pacific'. Under this treaty, Australia would get to buy three American Virginia class SSN submarines. These nuclear-powered fast-attack subs are armed with cruise missiles. This pact has enhanced the deterrence capability of these nations, raised the costs to China, and thus, contributed to stability in the Indo-Pacific. Simultaneously, West European powers plus Canada and littoral states like Vietnam, South Korea (ROK) and New Zealand have been involved in QUAD discussions for a QUAD plus grouping.

ROK-Japan Rapprochement: Continuing Chinese aggression and North Korean belligerence also instigated the historic rapprochement between South Korea (ROK) and Japan. ROK had been demanding reparations from Japan for its forced labour and comfort women during WWII colonisation by Japan. Setting these aside in a brave political decision, on 16th March 2023, ROK President Yoon Suk Yeol travelled to Tokyo to meet the Japanese PM. This assumes great significance in the overall security scenario in East Asia and the Indo-Pacific Theatre.

Japan: In view of increasing belligerence of China and North Korea, former Japanese PM Shinzo Abe had striven to make Japan emerge from the shadows of its post WWII 'pacifist defence policy' by taking charge of its own security. Now, as a consequence of the Russian attack on Ukraine, plus contingencies on Taiwan, Abe's initiative has been realised. On 17 December 2022, Japan adopted its National Security Strategy. This seeks to make a 'Proactive Contribution to Peace' and reduce Japan's dependence on USA for its security.

PRC Belligerence Against India

Tibetan Plateau

After Xi became PRC President in 2012, Chinese hostility increased progressively. In May 2020, PLA's transgressions in East Ladakh flagrantly violated the 1996 Border Agreement with China (among other agreements) and instigated the first fatalities among troops in 45 years. In response, Indian Army occupied the Kailash Range overlooking PLA's Moldo Garrison and the Spanggur Gap. A rattled China agreed to pull back, on the condition of the Indian side pulling back first.

After we pulled back, PLA vacated only one of the transgressions in the Pangong Tso area, where too our Patrolling Points (PP) were pushed back to the Indian side of the LAC. Thus, PLA continues to occupy some 2,000 square km of Indian territory with as many as 26 of 65 PPs firmly under Chinese control. Next, China embarked on cognitive war of giving Chinese names to 11 existing places within Arunachal, and stated that the Indian Ocean is not India's ocean just because of its name and went ahead to Sinicise 19 location names in IOR. These were promptly rejected by India.

Indo-Pacific

Chinese aggression has pushed India to focus more on the Indo-Pacific theatre where we enjoy a countervailing advantage. Peninsular India, jutting out into the Indian Ocean, puts India in a pivotal position astride the busiest trade route on the planet. India's Andaman Islands control the north-western entrance to the Malacca Straits, the South China Sea and Pacific Ocean – one of the narrowest choke points in the world. Eighty per cent of China's oil imports – some nine million barrels per day (bpd) – pass through the Malacca Straits. This confers on us a major geostrategic advantage in the Indo-Pacific Theatre.

India is belatedly leveraging this advantage by building a mega International Container Transhipment Port on the Great Nicobar Island, just 124 nm from Banda Aceh, the mouth of the Malacca Strait. While PRC's 'string of pearls' seeks to encircle India and secure Chinese Sea Lanes of Communication (SLOC) through the IOR, China is also deploying cutting-edge disruptive technologies like Quantum systems and AI, and modernising its nuclear force. India has made robust responses, both on land and in IOR, as in succeeding paras.

Indian Response

Along LAC

India effected the largest ever high-altitude military deployment in the Himalayas to challenge Chinese belligerence. Shedding a conciliatory policy (despite Minister of External Affairs, Jaishankar, stating 'How can I take on China with a much bigger economy'), we have accelerated our military build-up through indigenous weapon system acquisitions, and enhanced border infrastructure and connectivity. India's resolute stand has confronted China with a two-front problem: facing India on its west and Taiwan in the South China Sea (SCS) to its southeast, thereby, imposing caution on any PRC attempt to 'reunify' Taiwan.

IOR

IOR has a number of choke points – the Mozambique Channel, the Bab-el-Mandeb, the Suez Canal, the Strait of Hormuz in the west and the Malacca Straits, the Sunda and Lombok Straits in the east. In order to enable effective control over these choke points plus the SLOCs, Indian Navy has a number of its own bases in IOR, besides the use of alliance partners' facilities.

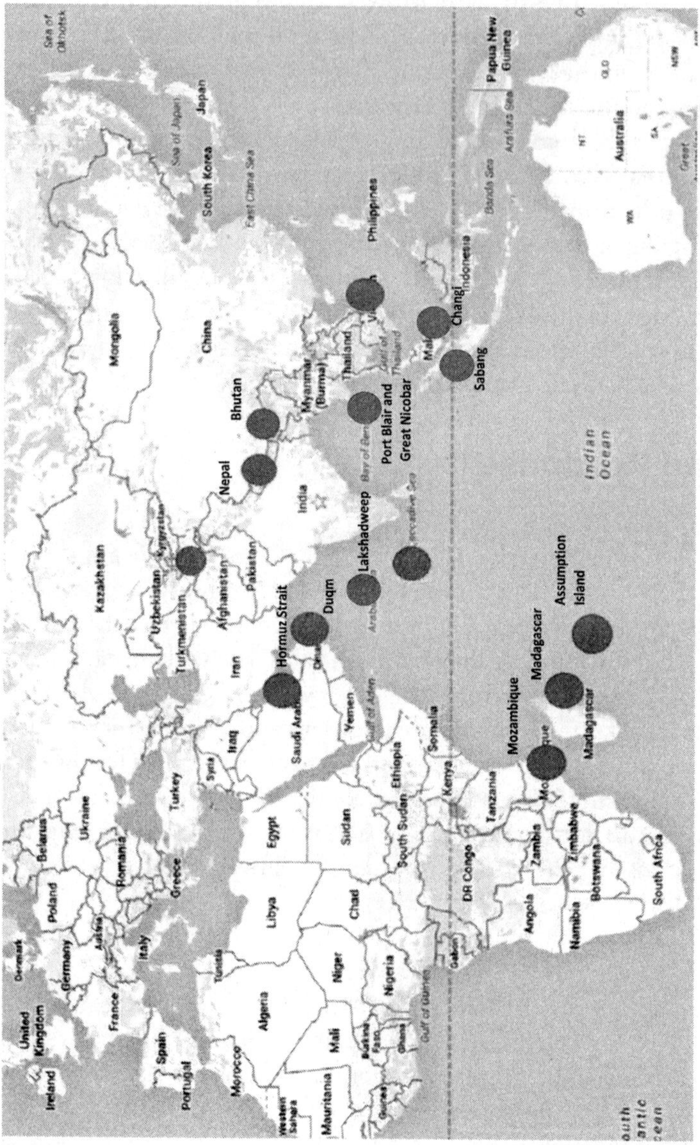

Hormuz Strait
Duqm
Lakshadweep
Nepal
Bhutan
Port Blair and Great Nicobar
Sabang
Changi
Mozambique
Madagascar
Assumption Island
Indian Ocean
India
China
Mongolia
Kazakhstan
Iran
Pakistan
Afghanistan
Saudi Arabia
Yemen
Somalia
Kenya
Tanzania
Ethiopia
Sudan
South Sudan
Egypt
Libya
Chad
Algeria
Niger
Nigeria
Mali
Mauritania
Morocco
Turkey
Ukraine
Romania
Greece
Poland
Germany
France
Spain
Portugal
Italy
United Kingdom
Ireland
Belarus
Iraq
Syria
DR Congo
Angola
Zambia
Zimbabwe
Botswana
Namibia
South Africa
Myanmar (Burma)
Thailand
Philippines
Indonesia
South Korea
Japan
Papua New Guinea
Australia
Turkmenistan
Uzbekistan

PRC Economic Problems

Even as PRC continues its belligerent actions against India and its neighbours in South and East China Seas, it is facing severe economic issues.

China's 10 per cent plus growth was fuelled by huge government-funded infrastructure projects, including global BRI schemes. However, many of the BRI beneficiary nations have defaulted on their repayments. Simultaneously, there was a glut of domestic infrastructure, particularly housing, resulting in many ghost townships with no takers. As a result, Chinese banks have been saddled with huge NPAs.

Chinese economy was largely exports-led with USA accounting for more than a third. However, recent Fed rate hikes have impacted American consumption. This has hit Chinese exports and affected its manufacturing sector, especially SMEs. Falling growth rates have also turned market sentiment negative. Therefore, already saddled with unsustainable NPAs, banks are unable to lend money for reviving manufacturing. Thus, tax revenues have also dropped, a problem aggravated by an ageing population profile. Hence, China will have to either increase tax revenues or fall into a debt trap.[4]

Indo-Russia Ties

In the backdrop of Xi's Moscow statement fully supporting the Russian position in the Ukraine conflict, there were serious concerns in India if we could continue to count on Russian support during the ongoing Sino-Indian tensions. As if in response to these concerns, on 31st March 2023, Russia published its new Foreign Policy strategy, which identified China and India as its main allies. The strategy mentions that Russia will build a 'particularly privileged strategic partnership' with India and seek to enhance bilateral trade, strengthen investments and technological ties, and ensure (the two nations') resistance to destructive actions of unfriendly states and their alliances (read the West and NATO). This has somewhat allayed India's concerns that Russia's growing dependence on China could constrain India's geostrategic space, and more importantly, impact Russia's sales of military equipment and spares to us.

Sanctions on Russia

The West had responded to Russia's Special Military Operations against Ukraine by their harsh economic sanctions on Russia and Belarus.

However, India has strong ties with Russia, and is extensively dependent on Russian military equipment and spares (about 86 per cent weapon platforms are of Russian-origin). Therefore, India (and China) ignored the US economic sanctions, mainly by buying Russian oil (at concessional rates), thereby, providing it crucial economic support. India also refused to join diplomatic efforts to condemn Russia for the Ukraine war. USA was forced to 'understand' India's dependence on Russia. US is trying to woo India away from Russian dependence by persuading it to seek alternative sources of military equipment, and promising help in developing its own cutting-edge military technology.

Geoeconomics

Responding to the West's stringent sanctions, Russia turned to China and India. Thus, for the first time, with a 22-fold increase in oil sales to India, Russia emerged as a top-five trading partner – $38.4 billion in 2022. In March 2023, India became the largest buyer of Russia's benchmark Urals grade crude, which accounted for over 50 per cent of all sales. (Urals grade crude is an important benchmark for the medium sour crude market in Europe). Consequently, Russia's Energy Tsar, Igor Sechin, visited Delhi at the end of March 2023, following which Rosneft and IOC signed an agreement to substantially increase oil supplies and diversify grades to India. Sechin also discussed ways of expanding cooperation in the entire value chain of the energy sector as well as payments in national currencies.[5]

Indo-Russian Partnership for its Far East

As global warming melts the Polar ice caps, it exposes vast deposits of hydrocarbons and other valuable minerals for exploitation. Hence, the recent visit of Aleksey Chekunkov (Russian Minister for Development of the Arctic and Far East) to India assumes great significance. India announced that operationalising the Vladivostok-Chennai maritime corridor and cargo transportation by the Northern Sea Route were discussed.

This signifies that Moscow is prioritising India as a key development partner for its Far East despite China being keen to connect the Arctic to its BRI.[6] These developments suggest that Russia could be viewing its Indian relationship outside the Sino-Russian prism. Russia would also be wary of exclusive dependence on PRC, with whom it has had past tensions, which include the Sino-Soviet ideological rift (1961–1989) and the 1969 Ussuri River border clash.

Petroleum Exports

Bloomberg reports that India is playing an increasingly important role in global oil markets, buying ever more cheap Russian oil, and refining it into fuel for Europe and the US. India's refined oil exports of 11.6 million tonnes to EU countries were up 20.4 per cent year-on-year during April-January, while USA imported some 2 lakh bpd from India. Thereby, in 2022, India's petroleum exports reached $61.4 billion, and added great value to our Russian partnership.

Indian Actions to Emerge as a Powerhouse

The Autonomy Plank

Right through its diplomatic history India has consistently opted for strategic autonomy. Even as Pakistan, our principal adversary in the mid-fifties, had joined American alliances, India had striven to steer clear of either power bloc. However, with USA's hostility during Nixon-Kissinger years, India was forced to align with the USSR whose diplomatic and military support proved invaluable during the 1971 Bangladesh War right until the demise of the Soviet Union.

Indo-US 123 Agreement

After India's 1998 nuclear tests, PM Vajpayee withstood western sanctions with imaginative diplomacy, which culminated in the US-India Civil Nuclear Agreement under PM Manmohan Singh in 2008. This also facilitated greater civil as well as military cooperation with USA, which culminated in our signing the four foundational agreements on Indo-US military cooperation. The promise of assistance in developing high-technology followed. While Chinese hostility drove us closer to the US, India fought shy of an alliance to retain strategic autonomy.

Indo-Pacific Alliance

In the backdrop of Chinese belligerence and the Japan-India 'Special Strategic and Global Partnership', Japanese PM Kishida visited India on 20 March to deepen bilateral cooperation and spur Japanese-led efforts towards a 'Free and Open Indo-Pacific', geared to curb Beijing's growing assertiveness. Further boosting the Indo-Japanese partnership, he invited

India to participate in the G7 Summit in May. This also underlines India's critical role in sustaining QUAD while India is at the crossroads of the geopolitical schism between the Eurasian landmass powers on one hand and the West plus the Indo-Pacific partnerships on the other.

Staunch Opposition to PRC Hostility

Even as we continue to avoid alliances, PRC hostility has pushed us to rely more on the US, the QUAD-plus nations, and ASEAN to counter China. Dogged defence against LAC transgressions have imposed caution on PRC's hostility to Taiwan, which has lent India greater credibility as an emerging powerhouse.

Soft Power

India has been actively enhancing its soft power with a number of initiatives. These have enhanced our world stature and promoted our endeavour for diplomatic autonomy. Some examples are as follows:

Vaccine 'Maitri': India provided as many as 163 million doses of Covid-19 vaccine to 96 nations during the Covid-19 epidemic.

First Responder: In several disaster-struck nations, India became the first responder, Turkey being the latest example.

Financial and Development Assistance: In April 2022, India extended $3.9 billion financial aid to debt-crisis-hit Sri Lanka. In November 2022, India closed a $1.2 billion soft loan for building Mongolia's first Greenfield Refinery, which is scheduled to complete in 2025. Seychelles and Maldives, two Indian Ocean nations of great strategic significance, have also received significant financial assistance.

G-20 Presidency: India is exploiting its G-20 Presidency as an influential medium to get the leading economies to collectively deal with global challenges such as climate change, food security, health and so on.

India's Strategic Options

Although the geopolitical dynamics after Russia's 'Special Military Operation' are still unfolding, the conflict is emerging as a war between

Eurasian powers China and Russia, and the West (US or NATO and Japan). The West is engaging China in a pincer—actively on Russia's west through its proxy, Ukraine, and by deterrent naval manoeuvres in the South and East China Seas, most notably in the Taiwan Straits. In this context, our robust stance against PRC on our Watershed/LAC assumes greater significance.

While our neutral stance *vis-a-vis* Russia and the West has gained us greater leverage with Russia, whether this would help in restraining Chinese aggressions against India in Tibet is an open question. Concomitantly, the QUAD and Indo-Pacific nations seek greater Indian participation to help balance Chinese belligerence in the East and South China Seas. Therefore, India could seek to retain Russian friendship while relying on QUAD to countervail Chinese aggressions along our northern frontiers.

However, due to ongoing geopolitical dynamics, India's desire to retain diplomatic autonomy could prove problematic. Continuing Chinese aggression may force us to make a choice—strive for autonomy by banking on our friendship with a beleaguered Russia, or finally push to counter China by joining a militarised QUAD, and Indo-Pacific Alliances.

Major General Pushpendra Singh is a graduate of National Defence Academy, Defence Services Staff College, Wellington, and the Kalinin Military Academy, Saint Petersburg. He commanded an Independent Artillery Brigade, and was GOC Madhya Pradesh, Bengal and Orissa Area. Post retirement, he assumed charge as the DG, Disaster Management, Madhya Pradesh. He has authored several books, including a much-acclaimed historical novel, *Hawk Hunters*.

Endnotes

1. World Bank figures in Global PEO Services.
2. Financial Express. 29 March 2023.
3. Saran, Sham. Indian Express. 6 Apr 2023.
4. With inputs from managementstudyguide.com.
5. Bhadrakumar, M.K. The Tribune, March 2023.
6. Ibid.

Membership of the **GYAN CHAKRA** THINK TANK is open to all serving officers and veterans.

Membership is also open to prominent scholars, scientists and academicians from affiliated universities and eminent media personalities and retired civil servants.

Corporate houses desirous of becoming members to facilitate research on defence related issues can also be permitted on approval from the Executive Council.

Please contact the Director's office for more Information.

Gyan Chakra, Senior Veterans Home
Sector-2 Panchkula, Haryana, India
t: 0172 2587305 **e:** gcttch@gmail.com
w: www.gyanchakra.org